Help Yourself
to a Blue Banana

• This book is easy to understand even for people who rarely read anything.
• Reading comprehension: 11th grade→adult, or very bright 9th grade→adult.
• It's assumed that readers have no previous art training and no ability to draw.
• Help Yourself to a Blue Banana has only three pictures (see page 7).

– The book title relates to appropriateness of color (see page 147, 6th paragraph).
– Units of measure within the text are stated in both U.S. standard and metric.
– Book design, jacket design and illustration ©Michael Adams MMV-MMVIII

Library of Congress Control Number 2005906025

ISBN   0-9770879-0-5

Help yourself to a blue banana™
The nine lessons of light™
The sources of visual experience™
Visual living™
The smiling blue banana™
The one, two, three rule™
The clutter rule™
The visual boundaries™
The scale of just us™
Art anxiety™
Unseeing™
The Curse of Graphula™
The separation trick™

BEHIND THE SCENES BOOKS
PINE BROOK, NEW JERSEY, USA
973 276 9472

© Michael Adams MMVIII

10 9 8 7 6 5 4 3 2

Help Yourself
to a Blue Banana

Awakening your eyes to art,
design and visual living

AN INTRODUCTION TO
THE NINE LESSONS OF LIGHT

MICHAEL ADAMS

BEHIND THE SCENES BOOKS
PINE BROOK, NEW JERSEY, USA

Acknowledgements

THANK YOU TO INDIVIDUALS who contributed to editing
this book and/or provided criticism. Some strengths of the
book are due to their interest. All its weaknesses are my own.

In alphabetical order: Jeanne Adams, Firth Fabend, Jared Garaci,
Francis Kerrigan, Jackie Mazzola, Penny Nichols, Guy Parker,
Mircea Ploscar, Catherine Reed, Chris Sadowski,
Ann Schear, Erika Schnatz and Beverly Weiss

In addition, thank you to anonymous professional readers
who, at a critical point in its development, favorably reviewed
the manuscript for several publishing companies. On some editions,
their wonderful comments can be found on the back dust jacket.

- and -

John Luttropp, Chair, Dept. of Art and Design, Montclair State University
Arline Lowe, Chair, Dept. of Art and Design, Seton Hall University
Dr. Terry Wilson, PhD, Chair, Dept. of Business Management
East Stroudsburg University
and students in my graphic design classes at
Tampa Technical Institute, The Center for Media Arts
and Montclair State University

ALSO ACKNOWLEDGED ARE friends, teachers and colleagues
who influenced or inspired over many years with their work
or professional support, often without realizing it. Among them:
Ernesto Barba, Don Ervin, George D'Amico, Roger Ferriter,
Jacquelyn Low, Linda Paternoster, Alan Prescott,
Josh Schwartz, Richard Stack, Robert Weaver and
Bernice Wiese (eighth grade art teacher, T.M.Wilhoite JHS,
Port Lyautey US Naval Air Station, Kenitra, Morocco)

LASTLY, THANK YOU to the booksellers, teachers,
librarians and museum/gallery managers who
help bring this book to a fresh generation
of readers and young artists.

❖

Your thoughts are also welcome.
Please send them to:

info@behindthescenesmarketing.com

Artists, art teachers and
other visual art professionals
are especially asked
to comment.

TABLE OF CONTENTS:

Illustrations: Following page 68 and on pages 115 and 268

*– A MAN SEES WHAT
HE WANTS TO SEE
AND DISREGARDS THE REST.*

PARAPHRASED FROM *THE BOXER*
BY PAUL SIMON

"HELP YOURSELF TO A BLUE BANANA"
HAS ONLY THREE PICTURES.

Instead of seeing pictures, as you read you'll be
taught to look directly at the world around you. You'll
find your own examples of what the text is saying.

In the text, you'll find references to hundreds
of everyday things that are inside your home, outside
your window or maybe just down the road.

Wherever you are right now, wherever
you are reading this, there are visual
discoveries to be made all around you.

About drawing skills

*The text assumes readers have no previous art training,
and that you have no ability to draw.
In fact drawing skills are not that important.*

See page 49.

*However, individuals with advanced artistic and/or
drawing talent are also invited to explore this book.*

Alvar Aalto – architect
Jean-Michel Basquiat – painter
Harry Bertoia – furniture designer
Leonardo da Vinci – artist
Roger Ferriter – graphic designer
Antonio Gaudi – architect
Al Hirschfeld – illustrator
Matt Hotch – motorcycle designer
Jean Auguste Dominique Ingres – painter
Donna Karan – fashion designer
Thomas Kinkade – painter
Gustav Klimt – painter
Mark Kostabi – painter
Roy Lichtenstein – artist
Raymond Loewy – designer
Liza Lou – artist/sculptor
Rene Magritte – painter
Michelangelo – artist
Isaac Mizrahi – fashion designer
Henry Moore – sculptor
Claude Monet – painter
Grandma Moses – painter
Louise Nevelson – sculptor
I.M. Pei – architect
Pablo Picasso – artist
Jackson Pollock – painter
Paul Rand – graphic designer
Auguste Renoir – painter
Norman Rockwell – painter
Cindy Sherman – photographer
Joan Steiner – sculptor
Vincent Van Gogh – painter
Andrea de Verrocchio – painter
Robert Weaver – illustrator
Andy Warhol – artist
Frank Lloyd Wright – architect
Andrew Wyeth – painter

Preface

After you open these pages . . . you'll know what artists know!

Welcome to my book.

If you have visual imagination I'm sure you'll like it!

This book is about art, design and visual living, three closely related things, things artists and designers are very familiar with.

"Visual living" is something enjoyable, a lifestyle that happens when you become aware of how your eyes see and understand the world. Visual living is fun! On the following pages, in addition to learning about art and design, you'll learn ways to try out visual living, and maybe make it a part of your own everyday experience.

Even though art, design and visual living are closely related, trying to define them is hard to do. But here's a way to explain what we mean: to start, try to remember if you've ever seen a statue that you liked (or hated) in a park, in a museum, on a fountain, or decorating the front of a building. Take a moment to do this. If you can remember that you once liked or hated a statue, then you probably know enough about "art" to read and understand this book.

Now consider this: Have you ever worn a shirt that made you feel good, or did you ever try to draw an eye-catching poster? If your answer is yes, then you probably sense enough about design to begin turning these pages. And lastly, if you ever said, "Wow, look at that!" when you saw a pretty sunset, or a full moon, or a beautiful cloud, well, that's a start to visual living.

Visual living is a frame of mind that lies somewhere between living your life as a non-artist (possibly where you are now), and living a life in which you express yourself visually to others (which is where you'll be if you become an artist).

It's an easy frame of mind for anyone to enjoy.

It's between *not* being an artist, and *really* being an artist.

In visible matters, you could say that art is the serious stuff, design is the cool stuff and visual living is the *fun stuff.*

We're going to learn about all three.

* * * *

    I said above that this is a book about art, design and visual living. True. But there's one more thing you're going to read about also. Actually, although art, design and visual living are important parts of this book, they are in fact not the primary topic here. The primary topic here is the thing that *connects these ideas together*. And the thing that connects art to design, and design to visual living, and then visual living back to art again is the visual language. It's the common thread. When you understand the visual language, then art, design and visual living begin to define themselves. All this connecting of visual things is a process which, all during your life, from cradle to grave, as they say, keeps going on and on and on.

    The funny thing is I'm sure you use at least parts of the visual language everyday, probably without realizing it. Here's why. It may sound too simple to be true, but I would guess that *no one ever told you you're using the visual language*.

    So let me tell you now. There are parts of the visual language that you are already very familiar with, and all through this book you'll read about surprising ways that you're *already* living with and using this unique kind of communication.

    This book picks up from wherever you are now in your familiarity with visual things. From that point, it leads you to knowing visual things even better. How far you go is up to you. You can use what's here to brighten up your bedroom, like they do on TV programs about interior design, or you can plan a whole way of life around it. If it really appeals to you, you can even explore a professional career in art or design using the information you'll read here. (Much more about this is coming up.)

    To summarize it, this book is about understanding art, design, visual living and the visual language, which is what connects them all together. It's about bringing these things more fully into your life. On top of that, if you like being around art and design or you like being around crafts, or you like having these things in your home or making them yourself, or even if you're just curious about why *other* people enjoy these things (including any artists you may know) then you'll be happy with this book.

Since this book is primarily about the visual language, you should know right from the start that the visual language has nine parts, called the nine lessons of light. You could call them the *secrets of visual expression*. The following chapters will introduce them to you. You'll read simple explanations of what the nine lessons of light are, and how they interact. To make it easy, there's nine chapters here, and each chapter looks at one lesson of light.

To show you what I mean, here's an example: in just a little while we'll read about color, the fourth lesson of light. In that chapter, we'll talk about things you already know about color, like how it influences the visual appeal of everything (including, for example, bananas). And we'll also talk about things you probably don't know about color, like how colors always strongly interact with other colors that appear nearby. The color chapter (and every chapter) is written in easy-to-understand words, and it's all fun to read.

*More about visual living
and the nine lessons of light*

The visual language and the lessons of light are the keys to visual living, which becomes the habit of using your eyes to explore and enjoy the visual characteristics of the world.

This isn't something you hear much about.

What I mean is, "visual living" isn't very widely discussed or practiced. People generally use their eyes for more ordinary things, like watching TV, looking for light switches or just taking out the garbage. I suspect, whether you're at home, at school or at work, you very likely use your eyesight primarily to help carry out common everyday chores. That's what most people do with their eyes.

Since visual living is not very common, the things that are usually said about art and design are often pretty superficial.

For example, you might hear an opinion about a new exhibit at a local art museum. A friend might say, "I really liked the art show. It was cool!" Or you might hear someone's evaluation of the dress an actress wears to the Oscars, like, "Oh My God! Kirsten Dunst looked *sooooo* beautiful!" Or you maybe you'll catch a comment about the design of a sports car ("*Awesome 430!*") or the layout of a web page, or the arrangement of table flowers at a wedding. Someone may compliment you on a scrapbook you created.

However, it's pretty extraordinary to hear anything said out loud about these things that's actually *visually* meaningful.

As a case in point, you would probably agree that it's pretty unusual to hear anything like, "I really love the texture in your sister's bedspread. It reminds me of Pollock and Basquiat." (Jackson Pollock and Jean-Michel Basquiat [pronounced *boss-kee-yot*] are American artists who used texture as an element in their paintings. More about them later.)

A comment like that would mean someone is thinking about texture. *And* about Pollock. *And* about Basquiat. And *relating* them. And *enjoying* it all. Wow! That's visual living. Usually, people don't think about how they're experiencing texture (even though we all continuously evaluate it subconsciously). And most people don't realize that artists know how texture can impact visual expression, whether it *is* a real Pollock or Basquiat painting or only a bedspread.

Looking for the right book

Before "Help Yourself to a Blue Banana," was written, when you looked for books about art or design, or about crafts, you'd find two different kinds.

Either they were "how to" books, showing you ways make or design things, or how to decorate your home or to do other "visual" things. Or they were "touchy feelie" books that might use beautiful words along with pictures of existing art and design to show you "what to look for," or to help you "get in touch with your emotions." Those kinds of books frequently have pictures. They say, "Here's a good example of art." And they might say, "Let your emotions guide your visual curiosity and everything will work out fine."

Actually, there's a lot of truth to that, and both of those sorts of books can be helpful.

But this book is not like those other books.

It's not like other art books. Not like other design books.

And it's not like other crafts books. I'll tell you why.

Unless you're reading "Help Yourself to a Blue Banana" on a computer, or you received it as a gift, you are probably browsing through it right now in some bookstore or library. Most likely you've found it next to other books about art and design. And again, some of those other books are probably filled with pictures of things to look at along with examples of colorful artwork or designs to examine, or instructions for projects to do.

Those books might be called, "How to Look at Art" or perhaps, "Expressing with Flowers" or, "Drawing People." Maybe the title is "Understanding Architecture" (or sculpture or graphic design) or, "Designing a Garden" (or your own wedding dress) or, "How to Paint Horses" or, "Creating Logos" (or packages, or ads, or hot rods, or web sites). If you're interested in design or crafts, I'm sure you've seen books like these, each one full of all sorts of things to look at and examples to follow.

In other words, it's common for beginners' books about art to show you *other people's art,* or *other people's designs.* Then they say, "You can do this too!" or, "You can learn to appreciate art like this!" But let me say it again, this book is not like that. This book is not about other people's art and it's not about other people's design. It's not going to show you art and design that other people created. That's why there's no pictures here of sculpture, or dresses, or pretty gardens, or stained glass, or logos or living rooms or clever layouts for advertisements. And despite the title, there's not even a picture here of blue bananas. (But more about blue bananas later.)

What I mean is, this book is not about visual living in someone else's life. Instead, it will tell you about these things *within your own experience.*

Everyone's first book about visual living

This book will tell you about these things by introducing you to the nine-part visual language called the nine lessons of light. It's a language made up of some things you may already know a little about, like color and texture and form, and several other things that are possibly all new to you, like scale and space. You will also learn that in its most effective and amazing expressions, the visual language *becomes* art and design.

There are two ways you can experience the visual language.

The first is to have a beginner's understanding of it.

When you do, it means taking a trip to a museum, for example, or just glancing around your everyday environment, is more interesting and more engaging. And as I mentioned earlier, watching interior design shows on TV may become a little more exciting, and any weekend craft projects you undertake may look quite a bit better when they're finished. When you know just a little something about the visual language, these things become more fun.

To compare this to a more commonly studied language, having

a beginner's understanding of the visual language is like maybe knowing how to speak a little French on a trip to Paris. If you know a little French, a trip to Paris is most likely more fun.

The second approach to experiencing the visual language is to begin using it yourself in ways that communicate feelings to other people. In this case, you begin to create your own expression, and maybe even your own art and design. That's fun also, but it can likewise be very, very serious. When you are fluent in the visual language, and expressing with it, you might compare that to knowing enough French to compose new words for the French national song.

In other words: If this were a book about speaking French, it would be the right place to start whether you want to get around Paris in a taxi, or you hope to write a new French novel. It's the right book to introduce you to *either* the playful side *or* the serious side of the visual language and visual living.

Your mind's eye
will provide the pictures

Unlike other art books that present things to look at, you've probably noticed already that "Help Yourself to a Blue Banana" has only three pictures.

As you read, instead of seeing pictures, you'll be told to look at the world around you. In the following chapters, you'll find references to everyday things that are inside your home, outside a window or maybe down the road. Wherever you are right now, wherever you're reading this, there are visual discoveries ready to enjoy all around you. Each chapter will help you find them.

From time to time, you'll take a break from reading and just look at everything nearby. The visual information that you'll need is taken from the everyday world, and it's a world that's *full* of exciting examples of the nine lessons we'll learn. The wonderful thing is, the examples you will explore while reading "Help Yourself to a Blue Banana" are *your* examples. You'll find them all by yourself.

To see what I mean, try it right now.

Get visually interested in *everything* around you at this very minute. Wherever you are, stop reading, look up and search for the most appealing thing that catches your eye. Is it a pretty color?

An unusual shape?

A bouquet of flowers?

A good looking chair?

An attractive person? An unusual carpet?
A pretty light fixture above you?
The watch on your wrist? Your new shoes?
The cover of this book?

When you have noticed something around you,
make a note about it in the blank space here.

The most visually interesting thing around me is:

_____

Then, also stick some *visual memory* of it in the back of your mind, a place inside your head where you'll remember it a few days from now. We will refer to it again later on in the book. As you read "Help Yourself to a Blue Banana" you'll see that *anything* that looks interesting has the seeds of visual expression.

The process of going back and forth between reading and looking at your actual environment is the way learning will happen as you progress through the book. At the end, when you look up from reading the last page, at that moment your eyes will awaken *permanently* to art, design and visual living. Your ability to see the lessons of light will replace the process of reading about them.

In addition, there are references throughout "Help Yourself to a Blue Banana" to searching the internet for background on some material that is mentioned. Your learning will be greatly increased if you use the internet to discover more about art and design.

However, and this is *very important*, except in those places specifically described as an exercise to carry out while you read, I advise that you do not look at other visual material, including artwork and web pages, before you complete the last chapter. At that time, your visual curiosity will be ready to understand what the nine lessons of light are ready to tell you.

So instead, *bookmark the internet searches that are referred to* and come back to them on your second visit to each chapter. I am certain your learning will be noticeably improved if you just wait to begin exploring additional visual material until *after you've read the whole book.* In addition to that, when you've finished the book, for even more inspiration, you can also search the names of the individuals, artists and events that are identified in the reference notes you'll find after the last chapter.

Where you'll wind up
after reading nine chapters

Reading this book will provide a new feeling of freedom, and you will begin to appreciate the impact that art and design have on everything, which is part of visual living. You'll admire the simple visual pleasures of life as well as the work of artists and designers (including Mother Nature).

On the practical side, you'll go to art shows with more confidence, buy clothes that "suit" you better and probably take better vacation snapshots. When little children show you their school art, you'll know if it's good, and best of all, . . . *you'll know why.* If you want, you can tell them. When you know the lessons of light, you'll put into easy-to-understand words whatever it is that you like about the things you see. You'll put into *meaningful* words whatever you like about all the visual excitement that surrounds you.

In addition, you'll no doubt create more *origin*-ality in your living spaces, and more *individu*-ality in personal relationships. One possibility: while your visual life blossoms, you may decide one day that a clutch of wild flowers is a more meaningful gift for a friend or valentine than a store-bought bouquet.

(Wow, the spirit expressed by wild flowers!)

Visual living will become part of your life.

And for your artist within . . .

Beyond that, it may be that you have the ability to create art or design. You may have the skill or potential to create visual messages and expression that have an emotional impact on other people. Like thousands of visually sensitive people before you, you may feel the need to express yourself through the visual language.

Perhaps you have that special talent.

Perhaps you *are* an artist.

If that's true, this book was written equally for you.

If you are a beginning artist, this book may be only the start of your visual education. You may be someone looking for guidance to help you on your way. . . to broaden your visual instincts or boost your visual confidence. "Help Yourself to a Blue Banana" is the first step on that path also. Whatever direction your curiosity takes, by that I mean the fun direction or the serious direction, you'll discover this book can open that special door.

The lessons here are the foundation for every type of visual expression, for every type of design and art. They are also the foundation for every type of art or design career. They can lead you to the satisfaction that artists and designers find by living each day to its greatest potential. "Help Yourself to a Blue Banana" can lead you toward a lifestyle touched with remarkable beauty, emotional fulfillment and a sense of participation in the natural order that influences everything you see.

About your valuable time . . .

Is this book the best introduction to the visual language?

Is it worth your time to read it?

You should know I worried about these things because I know your time is valuable. But I believe the answer is yes, your time is *very well spent* reading this book. Here's why:

As we said earlier, this book is organized in a new way.

It explains the visual language using four new approaches.

First, it simplifies all this information into nine parts.

Putting these ideas together is a different approach to outlining the visual language. For the first time, this book writes about *all visual ideas together as one system.* And beyond that, this book finally gives them a shared name, "the nine lessons of light."

This has not been done before.

The second new approach here is the lack of pictures mentioned above. Discovering your *own* "pictures" within the real world helps you to develop your personal "visual curiosity," an important asset you will need in order to learn about visual expression.

We'll talk much more about visual curiosity.

Here's the third unique approach that's found only in "Help Yourself to a Blue Banana:" Everything written here applies to *all* visual activities. That's not true in other art books. If there was a picture of a new building somewhere within the following pages to help explain scale, that would pretty strongly link the concept of scale to the expression of architecture. Actually, there's no doubt, scale is a big (BIG) part of architecture, but it is also a big part of every other type of visual expression, including fashion design, photography, art direction and even any re-decorating you might do within your own home. When you're remodeling, how wide and tall is the opening you create between your kitchen and the family room?

That's a question of scale.

For that reason, none of the nine visual ideas we will discuss are linked to pictures of specific types of visual expression. Instead, you are guided to uncover these visual building blocks yourself, in *everything* you can see in the world that surrounds you. You'll teach yourself about scale, along with the other lessons of light, and you'll know it is part of *all* visual expression, not just architecture. All the information you'll read here is universal.

Fourth and last, this is the only book that describes a visual lifestyle that you can enjoy *separately from* the experience of actually being an artist or a designer. The satisfaction of seeing and understanding the world visually is available to anyone, not just to students and professionals of visual art. It's meant for everybody.

I named this lifestyle "visual living," and it's obviously growing in popularity, shown by the increasing number of shows, books, magazines and web sites that help people incorporate more visual awareness and excitement into their lives, their homes, their clothing and their vehicles. Or even to permanently change their faces and bodies with cosmetic surgery, adopting a process that's sometimes called extreme makeover.

Perhaps, at first, your interest will center more on exploring only the visual lifestyle, that is, visual living, rather than on the idea of creating any visual expression (art or design) yourself. However, having a visual lifestyle is the *first step* on that path anyway. So as things change, maybe you'll grow into a desire to actually create art. Either way, I am pretty sure you are going to love visual living.

Beyond these features, this book also introduces additional concepts for the first time. Among these are *visual curiosity, collecting visual experience, the visual boundaries,* the *separation trick* and the *Curse of Graphula.*

Opening your eyes
for the very first time

I have used this approach to understanding the visual world throughout my own career, and I have taught art and design at three schools. I believe this is the best way to inform you about the visual language. However, I am not the greatest living artist (probably very far from it), or the greatest teacher (again, probably not). That means there are very likely other artists and other teachers who may find weaknesses in these chapters.

I would be happy to know of any.

In the meantime, though, I consider this the best book available as an introduction to visual understanding. Even if you're an individual who rarely picks up a book, you'll never regret the time you spend reading *this* one.

One of my students once summed it up.

On finishing the last chapter, she wrote to me saying,

> "I felt like a newborn baby, opening
> my eyes for the very first time."

If you embrace these pages, I'm pretty sure you'll share that same beautiful feeling.

This book can make wonderful things come true for you.

And I know you're going to like it.

Foreword Some people are wrong about art

Although this book is about the visual language, let me ask you to start for a moment by thinking about . . . *food*. Imagine walking into a restaurant. The waiter hands you a menu which, oddly, looks like this:

Appetizer	Whipped chocolate fudge cake
Main course	Steaming hot coffee
Dessert	Braised duck under glass
Beverage	Baked potato

No matter how often you eat out in restaurants, you probably have two reactions when you analyze this menu. And I bet they are reactions just about everyone can agree with. The first thing you might notice is that the food items on the right are not opposite the proper menu category on the left. What I mean is, the cake should be the dessert, not the appetizer, and the beverage should be coffee, not a baked potato, etc.

And, if you look a little more at this funny menu, this is the second thing you might realize: None of the four foods listed on the right is food we could *even remotely* accept in the category it's listed in on the left.

In other words, if this menu said that the appetizer was "baked potato," (not cake) we could almost believe a strange restaurant is serving potatoes as an appetizer. Potatoes may be a funny appetizer but, hey, they *could* be an appetizer. But chocolate cake? Never! Never! Never! Chocolate cake can never be anything but dessert.

The same is true about the main course. Coffee is just simply not a main course. A main course is roasted chicken, or grilled steak or flounder, or braised duck, or a pretty substantial salad.

A main course is, after all, the main course.

So whatever it is, it better be *main*.

My guess is that it would be difficult to find anyone who did not agree with these criticisms of this menu. And that goes to show that people frequently share a common point of view about things, built up over a long period of time (or a long period of eating).

I am talking to you about this menu because there is another set of opinions, similar to these menu opinions, which many people also share. These are simplified opinions about visual expression. You could call them simplified opinions about art, opinions that people have built up over a long period of *seeing*.

Here's one of them: Just like the main course at dinner, lots of people believe (but this time by mistake) that there is a main part of visual expression as well. You could call it the *main course* of visual expression. And they believe (also by mistake) that there are other less important parts of visual expression, parts you might call the "appetizers and desserts" of visual expression.

That is, by mistake, some people think that in art, as on a simple menu, there should be a place for everything, and everything should always be in its place.

People who say there is a "main part" (a main course) of the visual language are speaking about content.

Content is one of the nine lessons of light, the visual characteristics of our world that are made visible by light. When the sun is out, or the lights are on, you can see these features of our world. They are all around us. The lessons of light *are* the visual language, and they're the principal topics of this book. They're the tools used by every kind of visual artist to express visual messages and emotional meaning and they are the keys to understanding visual living.

As I said, content is one of them.

And, like each of these tools, we'll talk much more about content later on. In fact, as previously indicated, each of the lessons of light is explained in an entire chapter in this book.

Also throughout this book, to explain things, we will call on many varieties of visual expression, including fashion, photography, advertising, architecture, web sites, illustration and even automobile design and tattoos.

We'll start with some examples of painting and graphics, but there's different kinds of visual expression discussed in the following pages. So if you like gardens or logos or interior design or motorcycles or flower arranging or cartooning, manga, cake decorating, or even dreaming up exciting visual themes for parties, keep reading.

In addition, we'll talk about crafts and about things that are visually beautiful or important in the natural world, things that are designed for us by Mother Nature.

But even though many people mistakenly believe content is always the main part of art, and although there is an entire chapter about content later in this book, it's never too early to start warning you how incredibly *unhelpful* this one lesson of light is when you try to grow more visually sensitive. For that reason, even though this is only the foreword of the book, let me start warning you about content right here and now.

Let's begin by imagining a pretty oil painting.

Imagine that it's hanging in a museum, or maybe it's printed on the cover of a new DVD. If this picture shows a beautiful young girl wearing a blue dress, sitting by a lake with mountains in the background, the content of the image (in this case) is the young girl.

The content is "what it's a picture of."

Content doesn't have to be a person. If a group of statues in a garden recreates a battle scene, the content is "war" or, as we will see, depending on your own opinions, it might be "tragedy," or it might be "senselessness" or "courage." Likewise, the content of a photograph or a drawing might be a building or it might be a fish.

Again, content is "what it's a photograph of," or "what it's a statue of," or "what it's a drawing of."

Now think for a moment about color and texture. Color and texture are also lessons of light. They are also important parts of the visual language. In the picture of the girl described above, the color of her dress may be beautiful, and the texture on the surface of the lake may be full of energy (waves and/or ripples, etc.), but for many people the young girl (as well as the war, the building or the fish in the other examples) remains the "main course." People will usually think of these things as the *most important part* of these paintings, statues or photographs.

There are, in fact, billions of works of visual expression in which content *is* the "main course," the most important part, and many show young girls, battles or fish. In some of these, in order to organize things in their "proper" place, it might even be helpful to say that texture is "the appetizer" and the colors are "the dessert."

But there is one GIANT difference between the things found on a menu, and how the visual language works. This is where it is common for people to make that mistake. And here it is: Although, in real life, chocolate cake can never be anything except dessert, in the special world of visual living, each of the nine lessons of light, the visual concepts you will be reading about shortly, can be *any course in a work of art.*

Any of the nine lessons of light, including color and texture, can be, shall we say, the main course for dinner on New Years Day.

Any of the lessons of light can be the "main part" of art.

This is important, and needs to be repeated. It's a principal lesson here, and it's central to understanding the artist's language:

> In the visual language, any of the nine lessons of light
> can be, in a manner of speaking, the "main course"
> for dinner on New Years. *Any of the nine lessons*
> *of light can be the "main part" of visual expression.*

So, in the picture of the young girl, ok, texture may be only the "appetizer," however in *other* pictures, *texture itself is the "main course."* Coffee can never be the main course for dinner, but scale (another of the lessons of light) *can* be the main course in the layout for an advertisement or in the design for a skyscraper.

And the same is true for the other lessons of light.

As you read, you will be constantly reminded there are eight parts of the visual language that can replace content as the main source of visual interest in the things you see.

That is to say, the "courses" (the lessons of light) that visually sensitive people "serve" in their work are not organized like the items on a menu. They don't have a "proper" place in art, like chicken soup has a proper place at the start of dinner on Sunday or on a big family holiday.

Instead, you could say our visual world is more like a splendid smorgasbord or buffet table, where the most appealing selection within view is the one that catches the eye. And that becomes the main course of what we are seeing.

In the visual world, there are nine equally powerful varieties of visual experience that can create that special magic, and they are called the nine lessons of light. Each of the lessons of light has a special energy and a special emotional significance.

Each is both a teacher and a tool.

As a teacher, each will continually inspire you with breathtaking discoveries you can explore within the world that surrounds you. And as a tool, each lesson of light attaches to your imagination and becomes a *partner*, helping you to understand how the wonders of art, design and visual living are expressed through the extraordinary visual language.

*What's the difference
between art and design?*

The title of this book invites you to "awaken your eyes to art and design." But is there a difference between them?

Before we continue, here's a way think about that.

To start with, you should know that the nine lessons of light are the foundation for *both* art and design, so there's no difference there. But sometimes you hear that art is a kind of visual expression that is, in a way, more serious or more valuable than something else that is "only" design.

Likewise it is sometimes thought that "art" represents visual expression that is a one-of-a-kind effort, like an oil painting, while design is more often a plan or guideline intended to be repeated, or even mass-produced, like a chair *design*. Then there is still another idea that art is somehow more difficult to create than design. In this case, it's implied that "artists," who are individuals with *real* visual talents, produce art (which has *real* visual meaning), while "designers" are only capable of producing design.

Of course, in this idea, the status of designers is lessened.

Actually, please forget each of those definitions, because they are all misleading or even wrong. None of these definitions provides any practical information about how art and design really differ.

So to make sense of all this, you should know, first of all, art and design are very similar words. They both describe visual expression and generally speaking, they're both just words that describe special experiences that speak to us through the visual language.

But there is one worthwhile distinction, one that makes art and design understandable as separate things. It has to do with problem solving and judgement, which are both part of all visual expression.

This definition, which I support, says art happens when artists apply their judgement toward solving their own visual problems. And design happens when *equally talented* artists apply their judgement toward solving the visual problems of others.

To put it differently, within this definition (which admittedly has exceptions) you need to remember just two things: The first is that art is (hopefully) created when an artist addresses his or her personal feelings using the visual language. And second is design is created when another artist uses his or her visual ability, and visual sensitivity, to address visual problems of *others*. Of course, those "others" are what we normally call clients or customers.

In addition, to overcome any implied differences between "artists" and "designers," I prefer to give designers the more understandable and appropriate title of "business artist." Art is created by artists, who are sometimes called "fine" artists, and design is also created by artists, who are often called designers. But in this book designers are usually referred to as "business artists."

In this book, art and design are *both* created by equally talented and equally capable artists.

Introduction PART ONE

Help Yourself to a Blue Banana
Awakening your eyes to art, design and visual living

On the following pages, you will learn about one of the most important languages the world has (literally) ever seen. But it's a language that throughout history perhaps only one person in five has had a meaningful understanding of. Even today I suspect many people, and often silently, wonder what they're missing.

You may be one of those of curious individuals.

If so, great! You've come to the right book.

The nine lessons of light
are the sources of visual experience

Every thought in this book leads to one idea: You can begin to learn about the visual language by understanding just nine concepts called the lessons of light.

The nine lessons of light are the building blocks of a wonderful kind of communication, one that is fully understood only by people who have a visual lifestyle. To say it simply, the lessons of light are the nine basic ways in which light makes our visible world visually understandable.

In fact, because they *are* the basic parts of visual experience, from time to time within the pages of this book, the lessons of light are called the *sources* of visual experience.

By reading about them here, you'll gain the insight needed to genuinely begin seeing. You'll open your eyes to visual meaning, possibly for the very first time. When you've finished reading, you'll look at your life with a new perspective.

You'll look at art and design . . . everything from the latest styles in fashions and clothes, to up-to-date paintings hanging in a trendy gallery, to the design of consumer products, to soaring modern skylines, to museums filled with Renaissance masterpieces, and even drawings you find in your local newspaper or the art made by you, your friends or your relatives . . . with a new confidence.

Believe it or not, you'll finally begin to understand.

What are the nine lessons of light?

The names of the nine lessons of light (the nine sources of visual experience) appear here. Remember, any understanding you now have of any of these words may be different from what it means as part of the system you will read about.

The nine lessons of light
(the sources of visual experience):

DEPTH
FORM
ANATOMY
COLOR
CONTRAST
CONTENT
TEXTURE
SCALE
SPACE

There is no "order" to these nine words, and they are equal partners in visual power and in their ability to anchor visual impact.

One of them, however, namely (again) content, is the most frequent source of visual experience. It is the most common lesson of light. In fact, content (unfortunately) dominates what we see hundreds of times more often *than all the others combined.*

Nevertheless, though it's more common, content is no more powerful than any of her eight sisters.

The only hard part of "Help Yourself to a Blue Banana" is to become familiar with these words. If you're like most people, before you can visually identify and explore these ideas, you will need to review them many times in your mind's eye.

You'll have to memorize this list.

You may find it easy to remember the first letters.

When they're all written together, they make the interesting word DFACCCTSS. Then, if you eliminate the repeating letters, this becomes DFACTS. It may help to think of it like this: $DFAC^3TS^2$.

Write this memory guide below, in the spaces provided.

This will help you to remember these nine words, and make better use of the material that follows:

Write the memory guide here: ____ ____ ____ ____--- ____ ____--

In many ways, these ideas can each be studied separately (and some often are). But while reading about all nine together, you will also learn them as a system. As you read, you'll learn each is always present in *everything you see*. And you will learn how to understand them together, and perhaps express with them together.

Even if you are a non-artist, only now intrigued by the idea of visual living, you'll learn the basics of visual understanding.

You'll learn the basic things all visual artists know whatever their interests, their profession or individual means of expression. Even if you're just a beginner, a curious bystander to art and design, you'll at least and at last begin to know the secrets artists know.

The one, two, three rule

When the sun is out, or the lights are on, visual information is available to our eyes.

When that information arrives in our eyes it is analyzed by our mind. During that process we evaluate it in nine separate ways. These are the nine lessons of light. It might help to think of them as the nine visual "parts of speech." Our initial reaction to everything we see (including our initial emotional response) is often triggered by just one of these parts; sometimes by two of them, and generally speaking by, at the most, only three of them. The remaining parts of everything we notice are usually neutral.

This is a basic principle of the system you are reading about. And, as you will see later, this helps explain why so much of the visual information passing before us is simply ignored.

You could call this the one, two, three rule.

It's important so it's repeated here:

The one, two, three rule:

Our reaction to everything we notice (including our
our emotional response) is often triggered by one of
the lessons of light; sometimes by two of them, and
generally speaking, at most, by only three of them.

The lessons of light are equal in their visual power, but that is where their similarity ends. That's one reason writing about them and speaking about them is difficult. Trying to find common ground among these nine ideas is hard to do. However, that should not be a problem. If I'm right, you'll need to gain the written understanding of these ideas only once or twice before their visual characteristics begin to become attractive to you. At that point, looking for and experiencing the lessons of light becomes fun.

Once that happens the written details here, I promise you, are boring in comparison.

But knowing at least the names of these concepts is necessary for anyone interested in visual living. How else can we finally sort out what we are talking about?

About reading this book

To help you to understand these nine concepts as a system, their names will always appear here in CAPITAL LETTERS. This way, you will recognize that any of these words may have a slightly different meaning than one you are familiar with. While learning the lessons of light, it is important to become familiar with each of these ideas as it is described in this book.

In addition, some chapters include more details than others. If a lesson of light can be explained more easily by dividing it up, these smaller ideas are also included. They're called "conditions." For example, shadow plays a role in our ability to see DEPTH. So, in chapter one, shadow is described as a condition of DEPTH.

Most of the lessons of light have conditions.

Every chapter starts with something called "Dialog," a section that describes visual ideas using simple words and situations from real life. "Dialog" will help you think about the visual language and about visual living in uncomplicated everyday English.

The dialogs are fun to read, especially if you never thought about art or design before picking up this book.

Each lesson of light takes up a chapter.

Although some of their names are probably familiar to you, there are two reasons you must read about each one.

First, because this is a system, you will need to know all the information in each chapter. Second, and again, describing the visual language in words is often difficult. But the impact of reading *all* the words in this book will be greater than just looking at individual chapters. If you read carefully, you'll discover that the total here is much (much) greater than the parts.

This book is a "translation" of the visual language into written language and into spoken language. It's a unified theory, or a Rosetta Stone of sorts. And it's a databased version of evaluating visual experience. It puts these languages (the written, the spoken and the visual) into a simple, understandable relationship.

In addition, you probably won't find words here you don't already understand. On purpose, I have used the easiest words possible to describe the lessons of light. You'll understand this book no matter how limited your vocabulary, and probably even if you speak English as a second language. Instead of wondering what the words mean, you can focus on the ideas behind the words.

Investing in your visual talents

To help you understand this system:

Before you continue to read you should locate some blank paper and a pencil. From time to time you'll want to visualize some ideas. Even if you can not draw (and I assume you can't), here and there your understanding will increase if you organize what your mind's eye sees with a simple sketch.

Get some plain paper and a pencil now, before you continue to read. If you are reading a hard copy of "Help Yourself to a Blue Banana," you'll also need a handful of cards or post-it notes to use as bookmarks. Also, feel free to write or sketch on the blank pages that appear between some chapters, starting on page 22.

Think of this book as a workbook.

Second, figure out how to highlight anything important.

(On your computer screen, you can change the color of important words or text, or underline them. If you are reading a regular paper book, then a highlighting marker is what you'll need.) This way, "Help Yourself to a Blue Banana" can be easily reviewed at a later date by glancing at the highlighted parts.

Third, plan to make some changes in the way you think as you read each page. Make room for nine new ideas in your "mind's eye." CLEAR OUT SPACE IN YOUR MENTAL GUEST ROOMS for nine important *and permanent* new guests.

Get ready to start thinking about what you see.

Lastly, expect to learn something! Expect to be able to think visually by the last chapter. In addition to exploring visual living, you can learn here to understand the basic concepts behind all the visual arts, including painting, graphic design, architecture, interior design, sculpture, fashion design, art direction, stage and set design, photography, illustration, and even "industrial arts" such as package design and product design. What about applying makeup? or throwing clay? styling hair? blowing glass? dressing windows? chopping rods? designing hawgs? tooling jewelry? sketching at criminal trials? staining windows? or manipulating images on your computer? Just keep reading. There are lessons here that apply to all visual activities. That may sound like a lot of material, but finding out how artists express in these situations may be less difficult than you imagine. Quite possibly, it's easier than you think.

On the other hand, you must take this book seriously. You'll need to think about what you are reading, and question some of it. You'll find that something that relates to every lesson of light exists practically everywhere. It doesn't matter where you are: your house, a friend's office, inside an airplane or on the backseat of a bus. Just look around and you will discover examples of the lessons you will read about.

From time to time, look up and become curious about what you see. To say it once again, a nice thing about "Help Yourself to a Blue Banana" is that the examples are *your* examples. You'll find them all by yourself.

If you are serious about learning, by now you should have blank paper and bookmarks handy, and you should have by now highlighted the first sentence of the last seven paragraphs (they're all very important).

Ok. I suspect you *didn't* highlight those sentences.

But summarizing information is very important.

So in order to show you how helpful this habit can be, here are those seven sentences again, repeated for your convenience at the top of the next page:

Go back and highlight these points (these are
the first sentences of the last several paragraphs:

1. Before you continue to read you should
   get some blank paper and a pencil.
2. Figure out a way to highlight anything important.
3. Plan to make some changes in the way you
   think as you read each page.
4. Get ready to start thinking about what you see.
5. Expect to learn something!
6. You must take this book seriously.
7. From time to time, look up and become curious
   about what you see at that moment.

Also, return to the "main course" statement (page 26), and the
one, two, three rule (page 31), and highlight them also. If you're
ready to learn, do these things before you continue to read.

Once you have marked important information, get ready to
review it. Give yourself time to practice having "visual experiences"
according to the lessons you will read about. Look around, explore
everything that you see, and study the material here until noticing
and *remembering* what your eyes discover becomes a habit.

Artists (and writers) have a special power

Everyone understands a little bit about writing, so, for just a
moment, let's compare artists to writers. Writers know how to use
words and language to create moods and emotional responses in
readers. Writers can make you feel happy, scared, stupid or angry.
It's a power that words have on people who read them. In the same
way, anyone whose eyesight is normal makes emotional judgments
about what they see. This book will show you how art and design
make people feel those same emotions, and thousands more.

It will teach you about the nine tools we rely on to create those
emotional responses in people.

These are visual tools of both fine artists and business artists
(who help business people make money). And for non-artists, the
nine lessons of light are the secrets to uncovering visual expression
and enjoyment. The secrets to visual living.

The information within this book can lead you to the habit of
"seeing" instead of "looking." Experiencing your sense of vision

rather than simply accepting it. After that habit is formed, you will probably want to put away the written lessons here, as you once put away the training wheels on your first bike. As soon as you understand the lessons of light, it's time to stop reading; instead it's time to start seeing, to be free, to *start living visually.*

I have been thinking about how we experience our vision for about twenty-five satisfying years. The result is the information written here. My wish is that the pleasure I have found as a visual artist and teacher of design comes through and, most of all, that you also find the inspiration to appreciate your eyes more creatively by reading these pages.

Welcome to "Help Yourself to a Blue Banana!"

Introduction PART TWO

FRAMES OF REFERENCE

The lessons of light are tools visually active people use to understand what they see, and to express what they feel. But there is one additional idea we need to also talk about briefly. It is not a source of visual experience (it's not a lesson of light), but it plays a big part in helping our eyes decide what to look at. What I am referring to is "frame of reference." Frame of reference is a part of visual perception that acts like a stage which catches our eyes' attention.

It's not a conscious process, but every time we look at something, our attention focuses on only a small part of the total field of view that presents itself to our eyes. That is to say, people almost never notice *everything* that appears in front of them.

Instead, our mind decides which area of a scene is "active."

It could be a poster on a wall at the other side of a room, a teddy bear sprawled on a nearby shelf or a box of cereal as you read the list of ingredients. But whatever it is, once your mind decides to notice something, it puts this in the center of your vision. From that moment on, you ignore less exciting things that are *outside this area.*

Instead, your full attention turns to this one spot.

This point of interest, this special area of information, is the "frame of reference" of what we see.

(Let me remind you to highlight this.)

A frame of reference can sometimes fill 100% of our field of view, for example, as it does when we look out at miles of country-side from the top of a hill. But that is rare. Instead, in our daily life, a typical frame of reference is more likely a much smaller part of a scene, like a clock on a wall, or a postcard as we hold it in our hand to read it. Or, in fact, it can become much smaller still. This special area of interest can be as small as perhaps one/500th of our field of vision (a tiny, tiny area) when we are, for example, threading a needle. Every day, all day long, our mind decides to notice some frames of reference, while billions of other ones, less interesting to the eye, *go completely unnoticed.*

Try this. You'll see what I mean if you stare closely at the point of a pencil. At the same time, allow yourself to become conscious of the "unused" area of your field of vision. This will include every-thing your eyes see at the same time they see the pencil point. Notice that once you have decided to focus on the pencil point, you automatically ignore everything else. Try this experiment now with a pencil point or a pen point before you continue reading.

Frames of reference are important because they are what we notice *first* about things. When our eye is attracted to something, that "something" is interesting first from the "corner of our eye," and then becomes more and more engaging when we turn our full atten-tion to it, by moving our head and eyes, or even our entire body.

We might even say visual artists (graphic designers, architects, illustrators, sculptors or photographers for examples) are concerned with how our eye reacts to a scene *before* we focus on it. Causing people to look at something (whether it's serious visual expression or, say, just the cover of a magazine) requires attracting people's attention away from everything else, and focusing it instead to a frame of reference you have created.

Whether frames of reference are giant or tiny, they are an important part of our sense of vision. Nothing can be visually at its strongest until either Mother Nature or a visually talented person tailors its frame of reference to the information being presented.

Some descriptions of frames of reference

Let's define some frames of reference.

Throughout this book, we will be concerned with how things look in two dimensions (like a design for the cover of a high school yearbook) and also about how things look in three dimensions (like a hat design or a dozen roses). So for that reason, some information needs to be said twice.

For example, SPACE in two dimensions is different in some ways from SPACE in three dimensions. And likewise, there are two types of frames of reference: two dimensional frames of reference and three dimensional frames of reference.

Beyond yearbook covers, two dimensional frames of reference also include things like a painting hanging in a museum, a "for rent" sign in a window, your computer screen, the front cover of a shoe catalog, a banner ad on a web site, a billboard along a highway, or a page in your local newspaper. All of these things have an easily seen boundary, or frame, or "edge," telling us where their frame of reference starts and stops. We can usually see the entire edge of a two dimensional frame of reference at a single glance. For example, the "edge" of the frame of reference of a newspaper page is the actual edge of the paper itself. Understanding where the edges of a two dimensional frame of reference fall is usually very easy. Generally speaking the edge of any two dimensional frame of reference will be the edge of the thing itself.

You can begin now to look at your environment for examples. Wherever you are, take a moment to look around. There are probably dozens of two dimensional frames of reference near you at this very moment. See if you can find one. Look for an example of something that has an easily seen edge where your visual interest comes to an end. Then make a note of it here:

A two dimensional frame of reference: _____

Three dimensional frames of reference

As a rule, three dimensional frames of reference also have physical boundaries, but they may *not* be completely visible all at one time. Three dimensional frames of reference are, rather, nearly always three dimensional FORMS. For example, a statue of a horse has a frame of reference which is the FORM of the horse itself. No matter where you are standing, part of the frame of reference (for example, the other side of the horse) is hidden from your view.

Other three dimensional frames of reference may be a tea cup, or the complete set of dishes it belongs to; a building, a tree, an electric hair dryer, a rabbit or an automobile. Three dimensional frames of reference also include such things as a wedding dress in a store window, or even the entire window display itself, or the inside of an apartment. A hard copy of this book has a front cover that is a two dimensional frame of reference. But the entire book is a three dimensional frame of reference. Take a moment now to see if you can identify a three dimensional frame of reference nearby.

A three dimensional frame of reference: _____

Choosing frames of reference

The influence that frames of reference have on the way we perceive the world is almost limitless.

Frames of reference are sort of like compartments we call on to store temporary bundles of visual information. Once we're done thinking about one bundle, we usually ditch our interest in it, ending our experience with that frame of reference, and move on to the next one. Whatever catches our eye fits in its own frame of reference only as long as we are visually engaged with it.

Sometimes we may accept a frame of reference for only an instant, before revising our decision (perhaps unconsciously) so we can select another frame of reference to concentrate on, still within the same field of view. That change of decision could be compared to holding up *two* pencil points side by side, then deciding which one to stare at.

A day of shopping might provide another example. Walking by a store window, a person may be attracted to the entire window display of out of the corner of her eye. But, turning to see it, she may then decide to refocus interest on a single suit of clothing in the window, and then perhaps *again* (instantly) to a detail of a belt buckle.

In other words, someone's attention can be attracted first to a store window, then to the clothing in it, and then to a buckle by three separate frames of reference. This is an example of how a window designer may work to control our interest in the merchandise displayed, but the ability to effectively manage frames of reference is a talent called upon (usually unconsciously) by anyone who is working successfully with the visual language.

Frames of reference can exist one within the other (like a belt buckle exists "within" a suit of clothes) or they can exist side by side (like six playing cards side by side on a poker table, or two pencil points seen side by side as we examine them). Each of these possibilities suggests a frame of reference that fits well within our eyes' ability to see it (or them) all at once.

But other frames of reference are too big to be seen entirely at a single glance. Scenes like that are rare, but they are sometimes the most dazzling. Looking straight up from a hilltop toward a clear, star-filled evening sky is an example. That is to say, if you stand high on a hill and look up, the sky is just *too big* to see all at once.

As a rule, we are unconscious of a frame of reference, just as we are normally unconscious of the lessons of light. Although that's true, our interest in what we see usually ends at the edges of a frame of reference, no matter whether it's two dimensional or three dimensional. In either case, these edges, the boundaries of a frame of reference, are defined by one (or more) *conditions*.

These conditions inform our eyes that it's ok to restrict their attention to an area smaller than our entire field of view.

The four conditions of frame of reference are:

> Focus
> Light
> Preconception
> Intention

Here's some examples of each

Most naturally occurring frames of reference attract our eye by relying on the first three of these conditions. The fourth condition happens when one or more of the first three is adjusted, at times by an artist, in order to control the arena or "stage" for a "handmade" visual experience.

Focus: Frames of reference created by the focus of our eyes exist because we can't bring into clear focus all at once the entire DEPTH of field of our vision. Human eyes just can't put everything into focus at once from in front of our nose to the distant, far away horizon. That means, wherever you are looking, there will always be something out of focus.

If you have normal eyesight, you can prove this by holding up your left index finger at an arm's length in front of you. Point your finger into the air as if you are ordering one Coca-Cola from a waiter across the room. At the same time, hold the index finger of your right hand in a similar position, but only halfway between your eyes and your first raised finger. Be sure the wall you are facing is at least twelve feet (4 meters) away and the room is brightly lit. Then close one eye and focus your other eye on the tip of your up-pointed left index finger (your finger that's ordering a Coke).

OK, while still focused on your left finger, and without moving your eye, allow yourself to notice your right index finger (closer to you). If you are holding your fingers in the proper positions, your right finger will appear out of focus (fuzzy).

Now, again without changing focus from your left finger, and without moving your eye, notice something, some detail, on the wall at a distance in front of you, *beyond* your left finger. Again, if you are doing this correctly, everything on the wall (bookshelves or pictures or whatever) will be out of focus.

Now, without moving your eye or your fingers, and without changing your focus, see how clear the image of your left index finger seems in comparison to everything else that falls in your field of view, both in front of it and beyond. In this experiment, the clearly focused FORM of your left index finger creates the frame of reference of what you see, i.e. your left index finger. It's a frame of reference determined by focus, the first condition of frame of reference.

People tend to automatically ignore things that aren't clearly focused. We will concentrate on a frame of reference sometimes because we just can't focus on everything at once, even if we want to. One power of the nine lessons of light is their ability to catch the attention of our eye (causing a visual experience), which leads us to turn our eyes and to *focus* on that area of interest.

Light: Frames of reference that are created by light occur when our eyes are attracted to the lightest area within the field of view.

Where there is no light, there is no seeing. Light makes seeing possible by illuminating all the physical characteristics of the world. Light teaches us what our world looks like, so our attention naturally moves toward the concentrated light of a theater stage, a TV or movie screen, or a computer monitor. Our eyes look toward the most well lit area of a room or landscape.

And similarly, we can make *ourselves* a stronger frame of reference by wearing light-COLORED clothing when riding a bicycle at night, or *bright*-COLORED clothing when dancing in a club or performing on a stage.

Preconception: People store some frames of reference permanently in their mind's eye. These frames of reference are so familiar we can imagine them before they appear before us in reality. Then, if what we see does not match up with our remembered (that is to say, our "preconceived") frame of reference, our eyes will resist looking at it. There is a sense of "wrongness" we feel when our eye comes across any clash between judgment and reality such as this.

A case in point: package designers know everyone has preconceived ideas about how everyday packages should look. Things like milk cartons and soft drink cans are so standard that changing their shape may bother some shoppers. The FORMS of these packages, like our outstretched index finger, are their frames of reference.

That means, usually, business artists try to make them look like everyone's preconceived idea of how they should look. For a milk carton, a designer will usually accept the familiar wax-covered cardboard package with a pointed-top, and only change its COLORS, SCALE and SPACES. If it's whole milk, the primary COLOR on the package will most likely be red, because that's everyone's preconceived and widely accepted idea of the appropriate COLOR to represent whole milk. Light blue means it's reduced milk. (There's much more about appropriate COLOR in chapter four.)

Years ago, when a food company attempted to redesign old-fashioned narrow-top ketchup bottles, the idea was met with some consumer resistance. The new design had a wider opening so that a spoon could be used to get into the bottle, but some people would not accept it. The preconceived frame of reference for the old bottle was so strong that a new design just didn't seem "right."

Realizing this kind of buyer resistance was a frequent issue, Raymond Loewy, a design pioneer of the last century, suggested that the most successful product designs are always *MAYA*, meaning "the most advanced, yet acceptable."

Even when a new package's frame of reference *doesn't* change, designing new graphics for it is still not easy. A photograph or illustration of an orange on one side of an orange juice carton does not fill its frame of reference, which is the entire surface of the carton on all four sides, as well as the familiar pointed top.

Like a statue of a horse in a park, part of the three dimensional frame of reference of an orange juice carton is always hidden from our view. But because an orange juice carton is so familiar, as are many objects in daily life, we store a strong "feeling" for its entire frame of reference in our mind's eye. Neglecting to design the *entire surface* of a three dimensional frame of reference is often a mistake made by inexperienced graphic designers.

Now, consider this commonplace, widespread, and widely preconceived frame of reference: I am referring to the round face of an ordinary clock. If you don't think you have a strong idea of how a clock face should look, try this: Find one with big numbers and hold it up to a mirror. In the reflection, you will be surprised at how *poorly designed* and unbalanced the numbers will look when seen backwards, that is, when they are reversed from their normal, comfortable and *preconceived* frame of reference. Do this before you continue to read. (Find a clock and look at it in a mirror.)

Not all unusual frames of reference are bad and, in fact, people often do like common frames of reference that have been recreated in fresh and imaginative ways. Consider what happens when exciting changes are applied to the human body, a visual process that occurs every year throughout the fashion industry.

But be careful. Fashion designers know the human FORM is the *most* preconceived three dimensional frame of reference there is *now,* or *ever will be* (more on this later). So for that reason, fashion designers must be careful. They know most people, especially people who are living visually, just don't like fashions that ignore how human beings expect to look.

Fashions do change, but the changes are gradual, and there are lots of stories about new fashion looks that failed because they went way too far, way too fast. Furthermore, fashion styles eventually come back because, and make no mistake, people always want to look the way they think people *should* look.

Intention: Sometimes a new product, or some other original visual message, doesn't have a suitable preconceived frame of reference, or *any* existing frame of reference. An artist may decide that a common square or rectangular canvas is not right for an oil painting he's planning to create. And designers of new products need to decide how the new product is going to look.

When that is an issue, the only solution is to create a frame of reference "from scratch." The result is a frame of reference created by intention.

The design of music players, cell phones, personal computers and other electronic items are repeatedly subjected to this. Does the best design for a new computer combine the keyboard, processor and monitor together? Or should they be separate components? Should the keyboard and monitor be combined together, leaving the processor freestanding all by itself? One trend was to combine the monitor and processor together.[1] The keyboard was still separate.

And, of course, laptop computers combine all three.

Once there was a debate: Should personal computers be big, so they seem impressive (and valuable), or tiny so they fit in a pocket? Especially with early computers, most of us were simply stunned the first time we saw inside a processor cabinet. The inside of the original desktop systems was practically empty. But their outsides looked big, impressive *and expensive*, which was the whole idea.

Technology continues to create these questions by allowing just about anything to be possible. But imagine how surprised you'd be to go buy a car and have the salesperson ask which kind of passenger compartment you wanted, which outside body you preferred and which four-wheel engine assembly you'd like to buy.

That would be a surprise because we all have a strong feeling about the permanent frame of reference of a car, but none (so far) for personal computers.

For a long time, stereo equipment went through this evolution. Years ago, everyone agreed the parts of a music system should fit inside one unit. But no one was sure. I once had a stereo set that stacked in two pieces, but it was designed to look like *four separate components*. Now all popular music systems fit in your palm. I suspect that soon the size issue for personal electronics will disappear, because music will be sent by wireless signal, picked up by receivers that are inside our ears, or under our skin.

The process of creating intentional frames of reference can be as simple as changing the size or shape of a shopping bag so it fits the graphic design a department store wants to print on it, or as complicated as manufacturing a one-of-a-kind monitor for a very wide-angle multimedia show.

Whatever they are, when frames of reference are designed intentionally, they can give impact to visual expression that is nearly as strong as the lessons of light themselves (usually as FORM).

Working with frames of reference, artists can control visual experience from its beginning (when someone notices it, usually out of the corner of the eye) to its conclusion (when the viewer reacts to the lessons of light that appear within it).

It's a process that can take less than a single second.

The world is a stage

The words used here to describe frame of reference will fade from importance as you become familiar with the concept behind them. That is, everything we notice has a sort of "stage" on which it first appears. Anyone who explores visual expression can control not only that stage, but also the actors upon it.

The following chapters will introduce you to those actors: the nine lessons of light.

* * * *

Review: Before you continue to read, remember the nine lessons of light. Refer back to pages 29-30 for help. First, write the reminder:

___ ___ ___ ___--- ___ ___--

Then write the list:

_____

_____

_____

_____

_____

_____

_____

_____

Now let's look at the first lesson of light.

Chapter One

DEPTH as a source of visual experience

*Read the preface, foreword and introduction before starting
this chapter. The beginning of each chapter is called "dialog,"
and it discusses visual expression. After the dialog, each chapter
focuses on one lesson of light, which in this chapter is DEPTH.*

Dialog

AT SOMETIME OR ANOTHER, each of us comes across art we don't understand.

It may have happened to you only once or twice, or it may occur every time you visit a museum, art gallery or print store. If you live in a city, you may have seen a sculpture in a public park that seemed strange to you. Or you might wonder why a magazine or newspaper devotes several pages to an article and photographs of an artist's life work that is, in your opinion, *meaningless.*

No matter how often this has happened to you, you can be sure there are millions of other people who feel the same way.

And there are two good reasons why.

The first reason is that visual expression speaks a language most people don't understand. Look at it this way: It wouldn't be unusual for someone to pick up a book that's written in Latin and not understand it. In a similar way, if you don't know the artist's language, you won't understand most of the art you see. And almost certainly you'll never understand art the way the artist intends for you to understand it. (*If* he or she intends for you to understand it, which isn't always the case)

On the other hand, maybe there's a very smart, well-educated person who picks up a book written in Latin and *can actually read it.* Likewise, you yourself might really (already) have some understanding of the visual language. But even if that's true, there's still a second reason you may discover things in print stores, parks or museums that seem ridiculous, meaningless or awful.

The reason is simple:

Some art *is* ridiculous, meaningless and awful.

Sometimes when art offends us, or it bores us, and I am even talking here about art that we don't "understand," the reason is not complicated. It may be that the "artist" himself or herself is either not experienced in the visual language, or is not using it in a meaningful way. Visually sensitive people, including every kind of artist, as well as print stores, parks and even museums (sometimes) make mistakes. So, just because a design or work of art is in a famous place, doesn't always mean it's meaningful, or even good.

The reverse can be true also. Suppose some original art, like maybe it's a pencil drawing of somebody's girlfriend made by a 10th grade student somewhere in public high school, is hidden away or even lost in a crummy place. Imagine for example it's misplaced on a shelf in the back of an unused classroom. That doesn't mean it's bad art. In fact, it might be fabulous art, even valuable. After reading this book, you'll understand how that's possible.

And, more importantly, *you'll be the judge.*

Everyone is entitled to an opinion about art and design.

And it's just as logical to announce that everyone is entitled to their opinion of Latin. But if that's true, imagine this situation: What if someone is offended by some Latin words carved in stone on the front of a library. It would seem strange, wouldn't it, to find out the person doesn't even *know* Latin. The same is true about visual expression. You are entitled to your opinion of it, but before you can expect anyone to value your opinion, or even listen to your opinion, you'll need to learn about the language visually expressive people are using, defined by the nine lessons of light.

How do we use our eyes?

How do we use our eyes and what do people do with their eyesight? That sounds like a simple question, but it's important.

If you're fortunate enough to have no disabilities, you are no doubt aware we each have five built-in systems for perceiving the world: seeing, hearing, touching, tasting and smelling. For the most part, these five systems work separately, supplying information our mind can use to make decisions, and to help us enjoy our lives.

Each of our senses analyzes the world in thousands of ways that assist us in living and working. But one of these senses is much more valuable than the others. That's our ability to see, which we use maybe 100 times more frequently than all the others combined.

Perhaps 1000 times more.

That's one reason why, everywhere in the world, people give special attention to anyone who has the talent to use their eyes creatively. People have always admired someone with visual understanding, a skill recognized as one of the most special abilities. The names of history's greatest architects and painters and sculptors are known to many school children, and their influence is still an inspiration for lots of the visual expression that fills our lives today.

That makes it seem strange, doesn't it, that many people go through life with little thought about how sight actually works, even though it's knowledge that's highly respected. For example, it allows an artist to pick COLOR that can dramatically change the emotional impact of a dress, a mural, a package design or the interior of a church. Or, for another example, a knowledge of the visual language may help an architect create one SPACE where we feel like sitting down to relax, or another SPACE in which dancing seems like an excellent idea.

Although these visual talents aren't widely understood, they are nevertheless used every day by a staggering number of people, including thousands of fine artists (such as sculptors and painters) and perhaps millions of business artists (including photographers, art directors,* fashion designers, architects, set and interior designers, illustrators and communication designers).

People are hired and fired, business is won and lost, and fortunes are made and broken, all depending on the success or failure of understanding, or misunderstanding, visual information.

But what's the basis for all this activity? What is the basis for all this judging of right and wrong, visually speaking, making one oil painting, for example, worth a fortune, while another one is worth less than the art supplies someone used to make it? Also, what sorts of things happen to someone who has a more creative approach to using their eyes? On an everyday level, how can people use eyesight for something more creative, and more fun, than trimming their toenails or searching for car keys?

---

*Art directors don't work in museums. In the business world, all of the photographs, layout files, drawings, logos and typography, etc. used in marketing and advertising are collectively referred to as "art." If you're a business artist in charge of all this material, then you're an "art director."

To help us answer these questions, we'll describe the grass roots information understood by everyone who has visual curiosity. That includes everyone from weekend sketchers to top architects, from someone who does woodworking part-time to the rich and radical fashion designers of Seventh Avenue in New York City, from the hippest pop artists, to the fun loving free souls who create all those 3D sidewalk chalk images, from neighborhood florists, to the artists who conceive the stunning computer images, graphics and printed communications that help drive any thriving economy.

As this search unfolds, it will help you imagine how the impact of living visually can become a valued part of your own life. It's a lifestyle of emotional feeling shared by all these visually active people, and by millions of other non-artists who also use their eyesight for enjoying, that is for really exploring, the surprising visual excitement that is all around us everywhere.

These things are not really mysterious

One first impression that people sometimes have about visual expression, in general, is a sense of mystery. Carried to an extreme, you may be a person who thinks some of what artists do is a kind of magic. The magic I am talking about is separate from the overall emotional impact that art and design can have on us. What I mean is, many people don't have a clue even about the *very basics* of creating or recreating the images or objects of art and design.

For example, I made a drawing once when I was young. It was a picture of a girl and not very good. But a friend said, "how do you know how to do that?" I could barely draw, and the picture was not art. But that didn't matter. My friend was impressed that the girl had two arms, two legs and a head, all in relatively the right place.

Of course, getting that part of a drawing right is not much to brag about. But this illustrates how there are simple parts of understanding and creating visual expression, like getting the shape of a girl correct, that can seem difficult or even mysterious to non-artists. Generally speaking, for anyone who is living visually, these basics are important to know about, even if you are just beginning to be curious about visual expression. So, for just a moment, we're going to talk here about some *very* basic things.

When I suggested above that the picture I drew wasn't art, it seems to imply that the problem centered on my drawing skill. But that idea is too simple to explain anything. It's too simple to actually be meaningful about how the visual language works. The reason is: some people, including many experienced artists, do not allow *any* "inabilities," including poor drawing skills, to discourage their desire to speak to the world through visual expression. The urge to create can be that strong. That is to say, it's ok to allow inability to be a part of the process, and part of the outcome, of art.

In fact, this is not an exaggeration: some artists count on it, and even expect, that their artistic *inability* will be a very, very big and successful part of their work.

The truth is, it's possible to argue that some art *is* visually expressive mostly because it honestly springs from someone's emotions, regardless of technical skill. (In chapter five, in exactly this way, we'll see how events in China once brought to life a priceless visual icon.) That "someone" who accomplishes this may be simply flexing his or her visual muscles for the very first time.

In the world of visual expression, believing that you can't do something is at times surprisingly irrelevant. This is often proved by the simple realization that, despite your doubts, *you have actually done it anyway*. That's a satisfying reward of creating with the visual language. Your eyes may often see that something your hands did not believe they could do has already been accomplished.

Sometimes, drawing skill just isn't important

I am telling you that, so I can tell you this (which, after years of hearing otherwise, you may find difficult to believe): *Even people who can't draw can make art and design*, even *great* art and design. Even *valuable* art and design. People who "can't draw" can still create extraordinary visual expression. That's why we can't say someone, i.e., me and my poor drawing of a girl (see above) isn't visually talented just because their drawing skill doesn't seem developed.

In fact, some successful and experienced (and rich) oil and acrylic artists have a picture painting style that actually reflects an under-developed ability to draw.[2] You might even suggest they *can't* draw. But what they lack in drawing skill, they make up up for with expression (or determination, or passion, or spirit, or emotion, or even anger or rage). When you see their paintings, you might think, "I could do that!" And if you think that, then you probably can.

For whatever reason you're reading "Help Yourself to a Blue Banana," don't let anything prevent you from expressing yourself visually, in whatever way seems appropriate. That expression might begin in the unique appearance of your handwriting or signature, or in the style of your clothes, or in your selection of posters to put on a wall, or in the manner you arrange candles on a tray, or how you retouch computer files for your own personal web page. It might be found in the way you make yard sale signs, or layout a scrapbook, or fold napkins, or display model cars, or set up holiday decorations, or wrap gifts (which is where many young artists first express themselves), or in the beauty you'll bring to life by sending a handmade birthday card to your secret flame.

Each of these beginnings may foretell your aptitude to tap into the satisfying lifestyle of visual living, or even your ability to understand or even to create more significant art and design. The process may happen to you with or without any organized study of art or design in classes or textbooks. And contrary to what many people believe, the process may happen *without studying drawing*.

I put it like that because, again, many people, and especially beginners, think that not knowing how to draw is a more serious obstacle to visual expression than it is. I recommend drawing classes or even art school for anyone serious about art and design. But you don't need drawing skills to learn the lessons of light, and lots of artists progress just fine without them, thank you very much.

More important is learning how to understand the information that is presented to your eyes by the world around you. And then using that understanding to create visual expression.

For that reason, discussing drawing skills, or a lack of them, is only a very, very small part of "Help Yourself to a Blue Banana." Instead, we'll talk primarily about recognizing, understanding and creating visual meaning.

The surprising thing is this: Very few working visual artists actually rely on good drawing skills (and some of us have almost no drawing skills). Photographers, for example, rarely begin their work by drawing a sketch of what they hope to capture on film or flash card. And sculptors may begin their struggle with stone, steel or clay without first attempting to draw the FORM that's inspiring the effort (more likely, they'll make a smaller study in clay).

And for another example, a young person I know has immature drawing skills. But she still crafts wonderfully artistic miniature sculptures of human figures and vases and bowls. In fact, in high school, she won a district sculpture contest. She was the youngest of 300 artists in the show! Her drawing skills were not an issue.

To this day, she says flatly, "I can't draw."

There are opposite examples of this as well.

There are individuals who have excellent drawing skills, but lack sensitivity to other areas of visual expression. Someone may be able to make beautiful and realistic black and white pencil portraits of their friends and family, but not have the COLOR skills required to design a successful cereal package, or the familiarity with FORM to produce moving sculpture, or the feeling for SPACE and SCALE that an architect needs to carry out the work of designing successful buildings, parks or cities.

My point is, again, drawing is only a very small part of the visual language and the visual lifestyle.

Beyond that, when drawing skills *are* genuinely called for, professional artists including set designers, advertising art directors, interior designers, graphic designers, landscape designers, fashion designers, and architects generally rely on *other* artists (called illustrators, comp artists, or renderers) to create the final pictures used in their work. All of these talented people understand the visual language, but only a small number of them have drawing skills.

In fact, there is a man like this who actually creates paintings for galleries, museums and collectors. He signs them with his own name, *but he doesn't paint them*. He knows the nine lessons of light, but he doesn't draw or paint them himself. Instead, he supervises a group of artists in his studio. They all paint pictures that he has suggested to them. If he likes their result, he signs the canvas with *his* name, and these pictures sell for lots and lots of money. His assistants don't get any credit on these paintings (they are paid by the hour for their time and effort).

I don't know for sure, and perhaps at some level this artist can draw quite well, but in his professional life he often simply evaluates the nine lessons of light in the paintings his workers show him. When he likes a picture, he signs his name in the corner, packs it up, ships it out, and deposits that big check in the bank.

By the way, this isn't dishonest. Everyone knows he does it this way, including the people who buy and collect "his" art.[3]

Here are two more examples:

Another rich, successful pop artist was known for modifying existing photographs of famous people, and recreating them as oils or silkscreens on canvas. He didn't actually draw them, and for that matter, he didn't even take the photos that inspired "his" paintings.

But he knew the nine lessons of light – *cold*.

(As you can imagine, there are lawsuits about his work.)[4]

And last night on TV, there was a program that profiled one of the best motorcycle designers. When asked how he got started on a new bike he essentially said, "I'm not much of a drawer, so I just go at it with my torch and tools." Instead of drawing, like many true sculptors, he basically creates amazing three-dimensional FORM by simply bending, cutting and welding steel.[5]

On top of that, almost all business art these days is made by maneuvering with a computer mouse, or manipulating and changing images that are already in a computer. These talents still require a mastery of the nine lessons of light. But for most artists, our old fashioned pencils, charcoal and paint brushes (as well as erasers, smudgers and COLOR pallets) are now merely icons on a computer screen, not tools on a nearby drawing table, as they once were.

In the world of business, perhaps only 10% of the artists and designers who earn a living would say drawing is their most important skill. Furthermore, those artists who do draw on a regular basis usually draw things that *another* artist (who is often the "boss" and earns more money than they do) has designed or imagined. Every art professional needs an understanding of the nine lessons of light. But relatively few high paying business artist jobs actually require someone to draw images on a regular basis.

So where am I going with this? Just glance at the following imaginary quiz, in which I interview myself, to see my point. This is a summary about why you should be glad you're reading "Help Yourself to a Blue Banana" and not a book called "How to Draw:"

Pop (art) quiz:

Q. Michael, Do most working artists draw very much?
A. No, actually we don't usually draw very much
   while we're on the job.
Q. But, by comparison, do most working artists
   frequently need to evaluate CONTENT?
A. Do we ever! Absolutely.
   (For example, when choosing the CONTENT for the
   images to be used in an advertisement; or the CONTENT
   of the paintings or prints to display in a trendy restaurant;
   or even what the CONTENT should be for a new tattoo.
   This is *important*, it's imagery your customers must
   feel positive about for *the rest of their life*.)

Q. Do most working artists very often
   need to pick COLORS?
A. Well, you'd have to say the correct answer is *constantly*.
   (For example when specifying the COLORS for a new
   toaster design, or for a new automobile body; or the
   COLORS for a new brand of carpets or sheets or shoes;
   or the COLOR to use as the background for a web page;
   or COLORS for a new corporate identity program;
   or for the label of a newly shaped ketchup bottle.)
Q. Michael, do most working artists sometimes
   have to select TEXTURES?
A. Yes we do! You can be sure of it.
   (For example when deciding what's the best TEXTURE
   to use behind the product in a catalog photograph, should
   it be burlap or terry cloth? Or the surface TEXTURE to
   incorporate into the design for a ceramic vase.)
Q. OK, what about beyond that?
   What about the other lessons of light?
   Do most working artists regularly adjust SCALE?
   Tweak FORM?
   Modify SPACE?
   Make DEPTH more dramatic?
A. Yes, Yes, Yes and Yes.
   But draw pictures? No. No we don't.
   Not very often.

90% of feeling it

These above paragraphs refer to people who are working as
artists. But for individuals who simply want to live their life visually, with no concern for creating visual expression (this might be you
at this moment), of course that lifestyle also doesn't require drawing
skills. You can have a life of visual living without ever drawing *anything*. So don't let an inability to draw distract you from enjoying the
rewards of allowing your eyes to relish the visible world.

On the other hand, if you actually *are* a beginning artist, you
should realize that, frequently, creating successful visual expression
represents about 90 percent of feeling an emotion or an inspiration,
and perhaps only 10 percent of knowing for sure how to express it
(or how to draw it).

So even if your art "skills" (including drawing) are modest, *feeling the desire* to create art or design will frequently get you where you want to go.

If you really want to do it, whether it's making photographs, designing a garden, creating advertisements, working with computer graphics, designing telephones or dolls, or even drawing pictures with conventional pencils and charcoal, just do it. Usually, with just a little determined effort, your most important deep down emotions will eventually find their way to reality.

Sometimes all you have to do is try.

Follow your visual curiosity wherever it leads.

Experiment with a new wardrobe. Renovate your apartment. Model some clay. Build a miniature castle or a full-sized one. Snap some pictures of rubber boots. Pinstripe a dune buggy. Make an anti smoking poster. Knit a ski sweater. Decorate a Valentine's Day cake. Study ceramics. Do what inspires you.

Then, if you begin to grow in your desire to create more serious visual expression, the day may come (or it may not come) when you'll want to draw pictures.

That day may be years away. (Or it may be never.)

But don't wait.

Begin your adventure with the lessons of light *now*.

As we'll see in the upcoming pages, there are many wonderful ways to do it.

Getting started with the lessons of light:
Being not flat makes the world go 'round

Even if we're referring to the most serious visual expression, including the work of great artists found in prestigious museums, some of the "talent" that is apparent in their work could more honestly be called "technique."

That means, in visual expression, there are valuable ground rules about getting certain things achieved. You could call these techniques the "tools (or tricks) of the (visual) trade." Even the best visual artists use these kinds of shortcuts constantly.

For example, and I'm speaking generally, in visual expression *not flat* is often better than *flat*. In many cases, a visual message works better when it has three dimensions, or when *it looks like* it has three dimensions, meaning length and width and DEPTH, not two dimensions, meaning length and width.

That's true even when it is created on a flat surface.

Since this is important, the first question we are going to ask about the power hidden in the nine lessons of light is this: How is it possible to make something that starts out flat (let's say it's a blank canvas, a computer screen or a poster board) appear as though it's *three dimensional?*

How do you make flat surfaces look *not* flat?

That's a visual question to keep in mind as we explore the first lesson of light.

* * * *

Chapter one continued
AN INTRODUCTION TO DEPTH
The first lesson of light
How deep is a surface?

Here's what we're wondering:

How is it that a flat surface can look like it's *not* flat?

That's a pretty common challenge within visual expression.

Fortunately there are several ways we can make it happen.

We're going to look at all of them in this chapter by outlining the seven *conditions* of DEPTH as a source of visual experience.

To start with, our modern knowledge of perspective is a tool that visually sensitive people know about to help recreate DEPTH on a flat surface. Perspective is one condition of DEPTH. Each of these special varieties of DEPTH has its own strengths and weaknesses and we'll discuss all of them.

The seven conditions of DEPTH
as a source of visual experience:

Parallax
Perspective
Advancing or receding COLOR or tone
Memories
Circumstance
Shadow
Lightness and darkness of COLOR or tone

Parallax

Before we talk more about perspective, let me introduce you to a funny word called parallax. Here's what it means. When we say people can see in "parallax," it's another way of saying we use both eyes to help us see in DEPTH. That of course means to see with parallax requires that both of your eyes are healthy and alert. If they are, then parallax allows you to judge DEPTH which occurs within about fifty feet (15 meters) from your eyes.

Parallax helps us figure out, let's say, how far away we are from a can of Coke that is sitting on a shelf, or how far away a soccer ball is as we run up to kick it. We can use information from our sense of parallax to easily reach out, with only one try, to pick up the soda can from the shelf, or to connect the soccer ball with the toe of our shoe and send it flying.

We can judge distances (DEPTH) by parallax because each of our eyes sees a slightly different view. This is true because our two eyes are separated by a short distance (about 3"– 4" or 7–9 cm). Our eyes are sensitive enough to analyze the difference between these pictures. In addition, our mind can measure the tension in our eye muscles, and it uses that information to help judge how far they "turn inward" to focus on the soda can or the ball.

Here's two experiments that show how parallax works.

First, point your finger into the air, again as though you're ordering a drink from someone across the room. This time your finger should only be about 8"–10" (20–30 cm) from your eyes. Then pick a detail at the edge of your fingernail to focus on. If you close one eye and then the other, and carefully analyze what each eye is seeing, you can actually notice the difference between the two pictures of your fingernail your eyes are sending to your brain. Your mind is also aware that the backgrounds of each view, which are out of focus, don't line up with each other. That's another clue our eyes can evaluate to confirm that we're seeing in DEPTH.

Then continue the experiment in this way: keep both eyes focused on your fingernail and slowly bring your finger toward you. When your finger is five or six inches from your nose, you'll begin to feel muscle tension around your eyes. This tension signals your brain that you're looking at something that is very close. In fact, even the muscles we use to focus our eyes' lenses are sensitive enough to help determine the distance an object is from our eyes.

Here's another exercise: Look at a clock or small picture on a wall across the room from where you're sitting. Then hold out your left arm and make a "V" sign with two fingers, so you can see the clock or the picture *between your fingers*. With both eyes open, focus on your fingers and you'll see two clocks (or two pictures). Or, focus on the clock (or the picture), and you'll see two sets of fingers!

Try these experiments now and become aware of seeing parallax in this way, using the interaction of your two eyes. These simple examples are the basics on how parallax works constantly to provide your mind with information it needs to help determine the distances of objects that appear before you.

* * * *

Unfortunately, parallax is useful only for a short distance. When we look beyond that, the two pictures our eyes see, that is, the pictures they relay to our brain, are practically the same. And at one point our eyes begin to see in parallel (straight) lines, so the tension in our eye muscles also becomes much less noticeable. That means that judging distances beyond 100 feet (30 meters) is almost impossible unless there are other conditions of DEPTH to analyze.

To further explain it, imagine that there's a COLORful beach ball high in the air above you. If the sky is clear and the ball is more than 100 feet (30 meters) above you, you simply couldn't judge how far away the ball is. Beyond that, if there were *two different sized balls in the air*, at different heights, you would not be able even to tell which was closer to you. In everyday situations, beyond 100 feet (30 meters), we loose our ability to see DEPTH through parallax.

This limitation can directly impact our perception. Men and women who train to fly in SPACE are required to have excellent eyesight. But even though an American astronaut once spoke about a UFO seen from the U.S. space shuttle, he never described how big it was, or how far away he believed it to be. He told a reporter, in effect (and correctly), that when he saw the unusual object there were no useful conditions of DEPTH in SPACE to help him to accurately judge how far away it was. He was absolutely right.[6]

Parallax gives us a strong sensation of DEPTH because we can compare two different images (one from each eye). But most of the work artists create on flat surfaces does not provide this opportunity. Paintings, photographs and computer screens, for example, offer our eyes only one picture to analyze. We see these images with two eyes, but they receive identical information because there is no real dimension "to see around" on the surface of most paintings, photographs and monitors. So how do artists begin to overcome this shortcoming? That's where other conditions of DEPTH come into play (starting with perspective, which we'll discuss shortly).

However, still referring to parallax, perhaps most surprising is the way, over time, there have been a variety of methods discovered to "artificially" recreate it. For example, there is three dimensional (3D) photography, which was invented shortly after conventional photography was born (more than 150 years ago). 3D photos are made by setting up two cameras about 5" (12 cm) apart. The two cameras recreate what each of our two eyes would see.

To see the DEPTH in a 3D picture like this (actually two pictures), a special viewer is needed. The viewer causes each eye see a separate picture. When that happens, our eyes are fooled into seeing a normal lifelike view of that scene, including 3D DEPTH.

Some photographs that survive from the very beginning era of 3D photography are truly remarkable. Some present scenes like American Civil War battlefields, and even 3D photographs of U.S. President Abraham Lincoln.

Among other interesting images captured in early 3D photography are pictures of earth's moon shot through dual telescopes. Let me challenge your visual curiosity by asking you to think about this: Why bother photographing the moon in 3D if, generally speaking, parallax is not effective beyond 100 feet (30 meters)?

That's something to think about. (We'll get back to it later.)

For more information about three dimensional photography, you can search for "stereoscope" on the internet. (This is the first of many internet searches that are suggested throughout the book. But remember, please postpone all your searches until after you finish reading. Instead, bookmark this page and come back to it later.)

Just about fifty years ago, 3D comic books became popular. Comic book artists drew the first view of each scene in red (the view you would expect to see with your right eye), and the second view in blue (the view you would expect to see with your left eye). Both drawings are then printed inside the same frame of reference (which in a comic book is the little box that frames each scene). You could see the picture in 3D by wearing special glasses with red and blue lenses that allow each eye to see only one of the drawings.

At that same time, moviemakers began experimenting with a similar kind of artificial parallax, a process that required theatergoers to wear those same funny glasses as they watched the film.

These days, of course, we can go into a theater and watch a full-length movie wearing an entire helmet, which creates extremely lifelike illusions of DEPTH and dimension, again by recreating parallax. These movies are the visual side of "virtual" technology, which provides realistic artificial stimulus to all five of the human senses. Perhaps you have experienced one of these "virtual" shows at a Disney World theme park, where they are very popular.

A well-loved kids' toy, the "View-Master" viewer, also recreates parallax with images that are first captured with two cameras, just as our eyes would see them. Or else, an artist or cartoonist illustrates the two separate scenes that recreate, or exaggerate, the differences our eyes normally expect.

Lastly, "magic eye" pictures are a third variation of 3D parallax technology, developed in the 1980s. They use detailed printing on a poster, where the two pictures are miraculously hidden in a single TEXTURED image. To view the picture, you need to sort of cross your eyes. If you have not experienced one of these illusions, *keep trying*. When the image finally appears before you, it is a very rare and special visual moment which seems to appear from a wonderful new dimension of visual reality. Almost everyone gets a real thrill the first time a magic eye image appears before them.

In fact, I believe it's possible that magic eye pictures are yet to realize their full potential. Their rise and then their apparent fall from popularity surprised me. I once predicted that, because magic eye images don't require an extra viewer or glasses, everyone would gradually learn how to experience them. After that, so I thought, this kind of 3D image would become commonplace in printed graphics and on the internet.

But apparently I was wrong. I once created some promotional material (a poster and brochures, etc.) anchored by a magic eye illustration. To my surprise, and even after coaching, no one in my client's office could see the images correctly, and only half the staff in my own agency could do it. I had to ditch the idea.

Nevertheless, I suspect that anyone who's persistent enough to learn the simple trick involved in viewing magic eye images probably has the required curiosity to be successful at visual living. The small amount of effort called for is very well rewarded. More than ever, I continue to say, *keep trying*. Magic eye pictures are a genuinely groundbreaking visual innovation.

You can find magic eye illustrations to use for practice, and guidelines about how to see the pictures they hide, by searching pages and images on the internet for "magic eye." I just now did this internet search myself, and I can report that the three-dimensional effects work perfectly even on a computer screen. (Bookmark this page and come back to this search later.)

Although prints of some paintings have been converted to be viewed as 3D images, serious artists have mostly avoided this visual innovation. But there are possibilities. As far as I am aware, no artist ever created two original paintings of a still life composition (a group of objects such as fruit or bottles set on a table) so they can be seen in three dimensions through a viewer, or with a helmet. Creating these paintings would be difficult, but the chance to see a set of paintings such as this, brought to life by an experienced artist, would be a thrilling visual experience.

By the way, if you skipped bookmarking page 58, return to it now and begin a serious effort to learn from this book. You have the opportunity here, today, to welcome a new experience into your life that will enrich your days endlessly, and practically forever. Get a supply of bookmarks and markers *now*. Take this opportunity to grow in your understanding of visual expression. *Just do it.*

Welcome Bruce Willis to your living room

Although man-made images that incorporate 3D parallax technology aren't common, this is changing. The developments needed to bring 3D experiences to entertainment continue to become less expensive, and more effective. And at the same time, business and science innovators are finding more creative uses for 3D images.

Already, automobile makers create 3D simulations of new car interiors so engineers can study them before actual models are built. Plus, unmanned missions to Mars (and other destinations) now routinely use stereoscopic (3D) cameras to send back photographs of landing sites as well as other features of earth's planetary neighbors. These pictures allow scientists to see exotic places in realistic detail and dimension.

However, despite this progress, technologies we need to create flat images that look three dimensional *without* a viewer (perhaps 3D paintings or posters that you can just hang on the wall) are yet to be developed. On top of that, since so much communication is transmitted by computer and through the internet, that's another challenge we face. We are far away from developing genuinely 3D or "virtual" computer monitors.

Nevertheless, although there are genuine obstacles, you can expect this to change *big time.*

Just as no one can now imagine recording new music that is not in stereo or surround-sound format, you can expect that, probably in your lifetime, "flat" visual images will also become obsolete. If I am correct, science will find new tools for creative people that make 3D paintings and photographs the rule and not the exception. Everything we'll see, from magazine covers and business cards to museum masterpieces will appear genuinely three-dimensional.

A time will come when you may honestly mistake an artificial environment as reality. On an everyday level, actors on TV will perform "in" your living room. Virtual picture windows in family rooms will look "out" to any scene we choose, with changing weather, sunlight and seasons. And computer monitors will somehow surround us with information. Virtual visual reality will someday, and soon, be part of everyday life.

And all the glasses, viewers, helmets and other paraphernalia needed for current 3D technology will be no where to be found.

A three dimensional hero

But then, once again, maybe I'm wrong.

Maybe the future is further away than it seems.

Here's why I say that: A few days ago, I went to a fast food restaurant. On the wall was a very big poster that said, "See our new sandwich in 3D!" So I tried out their gimmick, and, sure enough, although I am not sure it made me more hungry, a giant meatball hero did nevertheless jump right out of the poster at me! To see that sandwich in 3D I had to put on some cardboard eyeglasses they had hanging on the wall next to the poster.

But here's why I say technology isn't changing so fast. Those glasses were exactly like the blue and red ones that were invented *60 years ago* for those first 3D comic books!

And similarly, there were 3D photographs of Mars published a while ago in an expensive coffee table book,[7] and, in addition, a sports magazine sometimes publishes its annual swimsuit edition in 3D.[8] And guess what. Tucked inside that book and the magazines are those same old-fashioned red and blue eyeglasses, ready and waiting to bring those Martian rocks and sexy bikinis into your living room in three dazzling dimensions.

Then, more recently, CNN announced it would broadcast the

first 3D *television* images. (Again, these were 3D photos from Mars.) It sounded new and exciting, but not really, because believe it or not, before the program aired, CNN posted information on the internet about how to *make your own* old fashioned red and blue cardboard glasses for viewing the pictures.

Although there are still real obstacles involved, I believe science will eventually bring monumental changes in 3D technology. And you can count on this: real or artificial, parallax will continue to be responsible for the most lifelike (that is, the most "believable") experiences of DEPTH.

In the meantime

Unfortunately for the time being (in case you didn't notice) recreating parallax (that is, creating artificial parallax) is a complicated thing to do. It requires that each eye receives a slightly different picture. And the truth is, throughout most of history (before 3D photography, 3D viewers, cardboard glasses and magic eye pictures, etc.) parallax wasn't just difficult to express with.

It was technically impossible (except for Mother Nature).

That shortcoming could make you wonder: does recreating DEPTH always require two images? That would be a problem and, worse, man-made visual experiences would likely be terribly boring. Art would be much less exciting. But fortunately there's good news: recreating DEPTH does not always require two images, or special eyeglasses, viewers or helmets. There are other ways, not related to parallax, to recreate the illusion of DEPTH on a single flat surface.

Unlike parallax, these remaining conditions of DEPTH are easily adapted to the many common flat surfaces of visual expression. They require only a single image to recreate the illusion of DEPTH. And they work equally well for paintings, photographs, prints and other kinds of flat artwork including illustrations, posters, web pages or even yard sale signs.

The remainder of this chapter is a summary of these easier-to-use visual tools we have for recreating DEPTH (the remaining six conditions of DEPTH).

If you're curious, there's much additional detailed and technical information about parallax available on the internet. You can search for "parallax," or for "parallax examples." Be sure to select "images" in your search engine, not "web pages."

(Bookmark this page and come back to it later.)

Perspective, the second condition of DEPTH
(and the art of motorcycle sales)

Now lets talk about the second condition of DEPTH.

The role played by perspective as a principle of visual perception is almost without equal. It causes objects to appear smaller and smaller to our eye as they move away from us, or as we move away from them. That's the way objects appear to behave in real life, and when objects are re-created that way on a flat surface, our eye sees DEPTH there also. By applying the principles of perspective to an image created on a flat surface, or exaggerating them in three dimensions (for example, to change the impact of an interior design for a room) any visually expressive person can produce or magnify the illusion of DEPTH.

For example, when it's necessary to make a railroad track that's drawn on a flat surface look as though it disappears over a distant hill, the two rails of the track are created (drawn) so they become closer and closer together as they move away from the front of the picture. Cars parked along a highway become smaller and smaller as the road moves away from the front, and telephone poles along the road become shorter and shorter, as well as closer together at the same time.

Of course, in real life, the railroad tracks don't become closer together. If you measured the distance between the two rails at one point, then walked 300 feet (100 meters) down the track and measured that distance again, of course, the reading would be the same. And the cars don't become smaller, and the telephone poles don't become shorter and closer together. They all simply *appear* this way. They appear this way both in reality and on the flat surface of two dimensional drawings, paintings and photographs.

I knew someone years ago who, after retirement, took a drafting class. He was surprised to learn these very basic facts about perspective. Since his childhood he had been a little mystified by the illusions of DEPTH he saw on flat surfaces. He's one of those people I mentioned earlier who thought it was some kind of magic. After he understood the rules of perspective he suddenly felt less intimidated by art in general. He was actually filled with a sense of pride and understanding.

These things weren't mysterious any more.

Perspective is used within visual expression everywhere. In one case, someone once painted a country road on the wall of a motorcycle showroom in the middle of a city. He started the painting at floor level, and he matched the paved surface of the painted road (which disappeared over a "hill" on the wall) to the COLOR of the carpet in the showroom. He used principles of perspective to recreate the road on the wall of the showroom. As a result, it's possible for people to sit on the motorcycles and imagine riding down that road into the country. Perspective is what makes it possible, and that's an example of how a business artist can help a business person sell motorcycles. Of course, if anyone tried to drive down that road, he or she would discover a very real brick wall, disguised by perspective and the other sources of visual experience.

Designers who create the sets for plays and musicals also use perspective, and they frequently exaggerate it. They know how to make the stage in a theater look larger than it is, and they can increase the DEPTH of a stage with the clever use of perspective.

I once saw a theater performance that used perspective to create the ceiling for a dining room that was the scene for one act. The ceiling was not a ceiling at all. Instead it was a sort of vertical wall (much like a large painting) positioned above the stage but hanging freely in front of it. This "wall" was lighted with spotlights and painted with the details of a ceiling in perspective. If you sat in the center of the theater, the illusion was excellent. The "ceiling" looked like it was over the actors. But I was sitting on the side of the theater. Because it was "artificial," the illusion worked *only when viewed from the center* where, of course, the expensive seats are. Anyone not sitting in the middle (me for example) was out of luck.

From the side, when the curtain opened, I couldn't understand what I saw. It was only a vertical surface above the stage painted with unusual boxes and ovals. Even though I'm visually oriented, it still took a few moments for me to "get it." But lots of people in that audience are probably still wondering what that thing hanging over stage and the actors was.

Here's another story about perspective:

When I was in ninth grade, my school held a poster contest to celebrate "Bicycle Safety Week." I entered with a poster that used an exaggerated example of perspective. I was a kid, barely an artist, but I managed to create a bicycle in perspective so it looked like it was coming toward you (with a big oval for the front wheel and a tiny oval for the back wheel).

You might say I used the technique of perspective to overcome the fact that I really could not draw very well. Then I scribbled "Be

Careful!" at the top of the poster and I won first place. What I mean is, it would be more accurate to say it like this: despite my poor drawing skills, *perspective won first place for me.*

(Sometimes all you have to do is try.)

You can easily see perspective working. Look out a window and notice how a road appears less and less wide as it moves farther away. Or notice how people and buildings appear smaller in the distance. Inside your home, try this: Glance at a door across the room. Then close one eye and hold your hand in front of your other eye so that the door is "covered up." In this example, perspective is allowing your hand to be *bigger than a door.*

That same illusion was immortalized for eternity by another American astronaut, Jim Lovell, who was definitely living visually on his 1968 Apollo 8 moon flight. Looking back at earth, he held up his thumb and effectively *blocked out our planet.* When he returned to earth, he reported in awe, "Everything I ever knew was . . . behind my thumb." Wow. The visual power of perspective!

Try a sketch on your paper. Make a row of flag poles down a sidewalk so they get shorter in the distance, and closer together as they move away. Or, try to draw a bicycle in perspective as it comes toward you. When you see a bicycle, look at it head on. Notice how the front wheel looks bigger than the rear wheel.

That's perspective.

For more information, search the internet for "perspective" or "perspective examples." Select "images" on your search engine, not "web pages." (Bookmark this page and come back to it later.)

Advancing and receding COLOR and tone

Here's how the third condition of DEPTH works. It's called advancing or receding COLOR or tone. You can see it in mountain country, or in photographs that show mountain ranges.

Because our earth has an atmosphere, everything we see is filtered through some distance of air. When we are inside a house or building, or looking at objects less than a few hundred feet (about 100 meters) away, the air does not greatly affect, or change, what we see. But at great distances, the influence of the atmosphere modifies the visual information that reaches our eyes.

One important change is how atmosphere influences COLORS, an effect that's even stronger when fog or rain exists. To understand what I mean, imagine standing on a hilltop or a mountain, with other hilltops or mountains rising up in front of you. If it's daytime, and the sky is bright and evenly lighted all the way to the horizon (the place in front of you where the mountains meet the sky) and with no clouds, the nearest hilltop or mountain will look bright and clear, with sunny COLORS.

The green COLOR of the trees will be rich and lively.

But the next mountain in line, farther from you, will appear slightly lighter and less bright. The changes will continue as each mountain rises farther and farther away. Each will have COLORS that look lighter and also less rich. Finally, the last mountain which touches the sky above the horizon will appear *much* lighter and far less bright than the one closest to you.

We know the lightest mountain is farthest from us. As result, we learn to believe a rule: When things get lighter and lighter, they are also getting farther and farther away. And that's an understanding about DEPTH we apply to every environment, not just mountain tops. And of course, that means an artist can express with this characteristic of DEPTH in artwork (or design) to give the illusion that things are far away.

But there's a surprising twist on this discovery.

A logical thought would be to assume things that become *darker and darker* in a frame of reference are getting closer. However all visual rules have exceptions, and one occurs when a mountain scene like this is seen in moonlight, or with skies that are overcast.

At those times, if you stand and look across the countryside, you'll notice a difference. Generally speaking, when mountaintops are seen in moonlight, or with skies that are overcast, the area of the sky just above the horizon (which is the last mountaintop) will be darker than the sky above your head. As the sky becomes darker in the distance, in the same way the mountaintops become darker (not lighter). The surprise is this: Our sensation of DEPTH isn't changed. This condition of DEPTH is called advancing *or receding* COLOR or tone, since we accept that objects are farther and farther away from us if they *either* get more and more light *or* more and more dark.

Furthermore, the sense of DEPTH we find in this scene is not changed even when we see it with no COLOR, as we would find in black and white photographs.

That means that advancing or receding COLOR or tone is very *un*-complicated. It's an easy-to-use condition of DEPTH. You can try this exercise to see what I mean: Find four pieces of colored paper. ("Construction" paper is good for this.) Pick four COLORS that range from dark to light. Browns and greens are best, but purple is ok too. Then tear each piece of paper on the long edge so it's uneven (that is to say, it's "jagged").

You can tear the paper as carelessly as you want.

Now stack the four pieces of paper with the torn edges on top of each other. Put the darkest piece on top and then the other pieces in order until the light one is on the bottom. After that, slide each sheet down about an inch below the next, and tape them onto a larger piece of light blue paper.

Find some paper now, or make a note to try this later.

Even with this simple effort, you will see that the four pieces of paper will look very much like mountains, one behind the other. The torn edges look like the ups and downs of a mountain range. You can see how your eye believes the light COLORED paper represents mountains that are very far away.

When art expresses using advancing or receding COLOR or tone in a painting of mountains, or when recreating the buildings on a city skyline (another place where advancing and receding COLOR is easily seen), it may exaggerate these changes in COLOR or tone (just as perspective was exaggerated on that bicycle poster). In fact, artists frequently exaggerate visual information to help bring frames of reference to life, and to overcome the truth, which is that flat surfaces don't really have dimension.

Back in the motorcycle showroom, the "country road" illusion, created primarily with perspective, is strengthened by a background of mountaintops. Of course, those mountaintops are painted according to advancing and receding COLOR and tone.

Memory, the fourth condition of DEPTH.
If it makes sense, see it

A child's drawing can help show us how memory sometimes works as the fourth condition of DEPTH.

Everyone goes through life remembering their experiences.

If something happens once, then we may expect it will happen again. It's natural to expect that what was true in one circumstance will be true again in similar circumstances. For example, imagine a child's drawing with these three parts:

a house
a pointy purple shape next to the house and
a yellow circle above the house.

Imagine the child draws a horizontal line across the paper, and the house and the pointed shape are sitting on the line. How would you describe the three objects according to their distance from the point of view of the child who made this picture? In other words, which is farthest away in the picture, the house, the purple shape, or the yellow circle?

>At right: *Look at the first drawing and decide the distance of each part. Which of the three parts of these two drawings is "farthest" away from the "artist's" point of view, and which is nearest? To see what some students and I learned, do this exercise before you continue to read.*

In a poll, most people said the house was closest, the purple shape was next and the yellow circle was farthest away. Some people said the purple shape was closer than the house.

That's interesting.

How can anyone say the purple shape is closer or further away than the house is? There's no parallax, no perspective (or is there?), and no advancing or receding COLOR or tone. Why would people believe the purple shape is farther away than the house?

One reason may be this. People guess that the child "artist" intended the purple shape to be a mountain. And because of memory (that is, let's say, a memory of a drive in mountain country) people will assume the mountain must be farther away than the house. Otherwise, the house is too big. Although this is complicated thinking, it results in people making judgments about DEPTH. People know mountains are much bigger than houses, so the mountain in the child's drawing must be farther away than the house.

That's the only way that a mountain could look smaller than a house (and, technically, that is because of perspective).

One person said the purple shape is closer than the house and was surprised to hear it was a mountain. She is not American and wondered why a child would believe mountains are purple. She has never seen the mountains in the western United States, which look purple-ish from far away. But, since *many* Americans have also

never seen those mountains, why do people commonly say mountains are purple? Another explanation is that they use memory to recall words from the inspiring song "America the Beautiful," which describes America's "purple mountains' majesty."

After this first exercise, a second drawing was tested.

This time, the "mountain" was replaced with a tree, and (different) people were asked, "How far away is each part in the picture?" What's your opinion? (Look at the second drawing to decide.)

People who see this second drawing offer three answers.

About one third say the house is closer, one third say the tree is closer, and about one third say it's hard to know *which* is closer. Everyone says the yellow circle is farther away than everything else. So, this time there's apparently no "right" answer.

What does this tell us?

In the second drawing there are no clues to help decide the question of relative DEPTH. The reason is that some trees are bigger than houses, and some houses are bigger than trees. If a picture shows us a tree that's shorter than a house, that tree might still be closer to us than the house.

That's because lots of houses are much bigger than trees.

In the same way, if a tree is taller than a house in a picture, that tree may still be farther away from us than the house. That's because lots of trees are much bigger than houses. Again, there is no parallax, no perspective and no advancing or receding COLOR or tone to help us see the picture "in DEPTH."

So, in the second version of the drawing, memory apparently does not help. There are just not any rules about how big a tree is compared to a house. We can't simply say that all trees are bigger than houses, as we did with mountains.

But memories are made from all the intellectual information we have, not just visual rules, such as mountains being always bigger than houses. Memories can therefore provide at least one possibility where we might know, after seeing this second picture, which is farther away, the tree or the house.

Suppose you are aware that the house in the picture is *your* house (let's say the drawing was made by your young nephew or by your baby sister). If that were true, you could determine, from memory, where the tree is. You'd know the tree is the tree in your own front yard. Because of that, you would know the tree is closer to the point of view of the picture than the house is.

These thoughts mean our reaction to what we see in DEPTH is affected by our previous experience in life. We can see DEPTH for no reason other than it makes sense to see DEPTH.

OK. How big is the sun?

In these children's drawings, people choose the yellow circle above the house as farthest away. What does this tell us?

You might state, quoting the paragraph above, "We can see DEPTH for no reason other than it *makes sense* to see DEPTH." People know the yellow circle is the sun, and since the sun is bigger than houses and mountains, it must be farther away in the picture than these other things because of perspective.

Otherwise, why would it look smaller?

At first, that sounds like it's making sense.

But the difficulty is this: How do we know, *visually speaking*, that the sun *is* bigger than houses and mountains?

Here's why that's an issue: In the first drawing, we can say the mountain is farther away than the house because we do know mountains are bigger than houses. We have seen houses next to mountains. In fact, we have seen houses *on* mountains, and in every case, the mountain is bigger. But we have never seen the sun right next to a house or a mountain. So how do we know, visually, that the sun is bigger than houses and mountains?

After all, our normal experience is to see the sun smaller than houses, just as it is in the child's drawing. But imagine for a moment one case where the sun actually appears larger than a house. Take a moment and try to imagine a situation where that would be true.

Try to recall a situation when the sun appeared to your eye to be larger than a house. Take a minute to do this.

Here is one way that could happen. Again, imagine you are standing on a mountaintop. This time it's late in the afternoon and sunset is approaching. You look out across the countryside and see a house on the western horizon (near to where the sun is setting). Perhaps the house is sitting on top of another mountain two miles (three kilometers) away. As the sun descends in the sky, you notice it appears larger than the house.

Of course, this could really happen. Since the house is so far away, because of perspective, it looks very small. So, in this situation, it's possible that the setting sun looks bigger than the house.

We might say this proves the sun is larger than houses.

But there is still one weakness, visually speaking, with this "proof." Visually speaking, before the sun touches the horizon during sunset, there is a possibility that perspective is working to make the sun look bigger than the house on the horizon. Again *speaking visually*, it is, after all, possible that the sun is actually smaller than the house, and only appears bigger because it is *closer to us than the house*. After all, the house in the first drawing appears larger than the mountain for the same reason.

So how is it possible, visually speaking, to prove that the sun is larger than houses? By using only information that's available through our sense of sight, how can we prove the sun is something very big, and very far away?

Circumstantial DEPTH

Fortunately, the fifth condition of DEPTH, a condition that we call circumstantial DEPTH, can prove this in a visual way. And it can do it using only information available to us through our eyes.

To see how important this is, imagine being alive before science accurately explained our solar system. Think of primitive people, thousands of years ago, using only their eyes to understand the sun, moon, planets and stars. How confusing it must have been.

Imagine yourself back on the mountaintop at around sunset. Suppose, as we said, the sun is descending and we notice it appears to be bigger than a house nearby on the horizon. How can we know this is not caused by perspective? How can we know this is not caused by the sun being closer to us than the house?

As we stand there watching, if we wait a few minutes, there will be visible proof. And this is it: As the sun comes closer to the horizon, one of two things must happen. The sun must either continue on its path in front of the horizon, or otherwise it must disappear behind the earth.

If you've ever watched a sunset, you were probably happy to see it is the second of these possibilities which occurs. That is, at sunset, the sun always disappears behind the earth. And as it does, we then see one of the two most startling examples of circumstantial DEPTH visible from earth.

Circumstantial DEPTH is the fifth condition of DEPTH.

It tells us that any object that's partly or entirely hidden from view by a second object is also *always farther away from us than the second object.* Of course, that sounds ridiculously simple. But in the visual order of our world, imagine how often you rely on that basic rule to judge the relative positions of things.

In these beginning efforts to learn about visual expression, you might think it is possible to reduce concepts to a level (such as this) that are just *too simple.* But describing an artist's life as a struggle to continually do *just that* is really not a bad summary of it. No matter what, simple sounding or not, circumstantial DEPTH settles objects in their proper places by helping to establish their relative distances (DEPTHS) from our point of view.

My point is, then, when the sun disappears behind the earth at sunset, we know it is farther away from us than anything else on earth, including the house on the horizon two miles (3 km) away. And the wonderful thing is, we know this from our eyes only! We know this without relying on scientific or intellectual information.

In the child's drawing, people guess the yellow circle is the sun. And they say it is farther away than the house or the mountain because, at sunset, the sun proves it is farther away than everything else on earth. Everyone's judgment about the sun in the child's picture is an example of a memory of circumstantial DEPTH.

Our memory of the sun as it disappears behind the earth during every sunset is visual proof that the sun is very far away.

A note to intellectuals

Ok, you might say: Enough. You might be thinking the last several paragraphs are just *too* simple. Perhaps you feel that talking about visual ideas with such primitive examples is too immature or too unsophisticated to be of real value in learning about art, design and visual living. You might say, "this can't possibly be the best way I can learn about the world of visual expression."

Along with that thought, you may feel confused with my talk of sunsets proving anything. On the contrary, you might remember you were *told* or *taught* the sun is very, very big, and very, very far away from earth. Someone may have told you this long before you figured the afternoon sunset had anything to do with it, if you ever figured that (and of course, most people haven't). Even for myself, as a child, I learned that the sun was very far away when a TV commercial said light had come 93 million miles (about 149 million kilometers) from the sun just to grow wheat for a certain kind of cereal.

It even said it takes the light eight minutes to get here.

(And, by the way, recently this was a question on one of the famous "millionaire" TV shows.)

But an apology isn't necessary for describing our environment, including the solar system, based only on what our eyes see. The ability to enjoy and create visual meaning starts with the knowledge of how we see the world with our eyes, *separate from the intellectual information that controls all our non-visual thinking.*

If you want to begin to explore your visual talents, or just to enjoy living visually, try to separate what you see from any intellectual understanding of it, as we've done here. You will find that making this separation completely is nearly impossible. But through the effort of *attempting* that mental separation, much of expressive visual meaning is brought to life.

Sometimes all you have to do is try.

That's a rule (call it the "Separation Trick")
worth repeating and remembering:

> *Visual meaning sometimes springs to life during an effort to understand what we see in a way that is separate from the intellectual information that normally controls our thought. (Sometimes, all you have to do is try.)*

An easy way to describe a successful work of visual expression *in words* is to simply say, "It accomplishes the separation trick."
(By the way, remember to never look directly at the sun.)

Another grand example of Circumstantial DEPTH

People whose workday centers around the visual language interact with visual ideas continually. It's part of our everyday life. But beyond that, our understanding of the visual language makes things interesting even when we're not working. A case in point: I am sometimes amazed at the visual power that leaps from an ordinary paper clip when it has been accidentally twisted into a meaningful FORM. And recently I was surprised at the energy I found in the curve of a garden path that was winding gently toward an arbor.

Yet people who have not developed a knack for enjoying the simplest visual pleasures do sometimes look forward with enthusiasm to larger, more well-known and widely publicized visual events. One of these visual happenings is talked about on TV, in newspapers and on the internet for weeks before it actually occurs.

Photographers shoot photos of it, singers sing about it, poets write about it, newscasters report it, and scientists analyze it.

In visual terms, it's just circumstantial DEPTH.

But that hardly describes it. In fact, it's a most amazing visual experience, and probably the grandest experience of DEPTH that we humans here on our home planet will ever see. It occurs every several years, and in case you have not guessed, I'm talking about the second startling example of circumstantial DEPTH we can see from earth (sunsets are the first). It's the awe-inspiring visual show that we call a solar eclipse, a moment when the sun slips out of sight behind our moon. No other event offers such an emotion-filled view of our solar system, and its immense size.

Imagine how people reacted to solar eclipses thousands of years ago! If you do, you will learn something about the power hidden in visual experience that has been separated from its normal, logical and understandable place in our intellect.

To say it again, making this separation (the separation trick) is frequently a goal of visual expression.

The sun is an inspiration

A solar eclipse provides such dramatic proof of the giant distances, the gigantic DEPTHS, that exist within our solar system! But visually sensitive people may also respond to the "poetic" idea, the "emotional" idea (you might even say the "artistic" idea) that for a few minutes during an eclipse the sun is actually blacked out.

To put it even more sensationally, consider it this way:

During a solar eclipse, the sun *disappears*.

You can understand why that's meaningful to an artist when you realize that the two most significant visual inspirations are life and light. And the sun is important as a beginning of both. As school children know, the sun is the primary origin of heat and energy, two basic ingredients for life. But the sun is also the beginning of almost all the natural light that illuminates our everyday world.

And that's even more important.

Everything we see is visible because light either reflects from it, or passes through it. The nine ideas we are talking about in this book are merely the parts of everything that are all *made visible by light*. Light teaches us how our world appears.

This important role that light plays is part of all visual experience. But it is especially interesting to explore what happens when things get in the way of light. You can see what I mean if you consider the unique contribution that light makes to the sixth condition of DEPTH, the condition we call shadow.

Here's how shadow works as a condition of DEPTH.

Shadow, the visual adhesive –
The sixth condition of DEPTH

It would be difficult naming anything so visually and so vastly important, yet so rarely noticed, as shadow.

Light gives us a picture of our world by lighting it.

And shadow also gives us a "picture" of the world by interfering with light. One reason we believe, visually speaking, that the world *has* physical characteristics is that we see how they stop the progress of light. When that happens, as it does all around us, all the time, the result is called shadow.

Shadow is a reminder that tells us, day in and day out, that all the things around us are obeying visual rules. It places things in believable positions in a frame of reference by showing our eye that light is acting in a predictable manner. Shadow shows us that light is acting the way light is *supposed* to act. Most importantly, shadow helps us see the relative position of everything in a frame of reference and that is why it is a condition of DEPTH. By giving objects dimension, shadow convinces our eye that objects are real, and that they are occupying SPACE at a specific place.

Furthermore, and not to be overshadowed by circumstantial DEPTH (excuse the pun) and solar eclipses, shadow also plays a spectacular role in our earth-based views of the solar system by presenting its own special show. Who hasn't watched the earth's shadow creep along the surface of the moon during a lunar eclipse?

I have come back to writing this page right now after watching a beautiful total lunar eclipse this evening. As I watched, someone commented the the moon looked *very* three dimensional, especially during the early part of the full eclipse.

Visual curiosity was triggered!

I looked again and the moon *did* appear much more spherical. Even after the full moon was completely within earth's shadow, during the early moments of the total eclipse, one side was in *more* shadow than the other. Because of the gradual deepening of shadow across its many mountains and craters, the moon's three dimensional roundness, that is, its spherical FORM, was quite dramatically more evident. Of course, normally we see the moon *evenly* lit by sunlight, or split by the strong line of lunar night and day. That means its spherical appearance is effectively much less obvious.

What a thrill! How rare and wonderful to experience such real dimension, and such incredible DEPTH, across such an enormous distance. Wonderful, wonderful night. (More about the moon and visual curiosity is coming up in the following chapters.)

You can search images for "lunar eclipse" to see a picture of the moon during total eclipse. (Bookmark this page and come back when you have finished the book.)

Incidentally, referring back to parallax and 3D photographs of the moon: If you are a photographer, you would do us a favor by shooting a full COLOR photograph of a total lunar eclipse in three dimensions. (Using two cameras, of course.) I'd love to see the finished picture(s). More about this in chapter eight.

Noticing Shadow

Lunar eclipses are relatively rare happenings, but discoveries to be found around you at this very moment can help you appreciate shadow and how mysteriously powerful it can be.

Although often overlooked, artists know that shadow is an amazingly expressive and important element of the visual language. In fact, one extraordinary artist, sometimes called the most important female sculptor of all time, once said, "Shadow to me seems more solid than the object it is a shadow of."[11]

Imagine such a sensitivity to shadow!

She will be mentioned again later on.

But if her comment inspires you, try this: Look up from reading to see the objects (FORMS) in the room around you. Hundreds of shadows are cast by the objects in any typical room. Introduce yourself to shadow right now by glancing at the things nearby.

Now, perhaps for the first time in your life, control the visual information that's reaching your intellect. Do this by overlooking the objects that surround you. Overlook the furniture; overlook the books; overlook the dishes and the dog, and even the people; overlook all the plants and the TV; in fact, overlook *everything*. Instead, allow shadow to become the most important part of what you see, let shadows become more "solid" than the objects they represent.

For the next few minutes, go crazy looking for shadows.

Do this now before you continue to read.

There are dozens of discoveries in this exercise.

You'll see that shapes of shadows usually do not match the objects casting them, except on flat surfaces. Instead, every object makes a unique shadow, depending on each object's FORM, where the shadow falls, the intensity and direction of the light, and the COLOR and details of the surrounding environment.

On curved surfaces, shadows blend effortlessly from dark to light. Shadow travels in a straight line, and a shadow falling across your lap may then fall to the floor and continue. If you are sitting in a room with more than one light (perhaps two table lamps) notice what happens when separate shadows cast from these two lights overlap one another.

Notice how COLORS and TEXTURES change as they move in and out of shadows. For a moment, imagine that all the light in your room is a *flowing liquid,* and the shadows are the places the liquid has not yet touched.

Notice the significant difference between the shadow on the back of objects and the shadow that is cast by those objects on the floor or table behind them. What you will see is that the shadow cast by an object is nearly always darker than the shadow which appears on the back of the object itself. This is an important visual rule that is central to successful painting and sketching.

To see this clearly, find a white coffee cup in your kitchen and place it on a table on a sheet of white paper. You will see the shadow cast behind the cup on the paper is darker than the shadow on the back of the cup itself. If you lay aside this book for several minutes in order to create this experiment, you'll learn one of the most basic lessons about how light behaves.

Once you appreciate these characteristics of shadow, imagine how significant it is for artists that "artificial" shadow, that is, shadow created on a flat surface or on a monitor, using pencils, paints, charcoal, cut paper, or a computer mouse, has the *same power.* Shadow created on flat surfaces can represent DEPTH with nearly the same power as real shadow.

What a great tool.

As we have said before, learning to notice and enjoy what you see is a process of forming habits. One habit that can surprise you with often unnoticed but exciting visual details is this: learn to notice shadow everywhere as it calmly goes about its job of bringing our world into DEPTH.

Lightness and darkness of COLOR and tone

Let's now look at the seventh condition of DEPTH, lightness and darkness of COLOR and tone.

The power hidden in this condition of DEPTH is triggered by a sensitivity inside our eyes which causes light COLORS to be seen with more emphasis than dark COLORS. At the same time, we normally assume that the lighter COLORED of any two objects is closer to us than a darker object, if there are no additional conditions of DEPTH that suggest otherwise.

Imagine two similar cars that are driving, side by side, and coming toward you down a highway. If these two cars are the same size and the same COLOR, they will appear to be traveling side by side. If, however, one car is dark and the other is light, the lighter car will seem to be closer.

For this reason, we often create two dimensional drawings, posters, designs and electronic graphics, etc. so that objects in the foreground are lighter in COLOR or tone than objects that are in the background. The result, once again, is that DEPTH, the first lesson of light, seems to exist on what is actually a flat surface.

The end of art anxiety

Like my friend who discovered perspective, it's not difficult to learn about DEPTH and the other "mysteries" of visual expression. When you do, it can be the beginning of the end of art anxiety, an uncomfortable feeling that people sometimes have in an art gallery or museum, or when art or design are part of conversation.

If that's an experience you are familiar with, as you progress through reading this book, it will gradually disappear.

You'll become comfortable with the visual language and its "secrets." If you're bothered with indecision, wondering "what to do first," or "what to look at first," or "what to say first," when you are faced with visual matters, the lessons of light provide the answer. Whether you're discussing an art show, designing a poster, photographing your car, patching a quilt, buying an antique or even studying masterpieces in an important museum, when you bring to mind the nine lessons of light, and some of these ideas that surround them, you will know where to begin those adventures.

Best of all, you may begin to look forward to those moments, instead of avoiding them.

* * * *

For review, here are the seven conditions of DEPTH:

> Parallax
> Perspective
> Advancing or receding COLOR or tone
> Memories
> Circumstance
> Shadow
> Lightness and darkness of COLOR or tone

Before continuing to read, take a moment to look for examples of these conditions of DEPTH. You'll find they are all around, no matter where you are.

If you can, take a look out a nearby window to see perspective working on the objects that appear before you. Look for streets that get more narrow as they move away from you, and cars that are smaller in the distance. See if houses or buildings appear darker or lighter when they are farther and farther away. Look for an example of Circumstantial DEPTH, where one object is clearly in front of other objects. This evening, if you see the moon rise from the horizon, experience the Circumstantial DEPTH it represents.

Notice the shadows cast by sunlight or the light from signs or cars or street lights, or from the table lamp next to you.

Lastly, notice how objects that are lighter in COLOR appear closer than similar things that are darker in COLOR.

———————

If you enjoyed evaluating the child's drawing
on page 68, there is an additional exercise relating
that picture to visual curiosity coming up on page 281.

Chapter Two

FORM as a source of visual experience

Dialog

IT HAS BEEN LARGELY FORGOTTEN, but long before 9/11, at the close of World War II, there was an earlier crash of an airplane into a skyscraper in the United States, this time accidental.

Flying through clouds on its way to landing in nearby New Jersey, an American military B-25 bomber crashed into New York's Empire State Building. The collision caused one of the engines of the plane to tear away from its wing. It fell seventy-nine stories outside the building and landed in the top floor (penthouse) loft of an apartment complex near the accident.

The loft, as it so happened, was the residence of an artist, a sculptor. He was not at home, but unfortunately the loft was also his studio and quite a bit of his work was destroyed. Many of his best sculptures were smashed and newspaper accounts at the time said the value of the lost art was about $75,000.

Soon after I read a historical account of the accident, I mentioned it to an illustrator I know. He was, likewise, the owner of a penthouse near the Empire State Building, where, like the artist in the story, he also maintained a studio. For that reason, I expected that he would be sorry to hear about this fellow artist and all the work that was destroyed in an apartment similar to his own.

Instead, hearing the story end with a mention of the $75,000 loss of artwork, his only reply was that the man must not have been a very good sculptor![9]

You can read about this crash by searching internet pages for "empire plane crash." (Bookmark this page.)

Working hard for your money

That comment made by my friend probably sounds funny to you, but it reminded me about the sometimes unbelievable amount of money associated with visual arts. Although $75,000 was a lot of money in 1945, when that accident occurred, it was small even then compared to the value of a more successful sculptor's work. Today, someone might earn a similar amount (that is, $75,000) just *preparing a study* for a public sculpture. The ability of a person to earn that much for everything he or she creates is rare, but it is not impossible. And consider this: in exceptional situations, some oil paintings are valued at more than $150 million.

In one spectacular case, after a painting was sold for $139 million, and just before it was delivered, the man selling it accidentally poked a hole in it with his elbow. The deal was called off, and the painting was revalued at $85 million. *A $54 million reduction!*[10]

If you are just now beginning to read about and look at visual expression, you may wonder, "What was so special about all that work lost in the airplane crash? Why would anyone assume it was worth *so much* money?" *What is so valuable about sculpture?*

If you asked a group of visually aware people that question, you would probably get as many answers as there are people. And each answer would probably have at least some truth in it. What I mean is, that's a hard question to get easy facts about.

So allow me ask you to think about it once more:

What *is* so valuable about art? How can a work of sculpture, let's say, become so priceless? What is going on here?

The truth is, for most people, including most knowledgeable people, trying to completely answer these questions is nearly impossible. There is, however, one explanation that seems simple enough, even though, as we shall see, it may not be. It's an explanation that gets to the bottom of what we are talking about when we say the visual language is a special way of seeing.

So here goes:

If the question is, "What's so valuable about sculpture?"
A simple answer could be:

> Some sculptures are priceless because
> they show off, in a pleasing way, the
> second lesson of light called FORM.

A thousand years of practice

Let me try to explain what that means.

Writers know that words act funny when they're used to talk about visual information. Words can tell us about the artist's language, that is, they can tell us about the nine lessons of light. But the closer they come to actually saying something meaningful about visual expression *itself*, then the more vague and troublesome words become. So, the answer above may get more complex because it suffers from this weakness that words have.

I said above, "Sculpture is sometimes priceless because it shows FORM in a pleasing way." Now, the way this sentence is written sounds as though it might very well be true. It sounds as though you should believe it even if you don't have a clue what it means. It sounds like *case closed*, even though it doesn't give you any information about *why* a FORM might be pleasing or interesting.

What is worse, if you don't enjoy seeing sculpture, you may believe that saying "FORM can be pleasing" is part of a big scheme. You may think, "For a thousand years these 'artist' types have been pretending that art has meaning. With such a long time to practice, they've got their stories straight, and now they can continue to pretend, in the same way, for another thousand years."

I hope that sounds crazy to you.

But it *is* how some people think. Since they have never been told the basics of the visual language, many people have never been able to appreciate what it's capable of "saying." So they think, and I don't blame them, that what it's saying is nothing.

If you share that opinion you deserve an explanation.

You need to hear how the habit of enjoying visual experience begins, how *visual living* begins; and you need to know that it starts the same way for everyone. It's how people begin to learn the special language of visual expression, the nine lessons of light, and it begins to explain why a FORM may be pleasing or interesting, and even enormously valuable.

Collecting is how it all begins

One way to explain how the habit of enjoying a visual life style actually *gets started* is to compare visually sensitive people to collectors. We'll do this because comparisons between collecting and visual living are easy to make.

However, when I use the word "collector," I don't necessarily mean someone who is rich and goes to galleries and auctions. I am speaking here about something more basic. In fact, I am imagining that you, yourself, may be a person who could start an interesting collection of *something*, perhaps without ever leaving your home. In fact, you may already have one.

A case in point: some people collect matchboxes or bottle caps. These can be found in just about anyone's house, and either one can be the theme of a great collection. And the same is true for such everyday objects as beer cans or ticket stubs. What else is just lying around that might be the beginning of a good collection? Take a moment to think about this, and then I'll list some additional possibilities. What's lying around your home right now that would be fun to collect? Think about this before you continue to read.

There are some characteristics that all collections have in common no matter what kinds of things they're made of. And there are always going to be some pieces in any collection that are more unusual than other pieces, even if the collection is only lead pencils, corks, marbles or candy bar wrappers.

And hopefully, you came up with other possibilities.

Different people have different opinions about what part of a collection is most interesting. And the pieces in a collection that people are attracted to frequently have very little to do with the amount of money spent on them, even if nothing was spent. That is to say, if someone collected 30 matchboxes by picking them up at restaurants over a period of several months, there would be one or two matchboxes I would like more than the others.

And you would probably have a favorite choice also.

But since every matchbox in the collection was free, there is no way our opinions could be influenced by the cost. Even if they weren't free, or if we take into consideration how much the restaurant paid to have them produced, price would still be of very little use in distinguishing between them, because even the most expensive matchbox is only a few cents worth of paper and ink. What I mean is, the value we assign to the pieces in a collection sometimes comes only from the *feeling* we have about them.

Because we like something, we feel it is valuable.

Suppose this collection went on for a number of years and increased to several hundred matchboxes, and suppose it was then shown to another matchbox collector. I suspect that he or she would probably have very strong favorites. In fact another collector might feel strong enough to offer money for one or two of them. The effort of collecting matchboxes over a long period of time might eventually pay off in some financial return.

Collecting sources of visual experience

We're talking about *that* kind of collection, so that we can talk about *this* kind of collection: There are many, many ways that visually sensitive people behave that are similar to how collectors behave. But unlike someone who collects matchboxes, antique cars or artwork itself, what artists and other visually sensitive people collect are *visual experiences.*

Just like someone who collects matchboxes, when a person has gathered together many visual experiences (most likely only in his mind's eye, but possibly in a scrapbook or a sketch book, or with a series of "preliminary studies," or even as a set of computer scans or files) he also begins to feel confident that some of them may have an intangible value.

We feel this way even though the *inspiration* for these visual experiences, which comes from noticing the everyday world, is just as free as the first hundred pieces in a matchbox collection. Just like other collectors, if you are living visually, you get the satisfying feeling that value might exist in something that costs nothing. An "artistic" value can be created from the unlimited supply of essentially free visual inspirations which surrounds us.

So here's my point: You can begin to enjoy that feeling yourself, to appreciate that artistic value, by beginning your own collection. We'll talk much more about *how* to do that in a minute.

First, we're still explaining why sculpture can be valuable.

When an artist has gathered together a collection of visual experiences such as this within his mind's eye, from time to time he selects a favorite one from the collection (or more realistically, parts from several) and recreates it (or them) within a frame of reference. He may then also bring in additional personal style or energy to this effort, and in that way a work of art is hopefully born.

It may be a simple FORM with added COLOR and TEXTURE (like many sculptures). Or it may be a SPACE with SCALE and DEPTH (as we frequently find in architecture and interior design).

Or in fact, it may be any one of the nine lessons of light, or any combination of them.

You would expect a rare matchbox to be more interesting to someone who also collects rare matchboxes and the same is true for any collection of visual experience. You won't be able to understand or enjoy the visual expression created by others until you, yourself, have begun to notice and appreciate (that is, to *collect*) the same kinds of things yourself.

You won't appreciate the value of visual expression, or why a sculpture or a painting may be worth a small fortune (or even a big fortune) until you understand how visually sensitive people can agree on which inspirations have visual meaning, and which do not have visual meaning.

Making something out of nothing at all

I like a song recorded during the 1980s by a group called *Air Supply*. You have probably heard the words which include, "I don't know how you do it, making love out of nothing at all." That song reminds me of a good way to think about visual expression, and it reminds me of a better answer to the question, "Why does a sculpture sometimes have great value?"

A sculptor sculpting a FORM is usually making something out of nothing at all. He or she is often showing us the most special example of this source of visual experience, this lesson of light, that he or she is able to imagine, inspired by perhaps years of observing (*collecting*) FORMS that came into view. If a person has been honest about evaluating the emotional meaning of the things in his collection of visual experience, this re-birth of inspiration may lead to the dawn of a new work of art.

And because other people who have collections of their own can recognize the special meaning that this process creates, it's very possible they will agree that visual meaning has, in fact, been discovered. People are frequently willing to find "value" in that accomplishment. In theory, this means the more of us who recognize this special meaning, the more valuable that expression is.

That's the theory.

In fact, however, it only takes the approval of perhaps several hundred of the best artists, art critics and art collectors to make visual expression valuable, even extremely valuable. These several hundred people understand the nine lessons of light. So, when they agree together that a meaningful work of art has been created, well, get out your wallet.

Asking visual questions

But, suppose you are not (yet) among those visually important judges? How can you know an artist has been "honest" in evaluating the art he or she shows you?

Again, although everyone is entitled to their opinion of art (remember the Latin displayed on the front of a building) an honest answer is that you really can't know this, at least until your understanding of the visual language is underway. At the very least, you will need to be aware that art is speaking a language that expresses meaning beyond the ability of words to fully capture.

If you come across an abstract FORM that's in a museum or a park, you may honestly wonder what the artist (or, for that matter, the museum or the park) found to be special about it. You may wonder why people went to the effort of actually making it, and moving it to a particular location.

If this has occurred to you, it's likely your ability to sense the visual meaning in FORM may not yet be developed.

An artist whose FORM is on display in some location where many people see it has usually spent many years looking at things, and deciding how he or she feels about them. But one thing is sometimes confusing: As a result of that process, it is not unusual for an artist to create FORM that is *based on reasons which may not occur to someone whose interest in visual expression is just beginning.*

For beginners, it is easy to believe that a sculptor is showing us a FORM because she feels it is beautiful. Creating beauty is frequently important. And because we all share similar visual lives in our mass produced culture, people can usually agree about what is beautiful and even what is ugly. But you should know there is plenty of confusion about sculpture, and frankly about visual expression in general, because of something that usually *doesn't* occur to people who are not yet visually sensitive.

What that means is, a sculptor (or a museum) may decide that a particular FORM has visual meaning for many, many (many, many, many) reasons *other* than beauty.

A FORM on display in some important location may only be asking us, in effect, "What if things looked this way?" Think of it like this: Just as a new book may describe a different way of living (even an "ugly" way of living), a sculpture may suggest a different visual reality. The sculpture may simply be saying to you (asking you a question such as):

"Did you ever think anything could look this way?"
        or
"Did you ever think you could *like* something
  that looks this way?"
        or even,
"Don't you hate looking at this?"
        (And, yes, that's a valid question for art to ask us.)

And of course, again, there are many other questions (many, many) that may be suggested by sculpture that can't be put into words. They are questions reserved for the visual language.

Furthermore, as a rule, the questions that art asks us in the visual language are considerably more important, and they're probably more profound, than any questions it may ask that we can put into everyday words. Again, that's one primary reason visual expression is so important. It allows us to ask questions and ponder experiences that the written and spoken languages cannot address.

Nouns, verbs, adjectives, sentences, paragraphs, and not to mention irony, hyperbole, rhetoric, sarcasm, poetry, narrative and prose. These are some of the tools writers use to communicate in the spoken and written languages, but they are simply not capable of framing the unique questions and experiences that are presented to us for evaluation by successful visual expression.

So when questions are asked by art, that's how we know the artist has been "honest" in deciding it has visual meaning. We know he has waited until an inspiration caught his own eye (by asking him a visual question), before it was transformed and then passed on to us by turning that inspiration into a work of visual expression. Because visually sensitive people usually agree when a FORM is asking a visual question, we know the sculptor has been honest in selecting it to show us.

Fortunately, as a rule, museums and parks exhibit abstract FORMS which they *already know* are able to ask visual questions. And although even museums make mistakes, when we go to a well-known museum to see well-known art, we are not so much interested in finding out if the work asks questions. It most certainly will because it has no doubt already proven itself hundreds of times before being accepted by the museum.

Rather, when we go to the museum, we can anticipate the excitement of discovering *which* questions it will ask.

When we come across art that asks questions, instead of *liking* it or *hating* it, it makes more sense for us to simply decide how we feel about the questions.

If the question seems to be, "How would you feel if things looked this way?" then it makes sense to just ask ourselves how we *would* feel if things *did* look this way. We may answer this question from dozens of approaches, but generally speaking, an artist's desire is simply to ask the question.

Once he discovers a FORM with this power, and creates art from it, he usually considers the job done. He doesn't bother over the many possible answers the question may inspire from the people who see it, whether they're critics in a museum, lovers in a park, students in an art class, or somebody reading this book.

As a result of "collecting," a sculptor usually hopes to find, and then recreate, a solitary (but perhaps complex) FORM which has the special ability to ask visual questions. In searching for this FORM, possibly over a very long period of time, he or she wants to create a visual question, an "artistic" value, from nothing.

We could say to the artist, "We don't know how you do it, making art out of nothing at all." Except that, once you have finished "Help Yourself to a Blue Banana," I promise you will begin to know how he does it.

Generally speaking, artists hope their efforts will be noticed by other people. They hope others will agree they have successfully asked a visual question. When this occurs, the aesthetic value of a visual experience can be translated into financial value, and in some cases, very big financial value.

A successful work of art can be worth lots and lots of money.

To simplify the last few paragraphs, allow me to say it like this: basically, artists are showing us their prized matchboxes.

And usually they hope we will like them.

Really collecting

The description of "collecting" that is outlined above makes a distinction between actually collecting *things,* and the different, often unconscious process that visually sensitive individuals have of collecting visual experience.

But here I must mention once more an innovative artist, the sculptor mentioned earlier, who actually *made her art* from things she did "find," sometimes from things she found just laying at the side of her street. Beyond collecting visual experience, she also collected *things*, and these things became part of her art. Many of her sculptures are complex arrangements of simple wooden boxes she found and painted black. Her first "discovery": a wooden linoleum shipping crate that measured 6' x 6" x 6" (2m x 15cm x 15cm).

Her work is a magnificent explosion of abstract balance, an important visual concept we'll explore again in chapter eight. If you bookmark this page, when you have finished reading you can refer to the notes at the end of the last chapter for key words to search on the internet to see examples of her breathtaking work.[11]

Awful expression

The last few pages present a simplified description of how visual expression is created and, as you might expect, things can go wrong. Just as there are bad writers, and bad cooks, there are also, of course, bad artists.

There are people who are unable or unwilling to start a collection before rushing to show us what they have found. In that case, what they have usually found is nothing. Or at least nothing new.

A bad artist may ask us a question, but not a *new* question.

Secondly, this whole process (described here in relation to FORM) must take place for each of the nine lessons of light. That is, everything we see has all nine of the sources of visual experience reflected in it, even the simplest sculptural shapes. Before someone can feel sure of his ability to select visual experiences that have meaning, and ask questions, he must understand all nine of these visual tools. Some people have a natural ability to do this, and you may say they're *born* artists, but for most of us, it's a learned ability.

And then there's this: unlike matchbox collectors, anyone who wishes to become an "artist" must also select at least one visual medium that will be used to express the work. That is, he must first understand, consciously or unconsciously, how to collect visual experiences, then how to choose which ones ask new questions, and then how to re-create what has been discovered, often combining several pieces from the collection.

Then he needs a "medium" to express what was found.

Among these media are the traditional disciplines of painting, photography, printing, cutting stone and drawing. And then there is architecture, expressing FORM and SPACE (with other lessons of light) in the design of buildings and environments.

And in addition, there are skills related to hundreds of commercial visual arts (business arts), including computer imaging, art directing, illustrating, sketching, designing, web mastering. flower arranging, applying makeup or air brushing, to name just several.

On the other hand, if your goal is merely to be a more visually sensitive person and enjoy visual living and all the great benefits we are discussing, then these tedious requirements about learning how to express yourself don't really apply. You can explore and enjoy visual living *as a lifestyle* just by awakening your two eyes and expanding your interest (by reading this book for example).

You can improve your wardrobe, paint your house or buy an abstract oil for your family room without following the more difficult path of making art, a path that serious artists accept.

Good hind-sight helps too

However, to actually be a fine artist or a business artist, one must actually *make* art or *make* design. So there's another responsibility that comes into play. This becomes part of the process for people who wish to have their visual work recognized within the body of visual expression that precedes it.

To create visual expression with an aesthetic value usually requires some knowledge of the *history* of visual expression. Re-discovering a previously explored approach to art is not a big accomplishment, just as running the *second* four-minute mile went largely unnoticed. A person needs to know where we were yesterday, and where we are now, in order to take us to some visually new place tomorrow. Anyone who explores unique areas of vision in his or her work may remain unknown unless the effort shows an understanding of what has come before it.

Above all, creating visual expression is often, plain and simply, hard work. Like all meaningful things to do, this process can sometimes require 10% inspiration and 90% perspiration.

Although some art explodes spontaneously from a person's soul (or at least from her hand), there is, more commonly, some difficult work needed. The hard part can mean anything from staying up all night long for six weeks at the side of a printing press checking COLORS on a new edition of prints (copies of an original painting), to developing a special metal alloy for casting a difficult piece of sculpture, or even mastering (or writing) a new computer program capable of creating the visual effects you can see in your mind. It is rare for anyone who does not have confidence in their ability to create meaningful visual expression (visual expression that asks visual questions) to accept the big amount of work that usually goes into its production. And when a person doesn't have that confidence, the result is often unprofitable as well.

This commitment is partly why the money associated with visual arts is justified and *earned*.

FORMING visual habits

My description above of artists as collectors needs one more modification. A person who collects things like old record jackets or picture sleeves (the printed covers found on small records) knows *consciously* what he is collecting. A big reason that people start any sort of collection, from bottle caps to artwork itself, is the satisfaction they get from displaying what they collected. But in this regard, calling visual artists collectors doesn't work.

Visual artists do not necessarily keep a permanent record of the visual experiences they "collect." Once the habit is developed, noticing the lessons of light as a way of life usually becomes second-natured. Unconscious even. For this reason, knowing exactly what inspired a work of visual expression is sometimes impossible.

If you put these thoughts together, a definition can be suggested that describes what a visual artist is:

> A visual artist is a person who has the habit of
> understanding life visually, the ability to process
> what is seen to create new visual expressions (ones
> that ask new visual questions), the need to actually
> create those expressions and the energy to do the work.

(Habit, ability, need and energy)

Where do visually sensitive people
look for expressions of FORM?

You might ask, "Where do visually sensitive people go to look for expressions of FORM and all the other lessons of light?
Where do they find these things to collect?"
Do the smartest artists spend all their time in museums?
You may say, "Museums have the most successful FORMS, so by going there something good is bound to rub off."

That's a logical thought, but almost nothing could be further from the truth. The visual information passing by an artist's field of vision is no different from the visual information that passes in front of any of us. But the habit that he or she has of *noticing* what is seen makes an artist's world considerably more interesting. It is this habit that supports the ability to collect, and the ability to create.

This book is written to assure you that everything you see, whether it's great art in the best museums, the view from an airplane window, or simply the clutter on top of your desk, is made up of the same nine visual building blocks.

Visually sensitive people will find exciting details in all of it, including that desk-top clutter. The world you see from your favorite easy chair, your living room window, the passenger seat of a truck or from a vacation cable car high up over the mountains is the same world that inspires people over and over to create moving visual art.

And it's a world packed with FORM.

* * * *

Chapter two continued
AN INTRODUCTION TO FORM
The second lesson of light
Expressing life in every dimension

It would be wrong to begin telling you about FORM in general, without first telling you how important human FORM, in particular, is to anyone who is living visually.

The human body is the most important inspiration for everything a visually sensitive person sees, feels and expresses. A separate book could easily be written about it. But to be brief, it's probably ok here to say only this: for many visually sensitive people, the human FORM is simply everything.

To put it another way, it's e-v-e-r-y-t-h-i-n-g.

As someone just now beginning to understand the lessons of light, when you read "the human FORM is simply everything" it's possible you'll think I'm referring to pictures of George Washington or statues of naked women.

It's true, visual expression is overcrowded with works such as those. But they represent only one small aspect of the importance human FORM has to all an artist sees, feels and recreates.

As this chapter unfolds, I'll try to explain why.

*Become a lean, mean
un-preconceiving visual machine*

Our body is an incredible machine that processes information that comes through the senses. Everyone is affected by the way their body and their mind uniquely process this data. And, anyone visually sensitive knows other people may (in fact probably) process the same information differently. Artists allow themselves to judge the world in an individual way.

You have that same freedom.

You can judge the world any way you wish.

The machine that allows this is your individual body.

The right you have to be an individual is a precious gift, but it is not always appreciated. Many people don't want to be individual. In fact, just the opposite is frequently true. There's plenty of evidence that *fitting in* can also be a very good idea (for some people). People who conform to everyone else, and "go with the flow" can sometimes be very successful.

But not many visual artists are traveling down that road.

More likely, they question and test all the information they receive through their senses. They try to understand it separate from all the preconceptions civilization teaches us. Those preconceptions include everything we learn in school.

For example, here are some "preconceptions:"

Do you believe 4 comes after 3? *That's a preconception.*
Is sugar sweet? *That's a preconception.*
Do you believe the earth is shaped like a cucumber?
　　That's a preconception.
Was Bill Clinton a U.S. president?
　　That's a preconception.
Does $e = mc^2$? *That's a preconception*

Of course, everyone knows these are intellectual facts (with the possible exception of the cucumber thing).

But we question them anyway.

Artists don't usually go with the flow. And they sometimes go strongly against it. You're free to question everything you're told. You're free to question everything you read.

And you're free to question everything you "know."

In other words, you can question e-v-e-r-y-t-h-i-n-g.

Since that's true, it won't surprise you to likewise hear that everything in this book is also a preconception. It's a preconception (basically it's *my* preconception) all about how the visual language works, and which words are best to describe it.

And like all preconceptions, you're free to accept or reject it.

But, you might ask: when schools try so hard to make us all think alike, why anyone would want to think differently?

Some of that answer has to do with FORM.

It's possible to make a simple case of it.

A visually sensitive person thinks differently than everyone else, including other visually sensitive people, because he or she *is* different from everyone else. For proof, he or she just looks at himself or herself in a mirror, using the observation skills we are talking about. At the same time, visually sensitive people are likely to wonder why you also don't think differently from everyone else, since in an artist's eyes, *everyone is as unique as himself* (or herself).

While discussing it, someone who is thinking visually might catch you off guard, speaking just four words that sum it up better than ten pages of theory.

Just what is so interesting about FORM?

He'll pause, take a breath, look you in the eye and explain:

You *are* a FORM.

The conditions of FORM

To be more specific, you are an *organic* FORM.

Organic FORM is the shape (or "energy") of things that are alive or things that seem to be alive. And alternately, there's another kind of FORM, called geometric FORM, and that's the shape (or the "energy") of everything else. Both these types of FORM can be either two dimensional or three dimensional.

There are two conditions of FORM:

> Organic FORM and
> Geometric FORM

It's important to know that classifying FORM into two categories, organic and geometric, is both a simplification and, again, a preconception. I doubt if prehistoric cave men knew there are two kinds of FORM, and there were thousands of visually successful people throughout history, artists and non-artists alike, before this idea came about and you could learn the visual language without it. But using these two names for FORM has the advantage of making a difficult distinction easy to put into words.

Serious artists may sometimes ignore the difference between organic and geometric FORM, but others can gain an insight from it about the role played by FORM in visual expression.

Organic FORM, the first condition of FORM
What do people look like?

There are not many subjects that ordinary people enjoy talking about (and thinking about) as much as the appearance of *other* people. But actually, most of us rarely take a good look at anyone. We're so concerned about how we *should* look, and how our neighbors *should* look, that we have, for most purposes, turned over the job of actually looking at each other to artists. We take our visual cues from professionals who are living visually.

Practically everyone who hears this statement considers it an exaggeration, or even a mistake in my opinion of how people see. But look at the evidence: business artists control the appearance of every person you have ever seen on TV, in the movies, or in advertisements, and in all the printed material you have ever seen. And before most of these people got to those places, another artist, at some point in the process, picked them to be there. Furthermore, a great majority of the people you see in your daily life have a "look" that has been largely decided for them by fashion designers, photographers, film directors, make-up artists and hair stylists and by *trends*. And, of course, trends are generally just a series of decisions that have been made . . . by artists.

I said years ago that one place that was somewhat isolated from this artist-dominated visual influence was the internet, where artists, if anything, were slow to get involved. I could see then that the net was being "designed" by millions of *non*-artists around the world; that is, by millions of everyday users who created and loaded their own web pages, pictures and sites. In the process they were uploading millions of pages of human experience that, generally speaking, were not first evaluated by artists.

I thought it would be interesting to see how the early influence of non-artists on the internet would develop, and how it would affect our idea of fashion and what people look like.

But everything changed. For better or worse, the majority of influential web sites were eventually re-designed by professional artists who gave them an appearance not unlike the over-designed look of everything in the non-net world. The first jury came in and again, for better or worse, there was not any big leap into new visual territory. (With one big exception: throughout all of communication, the look of *typography* was greatly influenced by the insanely word-heavy format of early web pages.)

Then, almost by surprise, we saw a second wave of raw visual imagery appearing on the internet, brought by the popularity of content internet sites like YouTube where, again, millions of *non*-artists began uploading how the world looks to them. And importantly, this time human beings in huge numbers are seeing it. This time it's likely that visual realities really may change. Someone on YouTube can wear an odd looking hat, or do a funny dance (like that guy who streams clips of himself doing the same jig in dozens of countries), and that can change fashion or choreography around the world.

To expand this phenomenon to issues beyond design and art (and dance), I likewise predict that soon a charismatic leader will introduce himself or herself to the world on a similar content site, using it to launch a low budget campaign that successfully wins the presidency of the United States or France or Pakistan.

But no matter what the future brings, in reply to my premise that artists are doing much of the looking at people for us, you might respond that yesterday you, yourself, looked at somebody, a *real* somebody, on a bus, or in a store (or on YouTube).

But even if you did, it is still my guess that you were only aware of the person's age and gender, or about how rich or poor they seemed, or how attractive you found them to be. But in the visual sense, this is hardly looking at all. Or you might say it is looking, but not *seeing*. Those opinions are intellectual observations, based on preconceptions tied to our learned habit of making value judgments about other people.

To be fair, each of these judgments does have its place in visual curiosity, because they are important characteristics of CONTENT. (Much more about this in chapter six.) But more important, and more difficult to see, are other visual features of people. What is the TEXTURE of a man's skin? The COLOR of his eyebrows? The proportion of his body. The message in his posture.

Or the FORM of his ear lobes? Anyone who sees people visually knows these are important observations to consider.

It's alive!

Then, there's another reason the shape of people is intriguing. In fact, it's a big reason: human FORM is the most important of all the possible organic FORMS, meaning, again, *living* FORMS (or FORMS that appear to be living).

I enjoy the scenes in horror movies when someone screams "It's alive!" It's always when a monster or alien comes to life unexpectedly. It's not only entertaining, but it's also a good dramatization of how differently we feel about something that is alive, especially when we thought it was dead.

It's hard (in fact it's probably impossible) to over-emphasize the significance that being alive has to visual living and the process of understanding, enjoying and creating visual expression. Having (human) life means having feelings. And the misery that sometimes comes from having strong feelings (which, for unknown reasons, may be stronger in the personality of a visually sensitive person) is possibly why people need to create art. It's possibly why some people have the urge to express what they are experiencing.

If you carry this thought further, it leads to the theory that maybe you have to suffer to be creative, a visual version of "no pain – no gain." And faced with centuries of evidence, we must conclude that suffering has certainly never hurt anyone's ability to be creative. One extraordinary artist, whose talent was never properly recognized during his lifetime, suffered debilitating emotional pain. He eventually cut off his own ear and later took his own life. His was just one of the countless historical suicides among artists, possibly brought on by the emotional torment they experience, or by depression they try desperately to work out or express in their art.[12]

Having life is a circumstance we share with other humans, and with all of the world's plants and animals. It's a circumstance that is extremely special, no matter what's alive. *Anything* alive is very different from something that is not alive.

To realize that some things have life while other things don't have life seems almost too simple to be important. But that plain sounding distinction is the basis for a sensitivity we must rely on continually to evaluate FORM. It is such an important distinction that putting it into these words is not an exaggeration:

> *The most important visual judgment a person can make about FORM is to sense how closely it expresses life.*

Getting over some old visual habits

This judgment about FORM is made continuously, although usually subconsciously, as we consider the scenes that come into our field of view. It doesn't matter if a FORM *has* life. It only matters if it *expresses* life. It doesn't matter if it is living, only if it has the energy of living. Wishing to create work that expresses life is one of the highest artistic ambitions. As a result, *observing* life can be an important exercise to practice.

A common way students are taught to see how living things express life (and therefore emotion) is by sketching human models. Students training as painters and sculptors are assigned to sketch models at classes throughout their schooling. But, although business art students can also benefit from this training, they are not always required to follow that strict discipline.

And as I said, many successful business artists never develop drawing skills *at all*. But this kind of training does have it's place because understanding how the FORMS of living things convey emotional feelings is one first step in knowing how to *recreate* emotional energy in a frame of reference, even if it doesn't actually represent living things. People who learn this process have spent perhaps thousands of hours observing (collecting) the visual information displayed by the FORMS of living things they see.

Seeing human beings as FORMS requires that we ignore the usual habit we have of judging people intellectually. Our intellectual judgments of people are not important factors in our opinion of people as FORMS. (But, to repeat, they *are* the building blocks of understanding the visual experience of people as CONTENT, as we will see in chapter six.)

To see people visually you'll have to learn to separate CONTENT away from FORM in your mind's eye.

One thing that helps this happen is to observe the human body naked. Anyone who seriously photographs the human FORM unclothed, or carves it in marble or wood, has advantages. First, when looking at a person with no clothing, there's no mistaking the emotional meaning hiding in human FORM because muscles, tension, posture, face expressions, complexion, even *aging* and build all help to express the model's emotional make-up.

And secondly, sketching nudes eliminates the distractions of CONTENT, COLOR, FORM (as style) and TEXTURE, all of which are normal visual characteristics of clothing.

Good evening, here's some news

This idea that a person's naked body represents some sort of a "picture" of their emotions may be news to you. Lots of people, including many visually sensitive people, go all through life without giving it much thought.

But it's not just the confusion of words that makes this emotional picture difficult to understand. What I mean is, it's *actually hard to see*. You have to somehow look beyond a person's FORM, into a kind of invisible glow that everyone has. That's where you find the energy of human FORM. Looking for that invisible energy is an important part of "collecting" FORM.

(Once again, words don't adequately describe this.)

On top of all that, the culture we live in can also play a role. Our culture works against us as we search for the truth about this kind of visual energy.

Since you are reading this book in English, it's likely you are part of, or at least familiar with, "western" culture. Western culture, like all societies, has evolved a set of ground rules for people within that culture to use in understanding life. Generally speaking, the ground rules of western culture are more *material* and less *spiritual* than, for example, "eastern" culture.

It's possible that this makes the statement "human FORM can be art" less easy to grasp for those of us raised in this society. That's because other societies often nurture ideas about the human body and human spirit that are more direct. Other societies sometimes take it more for granted that there is a link, even a *visible link*, between the body and the soul. They may accept that there's a relationship between the physical appearance of the body and the spiritual "glow" of the soul.

In fact, as proof, unless I am wrong, some societies, and languages other than English, have dozens of words that help describe this relationship.

Words that the English language simply does not have.

In some places, this link is part of mainstream thought.

It's familiar to people like, let's say, our own strong western belief in free speech. Since our own society doesn't make this connection between body and spirit a big part of everyday wisdom, and everyday language, then maybe it's understandable if you think it's odd to hear that a sketch of the naked body might reveal it.

It's understandable if that's news to you.

It's possible this makes western visual expression even more important. Generally speaking, western artists don't start with the idea (the *preconception!*) that body and soul are reflections of each other. Rather, western artists must actively look for evidence of this connection in the visible experiences they collect.

Suppose you glance at a woman who is carrying six bags of groceries. Something about her circumstance seems visually important. It might be how graceful (or ungraceful) she looks. Something about her character might speak (in the visual language) and inspire you to remember the details of this scene. How she seems to deal with the challenge of carrying all those bags is a clue to her being.

Of course, it's likely the woman would be wearing clothes.

But imagine, for a moment, a naked woman holding six bags of groceries. Her effort to manage the burden would be shown more vividly in posture and muscle tension, and even in her facial expression. By translating the visual language, those tiny clues can help us decide things. Is she strong? Is she weak? Does she take care of herself? And, of course, many other (and I'd say more engaging) nonverbal questions are also asked.

Questions that can't be put into words.

When a person's FORM asks us questions like these, it can make a very big impression. The impact can come without warning. You're just walking down the street. Everything is calm and nothing seems to be happening. You glance over there, and suddenly, Bam! Bam! Bam! Bam! . . . . from nowhere, a person's FORM is asking visual questions.

The energy of a person's FORM is revealed to you.

You could say a person's FORM is a sort of "window on their soul." If that window is open, discoveries are waiting to be made. When that window is open, it hits us like a ton of bricks, like a six alarm fire. Sometimes it leads to the irresistible urge to create art. Sometimes it inspires us to "tell" everyone what is seen through the window, to tell people about the magical link that has been discovered between body and soul.

This unique process of "telling" that I am referring to is done by creating visual expression.

That's what I have discovered about human FORM.

As the great dancer Mikail Baryshnikov put it in a recent TV interview, "The body never lies."[13] As you progress in visual understanding, you will discover your own truth and your eyes will help you do it. You must honestly evaluate whatever they tell you.

To make these discoveries for yourself by studying the nine lessons of light, you must accept that at some level, there are messages hidden in the FORM of the human body. Much of the greatest visual expression, art (and dance) comes to life when a person is inspired by these messages. To accept there's something there, to begin *watching for it*, is an important first step in learning the power that's hidden within living visually.

Turn around, look at someone

But even when a person is open to this, even if she starts by evaluating a naked model, seeing and *capturing* this energy is still hard to do. Seeing the emotional strength of human FORM and then transferring it to a lump of clay (let's say) is still a difficult process. In fact, I'd guess that most artists, even artists who are otherwise quite talented, *can't* do it. Human FORM and human emotions (let alone the human soul) are complex. Trying to make a visual statement of one through the other is where these complexities become most obvious. Trying to express life, that is, to catch the spirit of being alive (trying to capture the soul) by recreating human FORM is challenging, but it's not easy.

Nevertheless, when the goal is to create visual expression at one of it's highest levels, that challenge has to be met.

If there are interesting people near you right now (not necessarily naked), before you continue to read, take a long and careful look at them with these new thoughts in mind.

Once again, this is a simplified explanation of how visual expression works, and the last paragraphs have once again translated visual ideas into words. But, again, let me remind you, visually sensitive people don't usually bother with the words. If a sculptor has been inspired to carve a human FORM, it's safe to say he or she never stops to think, "I grew up in a western society, so this discovery process I'm beginning is more challenging because I don't have strong preconceptions about the relationship between the body and soul, a relationship that other cultures take more for granted."

If artists did stop to think like that, nothing would get done.

We're using words here to help open up your visual curiosity. But once that process begins, you'll realize these words are just the beginning. Even as I write this, I get a tingle of excitement imagining how wonderful you'll feel that day, during those special opening moments as these things I am explaining begin revealing themselves to you visually.

Sex lives and visual living

It would be nice if we could leave sex out of this discussion of human FORM.

But that's just not possible.

Sex is a dominant force in the life of every artist, and lots of visual expression can be traced to sexual experiences that inspired it. Some theories in psychology say that *everything* a person does is sexually motivated. So I imagine there are probably good arguments somewhere that all art is also sexually inspired.

I wouldn't agree completely with that. I wouldn't say sex is the only influence an artist reacts to. There are other common, emotionally charged inspirations like victory, murder, spiritual awakening, injustice or pain that can move a person to make art. But sex is nevertheless probably the biggest and strongest of them all. It's pretty well understood that, for most people (and artists are certainly no exception), sex is never far from the center of our thoughts.

Here's some evidence. When asked why almost all his work celebrated women, not men, a famous artist, generally considered to be the greatest sculptor of the 20th century, *didn't* say,

> "Women represent the nurturing mystery of humanity;"
> *And he didn't say,*
> "The complexity of female FORM is totally engaging;"
> *And he didn't say,*
> "My mother (or sister or wife or whatever)
> was the greatest inspiration in my life."

Instead, when he was asked why almost all of his work celebrated women, not men, the greatest sculptor of the 20th century replied quietly, "I like women more than men." At the time he was nearly 80 years old, but his attraction to women was, apparently, still his primary inspiration.[14]

Sex, love and romance are all very important issues in visual expression. And the sex part is quite visibly tied to human FORM. That means if an artist is using human FORM to bring life to a frame of reference, he or she is going to have to deal with the sexual messages that go along with it. Those sexual tensions in visual expression are among the more difficult to "translate" into words. Are they even part of FORM? There are obvious visible connections here. But it's also possible to argue that sexual feelings are more intellectual than visual. If so, maybe they're a part of CONTENT, the source of visual experience representing our thoughts and our logic (which is discussed in chapter six).

But either way, when sexual messages are present in a frame of reference, they'll probably overpower everything else.

The other organic FORMS

So the truth is, not all art and design is searching for the ultimate success of finding meaning in living human FORM. In fact far from it. In business art, to make my point, there is rarely the time, money or talent to pursue that high goal. As a result, lots of the "art" we see every day, including quite a bit found in galleries and museums, just reproduces human FORM "as is." In most cases, that's enough to bring emotional impact to a frame of reference.

For example, an art director for an advertising agency might load a picture of a pretty baby into a web site that promotes diapers. We see the image and accept that the child represents the emotional side of human experience. It would be unusual to find a baby picture like that that is, all by itself, genuine art. But it still speaks with organic FORM as a source of visual experience to help sell the product. (Even so, as we shall see, for a company trying to sell diapers, the CONTENT of an image such as this is even more useful than its human FORM.)

Therefore, to sidestep sex-related difficulties, and other problems of working with human FORM, artists employ other types of organic (that is living) FORM to do the job.

For practical purposes, the only other things alive are plants and animals. That means the shape of any plant or animal can bring life to a frame of reference. Again, it sounds simple minded, but anything living represents life.*

Imagine some students are asked to photograph a beautiful tree that's growing outside a classroom. Although they can create a

---

*Actually, there are thousands of species of life on earth that are neither plant nor animal. But the vast majority are microscopic, live deep in the oceans or underground (out of sight) and have negligible impact on our visual sensibilities. Surprisingly however, the *physical mass* of all that micro life may well dwarf all the plants and animals on earth *added together*, including forests and man. From *Beyond UFOs* by Jeffrey Bennett, Princeton University Press, ©2008, pp 68-70.

frame of reference (the photograph) that expresses life, they are not going to be bothered by the distractions that go with photographing a human model. For example, as they explore the tree, they are not tempted to wonder how rich or poor it is, or if it is happy or sad.

More important, and it may sound funny, but consider this other unique advantage: No one who ever photographed a tree ever daydreamed, wondering if the tree *liked* them. So, while shooting a giant oak, no normal person is likely to become sexually distracted, an obstacle that *can* sometimes be an issue when you are trying to express life through FORM by photographing (or drawing or sculpting) a living, breathing, perfectly proportioned naked human body.

Geometric FORM, the second condition of FORM
The soul of composition

We have been talking about organic FORM, which, in addition to the human body, includes all of the plants, flowers, trees and animals in existence. Each has the ability to express life. Each has its own kind of visual "glow." Human FORM is the most important of these, but at least in the decorative arts (such as book, wallpaper and fabric design) and in furniture design, there are many situations where organic plant life has served as an inspiration for artists wanting to express the energy of life through FORM. Who hasn't seen a table with legs carved like the roots and trunk of a large tree?

However, in many cases, organic FORM is not the only tool (or even the best tool) to carry a particular visual message. Not only are there eight additional lessons of light to bring emotional energy or "life" to frames of reference, there is also another kind of FORM.

We call that other FORM "geometric."

Geometric FORMS are the two or three dimensional shapes such as circles, squares, triangles, spheres, cubes and pyramids that can't be reduced to simpler FORMS.

Geometric FORMS are the workhorses of the visual vocabulary. They are the collection of common shapes that we call upon to organize our visual thoughts. Geometric FORM is, above all, the soul of composition, the superstructure that rivets visual experience into its frame of reference.

At a glance, we might say organic FORMS (living, life-*like* or life-*imitating* FORMS) are sort of round and wavy, while geometric FORMS (everything else) are straight and square. Speaking very generally, that's true (even though circles are geometric FORMS).

But the differences are more complicated than that.

The organic FORM of living things (plus all other FORM that imitates living things) can capture the spirit of our emotional human condition. By comparison, however, geometric FORM has the equal but different ability to attract our eyes to a frame of reference.

Humans love the emotional messages that we find in organic FORM, but we are almost powerless to resist *looking at* geometric FORM. So artists often rely on these individual strengths to create frames of reference that use geometric FORMS to grab our attention, and organic FORMS to keep our interest and move us emotionally.

The two conditions of FORM often work together like this.

Triangles, for example

Suppose that an emotionally strong organic FORM, a leaping whale, shall we say, is photographed in a frame of reference so that the whale and the frame of reference share a geometric relationship. (In this case the frame of reference is the rectangular edge of the photograph, or the image seen in the camera's view screen.)

One way would have the whale leaping along the diagonal of the rectangle. The diagonal of any rectangle is an imaginary line drawn from the lower left corner of the frame of reference to the upper right corner. (Here's another sketch to attempt: on your paper, draw a whale jumping along the diagonal of a rectangle.)

In this way, our eye is attracted to the geometric position of the whale in the photograph, and then entertained by the emotional strength of the leaping whale's organic FORM.

The rectangular shape (a frame of reference) is, to start with, a geometric FORM. By positioning anything along its diagonal, it is automatically divided into two triangles, and these are also very strong geometric FORMS.

Other formulas like this exist that help beginners understand composition. For example, a rectangle can be crossed with two diagonals; a square can be enclosed by a circle, a circle can be divided like a pie, any two geometric shapes can overlap, etc.

Try some sketches of these possibilities.

As you draw, allow your eye be attracted to the visual energy that's created by the relationship between the geometric FORMS you create on your paper.

Do this before you continue reading.

Generally speaking, the simpler the relationship is between geometric FORMS, the more eye-catching they are. But the goal of an artist is to sense the strengths of geometric composition without thinking about it. He can place emphasis within a frame of reference by understanding unconsciously how the geometric relationship of its FORMS works to attract the eye.

His eye tells him these things before he understands them "logically." An artist can, for example, modify the order in which the parts of a painting are looked at simply by alternating their geometric relationship to each other.

In business, advertising artists are experts at this. They can lead your eye around the many parts of a printed advertisement or brochure by planning their geometric arrangement. Without thinking about it, you might assume advertisements are designed to be read from the top down. But that is not true. In perhaps half the ads in magazines and newspapers, an art director or graphic designer first guides your eye to a place on the page *other than the top*.

In some cases, he or she wants you to first read the advertiser's name, even though it appears at the bottom of the page.

The way things are arranged within a frame of reference is called composition. Composition is not a lesson of light and it's not a source of visual experience. It is just one way geometric FORM is expressed to help draw our eye into a frame of reference.

Geometric FORM on its own

Geometric FORM has a sort of little brother relationship to organic FORM, but plays an important visual role anyway. It is the authority on visual organization. It's the everyday tool of choice for many working visual artists, the handmaiden of design in dozens of professions. You just can't imagine graphic design, product design or advertising without recognizing how they all rely constantly on geometric FORM.

In serious visual expression, geometric FORM has an equally large life. It was the backbone of modern art for a hundred years. And geometric FORM has dominated architecture since the time of the Greeks, three thousand years ago.

To demonstrate how great that role for geometric FORM has been for architecture, consider this: 100 years ago, when a Spanish architect used organic FORM as his primary inspiration (instead of geometric FORM), his last name entered everyday language around the world as a new word for *excessive*. To this day, Antonio Gaudi's work in Barcelona, Spain, is still considered amazing, extraordinary (and . . . excessive). I once traveled there only to see his work and was breathtaken for the entire visit.[15]

So how would life work without geometric FORM?

How would wheels roll? How would saws cut? How would buildings stand and carpets lie? How would pages turn and how would trucks pack? How would clocks tick, doors swing and elevators rise? What if skis didn't slide or drawers didn't pull out, or push buttons didn't press?

What if light didn't (usually) travel in a straight line?

If it simply wasn't so important to be alive, geometric FORM would proudly rule the day.

Be careful who draws you

Edgar Alan Poe wrote a short story about a painter who captures the likeness (that is, the energy) of his wife so perfectly on a canvas, that as soon as the painting is completed, the poor girl dies. The artist was so focused on the process of painting he didn't notice her life fading as he worked. It's possible that an artist may find this theory believable, but since I have never heard of it actually happening, to be practical, call it an exaggeration.[16]

But the idea that artists take energy from what is seen, and transfer it to a canvas, a block of marble or a web page is a valuable concept. For an artist, a photographer let's say, to successfully capture the essence of a model means to see it expressed through her FORM, and then to interpret that energy through the lens.

That's the power of the second lesson of light.

Cherish is the word
(Art is more than what an artist says it is)

The thinking process that we rely on to reach visual decisions (which isn't really "thinking" at all) is more complex than the familiar definition that says: "Art is what the artist says it is."

Artists use more than their status when they tell us, or show us, that certain FORMS are art, and certain other FORMS are not art. Instead, they call on their special ability to collect and identify which FORMS seen each day have visual meaning, and which are simply part of the clutter of everyday life.

As a beginning artist, or as someone interested in learning about the visual language, you'll have to do the same. You'll have to look at, and bring into awareness, the genuine visual character-istics of everything, separate from preconceptions. You'll have to look at the FORM of interesting people, separate from their person-alities, the TEXTURE of concrete sidewalks, separated from their function, and the COLOR of mouth-watering fruits separate from their delicious taste.

This exercise will build your insight into the lessons of light.

Eventually you'll begin to understand how they can each be collected, learned, renewed and *cherished*, . . . perhaps even with your own unique visual style.

* * * *

For review, here are the two conditions of FORM:

Organic FORM
Which means the shape of all living
things, plus the shape of any other things
that *appear* to be living

Geometric FORM
Which means the shape of everything else

Before continuing to read, take a moment to look for examples of these conditions of FORM. You'll find they are all around, no matter where you are.

So far

Some people have the habit of skipping over parts of a book, or skimming over certain paragraphs. This is particularly common among individuals who rarely pick up a book, and also among readers who are more comfortable with visual things than they are with words and writing (as some young artists are).

So allow me to encourage you otherwise.

If you arrived at this page after starting "Help Yourself to a Blue Banana" at some place other than at the beginning, please go back and start again. It's important to read this book from the first page, including the preface, foreword and introduction. They each include useful summaries of the theory you are reading about.

Also, this text is written so it presents information in the best order, and some text refers to points made earlier in the book.

If necessary, start again from the beginning now with paper, pencil, marker and bookmarks (see the introduction for more reasons why). And don't skip the dialogs. If you read carefully and do each exercise, you won't regret the time you spend learning about the lessons of light. This book can make a positive difference in the way you see the world. Even if you have no interest in creating visual expression of your own, it can still multiply many times the enjoyment you'll find in visual living. It's a pleasure you can count on for *the rest of your life*, and one that you can share with others who are close to you.

On the other hand, if you did start reading from the beginning, great! Please keep reading, marking, doing the exercises and placing bookmarks to remember the internet searches.

We're making progress toward the moment when you can look up from reading and understand the nine lessons of light!

Chapter Three

ANATOMY as a source of visual experience

Dialog

SUPPOSE YOU'RE WONDERING how, or *if*, the visual language influences your experience *before* you are living visually. After all, as we said earlier, lots of people go through an entire life without giving these ideas much thought. But, in fact, even a person who has never heard of the lessons of light will recognize, and react to, creative examples of these visual building blocks.

This happened not long ago in a popular American movie about space aliens. To help carry out the plot, the movie employed an interesting variation of ANATOMY, the third lesson of light. I'm sure you'll understand this example even before you read deeper into this chapter. Here's what I am referring to: The screenwriter for the film *"Men in Black"* saw the similar appearance shared between flying saucer UFOs and the two *plate-shaped* tower tops of the New York State World's Fair Pavilion. When the movie was made, those two towers were still standing in Queens, New York, many decades after the 1964 World's Fair for which they were built. Scenes from the movie were shot on the fair grounds there. To put it in visual terms, the screenwriter for *"Men in Black"* saw the similar ANATOMY shared between flying saucer UFOs and those two tower tops.

The visual idea worked because the top parts of the towers are sort of round and flat, just as we imagine flying saucers to be. *"Men in Black"* is a movie about aliens on Earth, so the writer, who is obviously living visually, wrote a plot twist based on this similarity between those tower tops and UFOs (flying saucers).

His leap of visual imagination became an important part of the story, especially at the end of the movie. If you remember the film you'll know what I mean. The writer, who I'm sure never heard of the lessons of light, knew we would understand when he suggested that the tops of those two towers could be flying saucers. He recognized that the twin tower tops share some ANATOMY of flying saucer UFOs and he used that clever understanding to help make the movie more exciting.

You'll see what that writer saw if watch *"Men in Black"* once again, or else search internet images for "1964 world's fair pavilion." (Bookmark this page and do this search after you finish reading.)

Here's a second example of ANATOMY. This is another one that is easy to understand and react to, a marketing promotion that was created to help sell beer. You may have seen it yourself.

Driving home the other evening, I saw a large billboard. It was an advertisement for a certain brand of brew. The billboard was divided down the middle, top to bottom. As I drove by it, on the left side of the sign I saw a picture of a bowling ball. In the picture, sitting next to the bowling ball, there were two 10-pins (bowling pins).

On the right side of the sign, there was a second picture.

This was a picture of a COLORful beach ball. It was resting in the sand on a beach, and behind the ball in the picture were two very pleasant looking palm trees. The trees were in the background and the artist had drawn the scene (using perspective) so that the beach ball was nice and big in the foreground (just about the same size as the bowling ball on the other side of the sign) and the two palm trees (which perspective made smaller), were just about the same size as the two bowling pins.

So here we have a sign where one side shows us a bowling ball and two pins, and the other side shows us a beach ball and two trees. Underneath the bowling ball was written the word "Them." Underneath the beach scene was the word "Us," along with the beer company logo.

Of course the meaning was easily communicated. The message was made clear using the ANATOMY of a bowling ball and two pins, comparing it to the ANATOMY of a beach ball and two palm trees. It was clear that the sign was saying, "Their beer is COLOR-less, dull and boring. Our beer is COLOR-*ful*, exciting and fun!"

Here's the point. The advertising agency that designed the sign could have just written the message on this sign using everyday words like so: "Their beer is colorless, dull and boring. Our beer is colorful, exciting and fun!"

But who would notice?

And who would believe them?

Instead, a clever advertising artist made me take very strong notice of this promotional message. He got my attention, *he created a visual experience*. He made me *understand* him, using the impact of ANATOMY. He showed me something he knew would get my interest and open my eyes. He attracted my eyes to a frame of reference (the billboard) by using ANATOMY to show me that, if they are viewed from just the right angle, "Hey, a bowling ball and two pins look just like a beach ball and two trees." Bravo, (with all proper respect to people who love bowling. Because generally speaking, and for better or worse, just about everyone thinks bowling is dull, especially compared to a day on the beach).

One more application of ANATOMY in advertising:

The cell phone industry invented an icon that indicates how good the signal is. It's five little lines that get taller as the signal gets stronger. One cell provider began "seeing" this icon in dozens of everyday situations. In some of their print ads, stacks of magazines get taller and taller, or five mountains get higher and higher. They use these images with a good slogan, "More bars in more places." In this way ANATOMY plays a central role in all their marketing.

"Hey, look at this! Stacks of magazines can look just like the signal strength icon!"

Before you continue to read, see if you can recreate on your paper the matching set of bowling/beach images described above. Don't worry about details. Just concentrate on getting the size (the SCALE) of the bowling image to match the beach ball and two trees. Try to sketch a bowling ball sitting next to two pins so they look similar to your second sketch of a beach ball and two palm trees.

When you're done, here's a second exercise that I'd like you to try. Glance around your room for something that also looks like something else. There are dozens of examples referred to on the following pages, but see if you can identify at least one before you continue to read. If necessary, get up and open drawers and closets to find more possibilities. Do this right now.

For example, I did this myself a minute ago in my own room. Guess what? I noticed for the first time that some slant-edged razor blades found in utility knives have a face on them, with two eyes and a nose (which are holes in the metal blade). Then there's three notches on top of the blade (which hold it in place in the knife), and the notches look like hair! Don't stop looking until you can make at least one comparison like this somewhere around you right now.

Chapter three continued
AN INTRODUCTION TO ANATOMY
The third lesson of light
Everything has a "ness"

ANATOMY is an easy lesson of light to understand.

In fact, visually curious people sometimes look forward to learning about it until they're disappointed to discover that the way people look when they're not wearing their clothes is only a very small part of what "ANATOMY" means to visual artists.

The idea that studying ANATOMY is like some serious medical requirement for artists, including big textbooks that illustrate all kinds of body parts, is a common misconception. It is true that once an artist becomes interested in the way human FORMS express life, he or she may find it interesting to study the details, both inside and outside, of those FORMS. In this use of the word, to study ANATO-MY means to understand how bones and flesh and muscle really look, and how they work to express emotion on the surface of, and in the posture and body language of, the human FORM.

Because the human body is by far the most important FORM (remember: we *are* FORMS), studying it up close, which can include dissecting a real human cadaver, sometimes has a role in advanced visual educations.

And for obvious reasons, a knowledge of human ANATOMY is helpful, or maybe mandatory, for sculptors and painters, who are sometimes thought of as our most serious fine artists.

But as a whole, and taking the broader view, visually sensitive people, along with most business artists, are more likely to be curious about the specific ANATOMY of *things* (like bowling balls and palm trees, or cell phone signal icons) rather than human bodies.

ANATOMY allows us to identify objects by details that make them different, and by details they share with other objects. Among other things, these shared details may include an object's COLOR, its SCALE and its TEXTURE. ANATOMY may also include the way an object performs a task (or the way it helps *you* perform a task) or even the way an object impacts our senses other than sight.

Normally, however, and for most evaluations, the common and everyday visual characteristics of a thing, like its COLOR or FORM, are the important characteristics of shared ANATOMY.

Everything has a "ness"

Years ago, I heard a typography teacher evaluate the design of a logo. It was the letter "M" intended to be a trademark for a new company. What he said was, "There's something wrong with the ANATOMY of this letter. It doesn't have 'M'ness."[17]

Every object has visual characteristics which we expect from it, including every letter of the alphabet. For example, bicycles have "bicycleness," eye glasses have "eye glassesness," and tennis rackets have "tennis racketness." When one or more of these characteristics are missing from, or misrepresented in, an object (or in a picture of an object), there will be a predictable, usually negative, reaction from people who see it.

It is not unusual to find even trained artists making a mistake in the way they recreate the ANATOMY of everyday objects, and this is frequently the cause of confusion in the impact of visual meaning. A tennis racket with a handle that is too short does not have "tennis racketness."

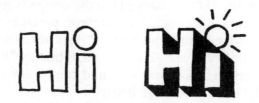

With the addition of the ANATOMY of a sunrise, the plain greeting (left) became a design with visual meaning (right). The modified greeting uses "sunrise-ness" to help make it appealing.

"Ness" usually means the simple shape of an object, and the shape of the *details* that make up an object. But it can also include less obvious characteristics, including COLOR and TEXTURES. For example, can you describe the way a red apple reflects light compared to the way red satin bed sheets reflect light? That may be difficult to put into words, but an experienced illustrator can express those differences using the visual language in a convincing way.

Details like this are part of the information artists notice all the time. It's what will make us familiar with how things *really* look. It makes us familiar with the ANATOMY of apples and the ANATOMY of red satin bed sheets.

Artists constantly notice the details of things that come into view. That's how the many visual characteristics of ordinary objects become part of an unconscious database of knowledge. Artists need this visual dictionary inside their mind to help them remember how things look. Some logo designers, for example, rely on it constantly.

Business artists who create trademarks and "corporate identity" (logos) need to be confident answering these questions: How does the letter "M" really look, and how may it be changed and *still* be instantly accepted by everyone as "M"? Or, to put it another way, what is the ANATOMY of an "M?" What is "M ness?"

And, by the way, that word *instantly* is very important.

In your own experience, I am sure you can recall examples of logos that substituted something for a letter, or perhaps you've seen this accomplished on a sign or a poster. A case in point is the logo for Staples, the office store, where "L" is replaced with a staple, a poor example because "L" looks only slightly like a bent staple.

Or maybe you have seen this more innovative one:

A logo designer once created a poster for his client IBM.

The image was a playful modification of the company's famous logo (which he also designed). He made the "I" an "eye," the "B" a "bee" and left the "M" unchanged (so the design is recognizable).

To be accurate, we could say his clever poster incorporated the ANATOMY *of sound*, since the letter "I" does not look like an "eye," rather, it sounds like "eye." And the same is true for "B" and "bee."[18] (To see this design, bookmark here and come back later to search images on the internet for "eye bee m.")

I once incorporated some more common ANATOMY in a logo design. When working in the Republic of China, I created a logo for the tourist magazine called "TAIWAN." It used normal letters, but substituted a Chinese pagoda (a building that has sort of a pointed top) for the second letter "A." It works because letter "A" actually looks somewhat like a pagoda, and a pagoda has some "A-ness."

You can visit my web site, behindthescenesmarketing.com, to see this design. Click on "our work," and then click #96.

(Bookmark this page and come back to it later.)

The conditions of ANATOMY

For anyone living visually, it's common to develop a curiosity not only about the details of objects, but also about what makes them different from other objects that may share some characteristics. This information is sometimes called your visual "repertoire" (Pronounced: rep-e-twa.) To have a strong visual repertoire means that you have memorized the visual characteristics of many objects that exist in our everyday world.

Once an artist has this visual reference material stored within her mind's eye, she can create visual statements whose strengths come from comparing what is similar and what is different, visually speak' about everyday things. In this way, ANATOMY is a source of vis experience, and one of the nine lessons of light.

Let's look now at the conditions of ANATOMY.

ANATOMY can make a strong impact
in a frame of reference in three ways

These are the three conditions of ANATOMY:

comparing similar looking objects
substituting similar looking objects
and
creating new objects by
combining familiar objects

Here's an explanation of how these conditions work within a frame of reference to create visual expression.

First, the similar appearance of any two objects can be compared side by side. That is, a frame of reference can announce (in the visual language), "Hey, guess what! This looks like this!" That's what the beer billboard shows us (mentioned earlier). For another example, chalk and cigarettes. Did it ever occur to you how similar they look? Some place, some time, a magazine may use that comparison to create visual interest. For example, it might illustrate an article about a kid who is caught smoking in grade school.

A drawing that somehow shows how chalk looks like cigarettes would be a good visual anchor for that kind of story. The reason is, visual curiosity is raised when we are shown that one thing looks like something else. It's a little bit like this: Did you ever meet a person who shares your exact name, but who is otherwise unrelated to you? I have a common name, and that has happened to me frequently, and it's an interesting sensation. It's the same way I feel when I see a frame of reference that points out that one thing unexpectedly looks like something else.

Second, an object can be *replaced* in a frame of reference with another object that has similar visual characteristics. (This is like announcing, "Hey, this looks like something else that you might normally expect to see here!") That's how the TAIWAN logo works (mentioned earlier). Another example might be an illustration for a different article; this time let's say it's a story about what football players eat for breakfast. It may show a quarterback with his arm back ready to throw a long pass. But in his hand, instead of a football, there's a large egg. Your reaction might be, "Hey that's not a football he's holding. It's an egg!" Of course footballs and eggs share some visual characteristics. Among similar characteristics: they're both sort of oblong, and they can both be brown.

The third way that ANATOMY works in a frame of reference is this: objects can be combined to look like other objects. In this case, a frame of reference may combine otherwise common things so something new materializes like magic. ("Hey! When I put this and this and this together, can you believe, it looks like this!") An overused example is that familiar image of a frying pan that looks like a face. The ANATOMY happens when two fried eggs are used for the eyes, and a strip of bacon is the mouth.

Putting things together to make a human face is a common kind of ANATOMY, very often used in children's books.

Whenever ANATOMY appears like this inside a frame of reference, it has all the power of the other sources of visual experience. Like the other sources of visual experience, it can ask engaging visual questions, and inspire us to imagine things that move beyond the ability of written words to express.

As this chapter continues, we'll look in more detail at all these visual possibilities and at the role they play as the conditions of the third lesson of light.

Comparing similar looking objects

Many everyday things look like other everyday things.

What would you notice if an appliance store displayed some old TVs right next to microwave ovens? If that happened, we'd see that some TVs and some microwaves share similar ANATOMIES. Generally speaking, they're both rectangular and box shaped. They both have a shiny dark rectangular surface on their front (the screen on the TV and the door on the oven) and they both have dials or controls. Some TVs and microwave ovens are also about the same size as each other. Of course we're talking about conventional TVs, not flat screen TVs.

When two objects are similar in size, that may help to show that they have similar ANATOMY. However, it is not a requirement.

Someone once pointed out the similar ANATOMY between a swirly blue marble, and the earth seen from distant satellite pictures. Even though the sizes of marbles and the earth are very different, the similar appearance of these two objects is easy to see.

For an even greater difference in size, consider our solar system compared to a simple atom. The atom may have at its center a single proton around which circle electrons, much like planets orbiting the sun. It's easy to see how the ANATOMY of an atom and the ANATOMY of the solar system are comparable.

The same is true for cannon balls and bowling balls, candles and dynamite, and white string and cooked spaghetti.

Imagine also how cauliflower is similar to the human brain.

Likewise, if you found a garden snake next to a garden hose, their similar ANATOMY would be obvious. The point is if you draw a picture of these sets (or photograph them) you will have a frame of reference with at least some visual interest.

To simplify, consider how obvious this sounds:

If you photograph a plate of cooked spaghetti that is sitting on a table next to a pile of string, you will have a picture that is more engaging than another photograph that shows only a pile of string. It would, in fact, be more engaging than another photograph that shows a plate of spaghetti next to a baseball. People are *naturally* interested in frames of reference that remind us that one thing looks like another thing. ("Hey! spaghetti looks like string!")

When I was a child, I watched an artist express ANATOMY on a kids' TV show. He'd invite a child from the audience to come on stage. Then he gave the volunteer a big marker and said, "Make any shape you want on this big drawing pad." No matter what the shape was, he could draw a picture using that shape as an important part of his sketch. His knowledge of how things looked (his visual repertoire and his understanding of ANATOMY) allowed him to imagine that original mark as part of dozens of scenes or objects.

On your paper right now, scribble a simple shape and visualize it as part of a larger picture.

Then attempt to draw that picture around your scribble.

Do this before you continue to read.

Each time you bring to conscious attention the fact that one thing looks like something else, you are helping to build your important visual repertoire.

Substituting similar looking objects
The eyes often have it

Illustrations whose visual strength comes from ANATOMY are common in newspaper articles, and are often found on pages where COLOR is not available. Many of these drawings are created by illustrators who sometimes get called by a newspaper just a few hours before the paper is printed. To solve such assignments, artists tap their visual repertoire, and apply it to current news events.

And of course they have to do it *quick.*

In fact, graphic designers who work on TV news programs sometimes create illustrations in just minutes (not hours) especially when there is breaking news. I'm referring to those picture boxes they design that appear directly behind the anchorperson.

As you can imagine, it's not easy to convey visual meaning under these kinds of deadlines. As a result, many news graphics are very simple, just a photo with a few words related to the story.

But, at times, visual meaning is beautifully captured. Last year, I remember, there was a snow storm that disrupted airline travel. Airports everywhere were closed. On one TV broadcast, behind the anchorperson, a beautiful snowflake appeared, representing the bad weather. But, taking a closer look, the snowflake was actually a *silhouette of five airplanes* parked nose to nose, with overlapping wings. The airplanes, of course, suggested all the airport closings. ("Hey, look at this! Five airplanes can look like a snowflake!")[19]

A strong visual concept. Like many successful expressions of ANATOMY, this one is easy to sketch. (Try it on your paper.)

Today however, I admit that I was wondering how original that snowflake was. Who knows? The designer who created it may have been inspired by *someone else's* snowflake. I say that because recently I was inside a FedEx office, and a holiday display on their counter was decorated with another snowflake, this time made out of five FedEx airplanes. This time, the artist added delivery trucks, parked between the planes. So how often has this happened?

Here is another description of a (newspaper) illustration that called on ANATOMY. In this case (in a drawing that appeared with no COLOR), a man's eye was replaced by something else. Before reading the details, try to think of things that look like eyes. Then make a list of them on your paper. You'll be surprised at how this artist approached that same challenge.

This artist was asked to create a drawing that would bring attention to an article about the cold war period of American-Soviet history, when the east/west military "arms race" was a part of everyday life. In those days, around the 1950s, everyone was afraid of an unexpected missile attack.

The final illustration showed a man's face in profile (from the side). He was looking from the left side of the picture toward the right. Flying into the picture from the other direction, toward the man's face, was a group of tiny nuclear missiles. Each was identical to the others and they were whizzing past the man's head.

The concept was ordinary except for one exciting detail.

The artist who drew this illustration substituted the shape of a missile *to represent the man's eye!*

Of course, from the side, a man's eye does look a bit pointed toward his ear, and flat near his nose, like a simple rocket. (Try a sketch.) But the beautiful detail that brought magic to the drawing was this: the tail fins on each missile were drawn so that, when a missile became the man's eye, its tail fins became his eyelashes!

No one can ever explain what a drawing such as this means in words. But it captured *something* about the arms race. Was it stupid? Was it silly? Was it self-destructive? Was it painful?

Words don't exist to explain the message communicated by the comparison of a man's eye to a nuclear missile. But if you imagine this illustration (or sketch it on your blank paper), you will agree there is a very engaging meaning there. And the meaning is greater because one of the nine lessons of light brought to our attention this interesting similarity of eyes and missiles.

Mother Nature is hiding in your closet

Because of ANATOMY, it's easy to make a mistake in understanding what you see. Sometimes those mistakes can be frightening. Many things look like other things, so you have to be careful as you evaluate the visible world.

In fact, the mysterious and scary possibilities of ANATOMY show up often in just about everyone's childhood. I'm sure, when you were young, at least once or twice you saw a "man" hiding in the shadows of a dark closet, or perhaps you looked up to find a "face" on the surface of the Moon.

Several years ago, when photographs were beamed back to Earth by an unmanned orbiter, we discovered still another face . . .

on Mars! (Apparently it's just a mountain on Mars that looks like a face.) As a little boy, I was once frightened by a small piece of crumpled wire on my bedspread. I finally ran for my life after lying there motionless under the covers *for an hour,* believing it was a spider.

And for one more unexpected ANATOMY: A climber at Mount Rushmore (near Rapid City, South Dakota) reported seeing a *fifth* face next to the huge carvings of the famous four American presidents. It's the head of an American Indian, which seems to appear within the natural rock in the side of the mountain.

ANATOMY is the reason for all these strange sightings.

In fact, as shown, Mother Nature herself serves up some of the most unique examples of this lesson of light.

Combining familiar objects –
Making ANATOMY out of nothing at all

These are mostly fun examples of ANATOMY.

But ANATOMY can be at play in serious visual expression also. When that happens, just like each of the other lessons of light, ANATOMY asks very thoughtful questions.

Try to imagine this inspiring art: It sprang to life from a combination of common objects we see all the time. An artist put together an *old bicycle seat* with a set of bicycle *handlebars.* You'll be surprised to learn that the result of this ordinary sounding effort is an amazingly realistic sculpture of a bull's head!

The seat is the bull's face, and the handlebars are his horns. A wonderful detail is that two screws, on each side of the seat, are in exactly the correct location to represent the bull's eyes. ("Hey look! If I put together an old bicycle seat with a set of handlebars, it looks just like a bull!") First fried eggs, then missiles, then screws. What else is out there that "looks" like eyes?

This sculpture of a bull was created from nothing at all.

It didn't exist until the artist allowed his eyes to realize that the parts of an ordinary bicycle could produce it. I don't know how his inspiration occurred. It may have happened when those parts were accidentally dropped side-by-side on the floor of a barn, or were displayed together in a bicycle parts catalog. But however it came to be, imagine the thousands of images like this that are yet to be discovered. Perhaps you'll be the one to find them.

And who knows? Maybe they will make you famous. The man who discovered the bull's head among his bicycle parts had a long, successful creative career. I guess so! He was Picasso, who TIME Magazine named "the most influential artist of the 20th century."

As you become familiar with modern visual expression, and visual living, you may discover a picture somewhere of that remarkable bull's head sculpture. Or in fact, you could make a plan to look for it in your library, a bookstore or, of course, you'll also find it on the internet. (Search images for "picasso bull's head" and include the quotation marks.) Bookmark this page, then come back and do this search when you have finished reading.[20]

When you see it, you'll agree it asks visual questions.

It will make you think more deeply about both ANATOMY *and* FORM, and for that matter, about bulls and bicycle parts. As a result, you may wonder, "Are bicycle parts just bicycle parts?" or, "Why didn't I ever notice that connection before?" or, "What other magic is yet to be revealed in the ANATOMY of common things?" And, of course, there are also many, many thought-provoking questions asked by this bull's head sculpture (and other examples of ANATOMY) that cannot be put into words.

As you react to ANATOMY, other thoughts may cross your mind. You may find that this is true: ANATOMY can lead you to investigate all visual experiences. You might say to yourself, "I can do that. I can find hidden expression in everyday objects. I can see how otherwise unrelated things are *visually* related."

As you look around your world for these visual links, your personal collection of visual experiences will begin to grow.

Talking beds and pleasant Sunday mornings

Rightly or wrongly, children's books love to show kids that anything can have a face. Children's books are filled with images of smiling houses, crying trains and talking coffee pots. For each one, someone has challenged his or her imagination to invent ways that the ANATOMY of the human face (that is, eyes, noses, mouths, ears, hair, and etc.) can be creatively combined with the ANATOMY of non-living things. And incidentally, this can be very easy to do. I gave a smiling face to a blue banana on the cover of this book, and his stem became a little green hat.

I knew ahead of time *positively* that you would like it.

"Hide and seek" illustrations, a picture game popular before TV and movies were invented, used ANATOMY differently. In those drawings, you'd search for pictures of animals and familiar objects the artist hid in the details of treetops and scenery. The game was to find as many hidden images as possible. (This wasn't Game Boy, but it did keep people amused 100 years ago.)

Following a similar idea, a successful and brilliant artist for many years drew pictures of famous people for newspapers, and he then concealed his *daughter's name* in the details of the drawings. He relied on the four letters in her name (NINA) to represent hair, or carefully drawn folds in a movie star's dress or other imaginative parts of the drawing. He sometimes made it all a game by including a tiny number next to his signature. The number told us how many times her name was hidden in the picture. For decades, newspaper readers enjoyed this playfulness within his illustrations, but it was only a minor diversion compared to the astounding genius of his drawing talent. Millions of people, including me, remember those drawings, and the whimsical game that accompanied them.

Pleasant memories of visual living on a Sunday morning.[21]

One surprise: you may gradually notice that the more simple a concept for ANATOMY is (like snowflake airplanes), the more likely it will be a strong visual statement.

And the more simple the concept, the more easy it is to put on paper. The "thinking" that goes into creating any visual expression made strong by ANATOMY might be more important than the technical skills needed to execute it. So your repertoire can be more valuable than an ability to sketch.

If an idea for ANATOMY is good, a sketch for it may be as plain as a few lines or stick figures. The drawing of the man with a missile eye (described on page 121) is so simple you could probably draw it. If you didn't already, try now to sketch that simple picture on your paper, even if you have no ability to draw.

The hard part about ANATOMY is knowing the details that make things visually exactly what they are. On a certain level, getting a good foundation in that is tough. I say so because throughout childhood, teachers and books often mis-guide children about how things really look. For one example, I recall seeing a kid's spelling book intended for pre-schoolers who are old enough to match an object to the word that describes it. It showed colorful pictures of things next to the written name for each one.

Not surprisingly, on one page there was a realistic drawing of a cat next to the letters C-A-T. But, on another page, S-U-N was printed in big red letters, and next to that was a bright yellow circle.

And in the middle of that circle – a happy smiling face.

How far can this go?

A book like that is a case of a careless (but probably harmless) influence on a young reader's visual education. Obviously, the sun does not really have a face. But there's another book, also published for kids, that is a fantastic celebration of fun ANATOMY, and a very positive influence on young visual curiosity. It shows photographs of perhaps a dozen miniature displays, similar to doll house rooms, that the book's author actually created by substituting *something else* for absolutely everything in each scene.

In one of these small rooms, a pretzel is used as the back of a tiny chair. If you think about it, or make a simple sketch, you'll see how the twisted FORM of a pretzel does look like the curved wood that you sometimes find on bent wood furniture. ("Hey! A pretzel can look like the back of a doll house chair!")

In the same scene, the cushion on that little chair is a round cracker. Another page shows a different scene. In that tiny room, a small tube of toothpaste is glued to the handle of a disposable plastic shaver, and it looks just like a miniature vacuum cleaner. This wonderful book presents perhaps 2000 examples of everyday things that look like other things in miniature. The book is such a success that several pages became available as posters, designed for kids' bedroom walls.[22]

A lesson here might be that, in some kind of a general way, everything on earth also looks like something else.

Unwanted ANATOMIES

Successful examples of ANATOMY can be fun or they can be serious. But ANATOMY can also be destructive. When that happens, it's usually because it has appeared in a frame of reference *by accident*, and that can have a very negative effect.

Just as it is possible to express ANATOMY to create visual meaning on purpose, it is also possible for some unplanned details to appear in a frame of reference. Good artists develop their eye so that, in just a few glances (that is, in just *nine* glances), they can be sure each of the lessons of light is working effectively. But mistakes happen. Each of the nine lessons of light must work as hard as possible to support the visual message that is trying to be born.

But at the same time, none of the lessons of light can be allowed to do unwanted work. That is, the nine sources of visual experience can weaken a frame of reference just as easily as they can strengthen it.

Suppose that an illustrator is asked to draw a picture for the cover of a cosmetics company's catalog. She first prepares a sketch of her idea (a pencil drawing showing only a few details). It suggests a woman sitting at a dresser applying makeup to her eyebrows. The sketch is approved, the drawing is finished and the catalog is printed. The next day it's mailed to customers before anyone notices that the finished picture looks a little like a *human skull*.

That may sound like an exaggeration, but there is an illustration like this sold in poster stores. The "skull" shape is created from a round mirror behind the woman's dresser. The woman's dark hair, and its reflection in the mirror, look like the "eyes" in the skull, and the lipsticks and cosmetics sitting on the dresser top are drawn in just the right place to look like the skull's teeth. Of course, that poster was created on purpose to look like a skull. But if you're curious (and I bet you are) you can see it by searching internet images for "skull mirror." (Bookmark this page.)

And more recently a well-known fragrance company used this same concept (again on purpose) as an advertisement promoting a perfume called Poison! The ad was inspired by the original poster.

"Hey, com'on," you may say. "You're making things up. No one could be so *un*-observant." Not true. Yesterday I came across a kitchen appliance whose design is hard to believe. It's a brand name electric grill with a pretty white flip-up top whose FORM is basically two geometric ovals. Attractive at first glance, but on second look its resemblance to a rest room seat is *way too close*. This unpleasant ANATOMY was apparently noticed by somebody, because the more recent models of that grill now look *completely* different.

That shows us how it is possible for *unwanted* ANATOMY, like this, to creep into a product design by accident.

For another example, buildings with noses

Illustrations (and snapshots) are typical places for unwanted ANATOMY to appear. But also common, and often funny, are the faces that somehow show up on the fronts of buildings.

If you leave out miniature golf courses and carnival booths, it is hard to argue that any building looks good with a nose. But a drive around almost any city usually turns up a building that looks like it has one, and usually with an entire face to go with it.

Some buildings are designed intentionally to look like faces (like one at Harvard College where their humor magazine is published), but many of them come to life unexpectedly as the result of poor design or renovations. They're the ones that remind us it's possible for ANATOMY to show up anywhere, even where it is least expected or wanted. (You can see the Harvard building by searching images for "lampoon building." Bookmark this page.)

Time flies: the ANATOMY of a kite's tail
(More ANATOMY in three dimensions)

Three dimensional ANATOMY includes Picasso's bull head sculpture that he made from bicycle parts, and buildings with noses. But here's another example of a successful use of three dimensional ANATOMY. It's a story of how a business artist (me) helped one manufacturing company sell more wrist watches.

I was asked to design a counter top department store display for a new watch.

It had to look exciting to buyers.

We wanted shoppers to say, "Hey, look at that!"

Lying on my table was a plastic triangle with an opening in the center. I glanced at the triangle, and then picked it up and looped the watch strap through the opening. Instantly . . . just like that . . . the ANATOMY of a miniature kite appeared before me. The plastic triangle seemed like the familiar diamond shape of a kite, and here is what surprised me: as it dangled from the triangle, the loose end of the watch strap looked like the kite's tail! I could see the possibility of making the display look like a kite.

That's how quickly a visual inspiration can come.

A more detailed model was presented to the watch company. We cut a diamond shape from plastic and strapped the watch through a slot in one of its points. The loose end of the strap became the kite's tail (to put it accurately, the watch strap had the ANATOMY of the tail of a kite) and the watch face was framed by the bottom point of the diamond.

The plastic kite was mounted on a short piece of coat hanger wire and that became the "string." The string was inserted into a paper weight, the base of the display.

The watch company liked the design so we produced them.

On the finished displays, we printed "Time Flys" (misspelled on purpose) across the plastic diamond, with the name of the watch below it, and ordered a supply of real paper kites, to be given away as a free gift to everyone who bought the new watch.

This design worked because a watch strap can look like the tail of a kite. That is, explaining it again, it can have the ANATOMY of the tail of a kite.

If you'd like, you can see this watch display on my web site at behindthescenesmarketing.com. (Bookmark this page and return to it after you have finished reading the last chapter.)[23]

The visual boundaries

Most of what we see every day is familiar.

For example, we know what cars look like and, day after day, cars keep looking that way; we know what trees look like and, week after week trees keep looking that way; and we know what people look like and, pretty much, month after month and year after year, everyone keeps looking the same way also. In fact there's a sort of relief we feel when anything easy to recognize comes into view.

In our everyday visual life, there are very few surprises.

The easiest way for people to visually understand something is to realize they have seen it before. Everyone analyzes everything, searching for that recognition. All that saved information we search through is in permanent "storage" in our "mind's eye." It's all part of our subconscious visual repertoire. When we recognize something, we search our memory for information that was true the last time we saw it. Then we call on that information once again (over and over) to help us take action on what we see. When we recognize something, we can put our mind on a sort of "automatic pilot."

Even at those moments when something *isn't* immediately recognized, ANATOMY still helps us classify new things. When you were young, I'm sure you noticed how those big pink pencil erasers look like bubble gum. When you see one of those erasers now, you can say, "that's not bubble gum, it's an eraser." And when you see bubble gum, you now know it *is* bubble gum and it's *not* an eraser.

You can relax. You have seen these things before.

You've got things well under control.

The trouble is, just when you think you are familiar with how everything looks, some frame of reference can remind you there are images that you have never imagined. Just when you think you are familiar with how every *thing* looks, those things are manipulated by someone who is thinking very visually.

First let's describe a situation where you may find a familiar image, one that's in fact so familiar, so predictable and so recognizable that you're most likely happy to see it: Think back to the many birthdays that you and your friends have celebrated. At one of those parties, possibly at many, a birthday card probably had that comforting effect on you or on someone you know.

Some birthday cards are so "friendly" that people actually do feel good just looking at them. That kind of familiar frame of reference can genuinely fill a person with happiness.

The images that represent most holidays, not just birthdays, call on this friendly familiarity to help us all, as Jennifer Lopez once sang, *get loud!* Bring to mind any holiday and the pictures in your mind's eye probably fall in that happy category.

The illustrations on birthday cards and greeting cards usually tap into that warm friendliness. They're covered with wonderful images of flowers, sunshine, pets, kids, families, rainbows, clowns and everyday people, etc, and usually the people are shown doing everyday things in a cute or amusing way, or saying cute and amusing rhymes. You don't need to be living visually to enjoy those kinds of pictures. Just about everyone reacts to them, and one much-loved artist had a long and profitable career just painting amusing pictures like this for magazine covers. Wonderful, happy pictures.[24]

Another well-known (very rich) artist mass-markets friendly paintings of very cozy cottages, winter villages, country gates and beautiful bridges all bathed in snow or sunshine. In other words, he explores the familiar and comforting territory of visual expression *on purpose.* Looking at his pictures really does give many people a satisfying feeling of well-being and contentment.[25]

And for one more example, perhaps you have noticed that some human smiles, *all by themselves*, have this same kind of wonderful power to make everything seem all right.

On the other hand, it's also possible to come upon frames of reference that are so *un*familiar that people are attracted to them in an unusual, almost nervous way. These may include evil images of monsters or demons, or terrible violence. One extraordinary young artist found a related style. He very often included images of strange beings and quietly disturbing details within his paintings.[26]

Those kinds of pictures can have a sort of hypnotic effect.

And on Halloween there are many exceptions to the "happy holidays" images mentioned above. To celebrate Halloween, everyday people and many very talented artists turn to the unfamiliar, or even the *very* unfamiliar. If you've attended the Halloween Parade in New York City you know *how* evil and unfamiliar things can get. You might even say the New York City street scene on Halloween is sometimes almost out of control, visually speaking. To see some of that scary visual chaos, search images for "New York Halloween Parade" or visit halloween-nyc.com. (Bookmark this page.)

It sounds odd, but sometimes people just can't resist looking at things that are scary or weird. Images of strange violence have that power also, and not just on Halloween. Most of us can't resist taking a quick look at violence or tragedy. For one thing, that's why traffic slows down around highway accidents.

Everyone has that built-in curiosity. And I discovered, it turns out, even me. As I wrote these paragraphs, I thought, "Maybe I am wrong. Maybe not all people are attracted to spooky and violent frames of reference. After all," (I thought to myself), "*I* don't like violence, and *I* can resist looking at it."

Then that offensive image of a boxer biting off the ear of the heavyweight champ a few years ago came to mind. Now *that* was a violent, *unfamiliar* picture. If you are like most people, it probably made you sick to look at it.

It made me sick too. But, no matter . . . *I still looked at it.*

If you don't recall seeing that bizarre spectacle, and you'd like to check it out, search images for "holyfield ear."

(Bookmark this page and come back to it later.)

The clutter rule
and the visual boundaries

I'm describing these things for you because these possibilities, called the *visual boundaries*, are useful tools in visual expression, useful for communicating visual meaning.

Each has its own power to ask a visual question, or to communicate a visual message. What that means is, it's possible to attract attention to a frame of reference both ways. An artist's work can attract interest by presenting "cute" and friendly images. Or else it can attract interest by filling a frame of reference with "strange," or even evil images. These frames of reference may rarely be art. To be sure, the holiday cards mentioned above are not serious visual expression, and neither is the boxing violence (although a talented photographer might have made art from that scene). Nevertheless, they can snap our attention into consciousness.

They can make us take notice.

This power that's found at the visual boundaries is at work anytime someone points a finger and says, "Wow! Look at *that!*"

Whenever those words are spoken, it means that something either very familiar or very unusual has caught their eye. Whenever an illustration, or architecture, photography, graphics, advertising, sculpture, painting, (or even some fashion model's crowd stopping / cutting edge designer shoulder bag, something that's wowing everyone along New York's Seventh Avenue) is successful at this, the reason is simple. It's because, for practical purposes, everyday visual clutter usually falls well within these two visual boundaries.

That's important because everyday visual clutter, everything that exists between these extremes, usually does *not* have the power to make us take notice.

To simplify, we could call that the "clutter rule."

The clutter rule suggests that lots of routine visual experiences, scenes that usually aren't visually stimulating, happen between the extremely familiar and the totally unfamiliar.

Repeated here for you to highlight:

The clutter rule:

Everyday visual experience usually happens between the extremely familiar and the totally unfamiliar; That is, visual clutter usually falls *between the visual boundaries, not at them.*

In fact, much of what we see is very near the middle of those limits. The result is that on any given day, our eyes are kept constantly busy processing an incredible mass of absolutely inane and boring visual gibberish, an avalanche of meaningless, but nevertheless *visible*, discord that makes no impression on us whatsoever.

A reason to become familiar with the lessons of light is that, once they have increased your awareness, you may sometimes surprise yourself by discovering an unexpected visual treat even in the midst of all that clutter.

That's another perk of visual living.

But it is still at the extremes of visible experience, where we find either the completely and totally familiar, or the completely and virtually unknown, that visual expression is often most irresistible.

* * * *

For review, here are the three conditions of ANATOMY:

        comparing similar looking objects
        substituting similar looking objects
        creating new objects by combining familiar objects

Before continuing to read, take a moment to look for these different conditions of ANATOMY. They may be all around, no matter where you are.

Chapter Four

COLOR as a source of visual experience

Dialog

WHILE CLEANING OUT A CLOSET, a young couple found an old art book. Inside were many prints, including one they liked very much. The COLORS were spectacular. Each was a soft pastel that swirled around another one. All the COLORS worked together helping each other be more expressive. The old print was so satisfying they framed it and put it in their living room.

Several weeks later a friend was visiting in their kitchen. The conversation turned to new apartments and they asked their friend if he planned to hang any pictures in a co-op he just bought. To their surprise, he said, "Probably. But no matter what, I'm not putting up images of naked people, like the one in your living room." It took a moment to realize he was referring to the print from the old book. And, still puzzled by what he meant, they went to the living room and noticed for the first time that the picture was an abstract painting of two young women, one of whom had no clothes on.[27]

The meaning of this story, which actually happened, is this: There are nine ways in which we understand the visual information presented to our eyes. They are the sources of visual experience, the nine visual "parts of speech" that I call the lessons of light. Because this couple was living visually, they were familiar with the lessons of light, and as a result, they found an emotional meaning in the way the old print spoke with COLOR as a source of visual experience. More important, this meaning was more engaging to them than the fact that the two FORMS in the print were people (CONTENT and FORM), including a girl who is not dressed.

Visually, the COLORS within the print were very engaging to them. The CONTENT and FORM were less engaging.

Allowing yourself to accept (and process) the strongest visual message that's directed toward your eyes, without requiring any intellectual explanation, is a skill you'll want to develop in order to explore the fun of visual living.

In this case, these artists lived with a print for a few weeks without being aware of its CONTENT, that is, without noticing or caring that the picture showed two women. The explanation is that this print's strongest source of emotional visual impact is COLOR.

How many COLORS are there?

Written and spoken languages make it difficult for us to use visual abilities to their fullest. Frequently, words just don't exist to describe the things that are most visually stimulating or important.

This problem is especially serious when we look for words to describe COLOR. To see what I mean, try to figure out an answer to this simple question:

How many COLORS are there?

A student once said this was a trick question. But my class that day class offered several interesting responses. Some of them show how difficult it is to think about this question visually. What that means is this: although the question is, "How many COLORS are there?," many perfectly intelligent people believe (by mistake) that it's the same as the more verbal (non-visual) question:

"How many COLORS *can you name?*"

So what's your answer? How many COLORS are there?

Take a moment to write your answer here:

The number of COLORS is: _____

Here are some responses my students offered that day.

See if you can guess who felt it was a trick question, and who answered from a visual point of view.

The answers ranged from "two," which the student named as black and white, "the only COLORS," he said, "because one represents all COLORS together, and the other one represents no COLORS at all." Another answer offered was "three," meaning the well-known, but usually misunderstood "primary COLORS" of red, blue and yellow. This student continued by explaining that, "These three COLORS can be combined into all the other COLORS except white, which is therefore not a COLOR."

Someone said, "There are four COLORS: red, yellow, blue and black, used by printers to recreate full COLOR pictures." Still another answer was that there are twelve COLORS, since that's the number found in a standard box of crayons. (Don't laugh, a student actually said that.) Several students listed each of the COLORS they could *think of*, starting with red, yellow, blue, green, pink, black, orange, etc. and came up with totals ranging from 21 to 33.

Unfortunately, each of these answers is incorrect and we're already seeing how hard it is to talk about COLOR.

How many people are there?

Asking how many COLORS there are is almost like asking how many people there are. There are two similarities to these questions, but one big difference.

First of all, no one serious about computing how many people there are would start by making a list of everyone they know. Although you could probably argue that everyone on earth has a name, the process of getting to know all the people on the planet would not be an efficient way of counting them. Second, no sooner do you count Mr. and Mrs. Jones as two people, do they get together and have a baby, which throws the count off.

That is pretty much how it is with COLORS also, except if you *did* decide to start counting up COLORS by making a list of their names, as several of my students attempted, you'd very quickly find out how useless the written and spoken language can sometimes be in the world of visual living. The reason is, there are simply thousands of COLORS for which we have absolutely no name. Probably millions. Everyone struggles through most of life not realizing there are practically no words that name COLORS. There are simply no words for many of life's most spectacular visual experiences, including many of the common COLORS that we find inspiring our emotional responses perhaps hundreds of times a day.

This is truly an *alarming* state of affairs.

So where does that leave us? What's the answer to the question, "How many COLORS are there?" Fortunately, there do seem to be two reasonably good ways to address this dilemma.

One answer is that there are an infinite number of COLORS. I say that because COLORS, like people, can get together to make new COLORS (by mixing together two cans of paint, for example), which can then get together to make newer COLORS, etc.

And the second acceptable answer, approved by the student who said it was a trick question, is that the exact number of COLORS (like the exact number of people) is for practical purposes simply unknowable.

Then there is this: Asking how many COLORS there are may not be a valid question for another reason. Instead, we should ask how many COLORS our human eyes can *distinguish*. That's true because there are probably more COLORS than any one person can see. To get an idea of how big the number may be, remember those early computer ads that bragged about processors and monitors that could reproduce millions of COLORS. On top of that, the ability to distinguish COLORS varies from person to person.

My point is that we can't rely on words to tell us what we need to know about COLOR.

What COLOR are people?

Another simple question: What COLOR are *you?*

Throughout history, people have been described according to the way their skin seems tinted with a certain COLOR.

But people are not actually these COLORS.

As a case in point, although people say I am white, I can easily see I am *not* white. My skin has a unique COLOR that has never been given a name. Someone might say that I am flesh COLORED, but that is just like saying that a barn is barn COLORED. Visually speaking, when it involves evaluating visual expression, neither description, flesh COLORED nor barn COLORED, is very useful.

And for another example, people who are Chinese have skin very similar in COLOR to mine, but people who don't use their eyes, and their language, effectively might say Chinese people are yellow. And you also hear African people are black, and American Indians are red. A terrible use of language.

In truth, none of these people has skin COLOR very different from mine, when you think of how many *possible* skin COLORS there are. For example, have you ever seen or heard of a green person? I don't mean they *seem* green (as you might say about someone who is very sick). I mean green like green peppers. Or have you seen someone who is blue? Not blue from being very cold, (or very depressed) but rather someone who is blue like a dark blue suit.

But if you red a book (see how confusing language is?) that said green monsters were having a war with blue monsters, imagine how bright the COLORS would seem. So imagine how unfortunate it is, visually speaking, to call American Indians red, or Asian people yellow. But if not, then what else? We simply don't have well-known names for all the diverse skin COLORS. And for yet another example of how inefficient language is, consider that even when I'm tanned dark brown, I'm still called "white."

In fact, in 1962, all this confusion about skin COLOR caused a toy maker to rename a popular crayon, one they originally called "flesh." (Now called "peach.") For many decades, "flesh" had been an innocent but obviously narrow minded effort to help kids draw.[28]

One requirement, then, for a person interested in using and enjoying COLOR is to accept that only a few well-known words exist that actually have value in describing most of the COLORS that surround us. Furthermore, the way we normally use those few words we *do* have is frequently misleading.

To be fair, it should be noted that a dedicated wildlife artist named Robert Ridgway once named approximately 1100 COLORS. Although that was 100 years ago, very few of his words ever became part of everyday English. They ranged from very simple names (like "bay" and "yale blue") to other unmanageable ones (like "blackish plumbeous" and "light brownish vinaceous").[29]

Here's how a great designer spontaneously
invented words to describe her COLORS

The problem is so bad that, at times, visually sophisticated people find there are *no* words that actually describe the most successful COLOR expressions. Artists are sometimes left speechless.

I once watched a TV program that presented the Spring runway show for a famous fashion designer. When a reporter asked her to describe what was special about her new collection she paused, grasping for the best words, and then said, "It's the COLOR. It's the vegetable, delicious, wonderful COLOR!"

Say what?
Vegetable?
Delicious?
Wonderful?
Excuse me?

I had no idea what she meant, but I was touched by the way she said the words. I sensed there was definitely something in the air, something about her fashions, about her new COLORS, and something different from fashion shows I had watched before. But unfortunately the typical COLOR reproduction on TV does not always do justice to the shades and nuances that are part of a great designer's repertoire (and I was watching a small old set). So after seeing about two dozen of her dresses on the TV show, I still did not have a particularly strong opinion of the COLOR in this new collection. Nevertheless I was impressed that the designer was genuinely excited by the impact COLOR was bringing to her work, and I could tell it was more so than usual.

I thought, "Well maybe that can be expected."

After all, the COLORS for Spring fashions change every year, and this was her day to show enthusiasm for them. And of course, you can't ignore the fact that she was there talking to the reporter, above all, in order to sell those dresses.

Anyway, the TV show ended and it slipped my mind.

Then a few days later I was browsing in a new fashion magazine. The COLORS found in printed magazines are usually more accurate and vivid than TV COLORS are, so the magazine showed clearly that the new fashion COLORS for that season were incredible. I thumbed through the magazine and was thunderstruck. I was amazed again that COLOR could be so original. I have been seeing and evaluating COLOR and COLOR combinations for many years, and you sometimes wonder if you haven't seen them all. But this was amazing. I turned a few more pages in the magazine, and . . . more of the same exciting COLORS!

Then a couple more pages and along came an ad for the dresses of that very designer whose TV show I saw. I was stopped dead in my tracks. Devastated. Knocked out. Totally out cold and down for the count. The COLOR of her dresses leapt off the page and left *me* sort of speechless, looking at the page. What was so special about it? What was so new? How could you describe it?

I'll give it a try.

More than usual, her COLORS seemed to be organic, that is to say, living. They all seemed perhaps to be growing, right there in the magazine. They were COLORS of damp green thriving earth, of fragile new life emerging, of brown soil yielding, of rosy infants nursing.

Then, as I continued looking at the page, all at once the designer's own words came back to me, and I saw what she saw.

I actually saw what she was saying.

The COLORS were vegetable, delicious and wonderful! What a revelation![30]

COLOR has the magic ability
to send us to a higher level of feeling

Business artists, fine artists and anyone living visually can experiment with words like that, doing our best to describe COLOR, but, unfortunately, you can't call a printing company and ask them to change the COLOR of your client's logo on the back of a brochure to something that is vegetable, delicious and wonderful. So the logical direction for this thought to go is toward an explanation of how a number system has been developed to help overcome the fact that we don't have names for COLORS.

Although that's true, and for any working artists the number system that's described below is important for day-to-day control of COLOR, it is far away from explaining the emotional impact COLOR can create, even when words can't describe it. It is more to the point here to tell you that even if every COLOR did have a name, even a beautiful name, words would still be of little help to convey how a visually sensitive person feels about it.

That's because, in many of its most expressive applications (especially when it is expressed with SPACE), COLOR may be nearly invisible to the conscious eye. Instead, it's the mood that COLOR creates that is "felt," almost not seen. For example, bright red is a COLOR we are usually conscious of seeing. But bright red is very likely *not* around when COLOR is creating a "mood."

Adding to the difficulties is the fact that a mood is usually cast not by a single COLOR, but rather by a *combination* of COLORS, like those pastels in the living room print (referring again to the beginning of this chapter). Even so, people who are living visually don't think of COLOR like car salesmen did back in 1958 when they were selling tri-tone Fords (that is, automobiles with three different COLORS of paint on the outside). That is to say, two COLORS are not necessarily better than one COLOR. And three COLORS are not necessarily better than two COLORS.

The point is, rather, that a painter who is creating a canvas is unaware of how many COLORS he has chosen. Instead, his eye tells him when and where COLOR needs to change to support the feeling he is trying to express. But, because these "feelings" are frequently created by a combination of COLORS, that means having a name for every COLOR would not provide any useful description of them. And for the same reason, it's curious to hear someone who is visually sensitive say he or she has a "favorite" COLOR. Generally speaking, people who are living visually search for meaning not in individual COLORS but rather in groups of COLORS, and how they interact and work together.

Imagine a restaurant where COLOR creates a good feeling of relaxation in people eating there. If COLOR has been chosen to create that sensation, it's true, it may be a single special COLOR (which is, of course, also modified by the other lessons of light). But more likely, instead it will be a combination of less eye-catching COLORS, each subtly working, and again further modified by the other lessons of light. But whichever it is, the goal of living visually is to understand COLOR so well that it can be brought along to create positive feelings anywhere, be it a restaurant interior, an advertisement, a photograph, a landscape painting, a package design, the walls in your home media room or even an arrangement of picture frames and candles set atop a white piano. (You don't have to be living visually to imagine how beautiful that can be.)

To make sense of all this, you could say it would be great if a word existed for every possible combination of COLORS. Then we could pick which word describes the combination we like best. But we'd need an impossible number of new words, one for every combination of COLOR.

That's a ridiculous thought, but that's what it would take before words became meaningful to describe all the subtle feelings that COLOR can create.

Since those words just don't exist, when someone chooses or creates COLORS that influence our emotions, it's something that words can not describe.

It means he or she has collected groups of COLORS, possibly over a long period, judging them for their ability to move us. Then at the right time they are brought together again, balanced with the other lessons of light and presented for the world to see. When this has been accomplished by a talented artist (or someone who is really living visually), the result has the ability to send us to a higher level of emotion and feeling.

In some industries, the chore of identifying and naming COLORS repeats itself every year. To help overcome the difficulties, there are several companies within the publishing profession that produce books that are filled with new names for COLORS. These books are rewritten every year, and are particularly liked in the fashion and automobile industries, where every year, every manufacturer must seriously promote their new COLORS.

The problem is, a dress company can tell retail store buyers that one available fabric is vegetable delicious green, but then what do they call blue? So instead of taking on the tedious job of naming every COLOR every year for every dress or every car, many COLOR names are now simply picked out of a book, used in ads, brochures and press releases, and then discarded at the end of the season.

Managing COLOR with the help of numbers

The emotional power of COLOR can inspire visually sensitive people to devote literally a lifetime to mastering it. But working artists, and especially business artists, require a streamlined under-standing of COLOR to carry on a realistic day-to-day workload. The stumbling blocks within language have therefore been neatly side-stepped by assigning numbers to COLORS.

This need for a numbering system presents another example of a difference between "commercial" (business) artists, and "fine" artists, including painters and sculptors. The difference is, business artists are usually very aware of how many COLORS they specify (in the graphic design for a poster, let's say). In the world of business art, each COLOR that's added to a design may mean there will be additional cost in any production or printing that follows. And, by the way, in the first years of web page design, before broadband became widespread, any extra COLORS also meant extra time was needed for customers or visitors to load a page.

All these cost and time factors are becoming less restrictive in business art as computer technology continues to make COLOR faster and cheaper to deal with. But it does illustrate one important point of view that a fine artist will have about COLOR, compared to a business artist. Since there are millions of COLORS, a fine artist will consider the entire range of possibilities and then choose exact-ly the right COLOR or COLORS that are needed to express the emo-tion he or she is looking for.

This freedom is possible because someone who paints land-scapes, let us say, can create unlimited (and basically free) COLORS simply by mixing them on his pallet. He won't consider the cost of adding more COLORS to a painting.

It's simply not an issue.

But, as we'll see on the following pages, within many areas of visual expression, especially within business art, using numbers to describe COLOR is unfortunately, and permanently, here to stay.

Although several number systems for identifying COLOR are in use around the world, the most popular format organizes more than 1000 COLORS in a simple-to-use reference book, similar to a loose-leaf binder. This book is called a COLOR specifier. Obviously, that's only a tiny fraction of the "infinite" COLORS that actually exist, but for business artists, is it sufficient to describe the basic COLORS people need to carry out their work.

The COLOR specifier has pages showing a printed sample of each COLOR. The samples are then usually perforated into smaller swatches. Each swatch is also printed with the number assigned to that COLOR. Swatches can be removed from the specifier and used to indicate the COLORS needed in thousands of applications within visual expression.

Swatches can be sent to printers to indicate ink COLORS, or to manufacturers to let them know the exact COLOR needed for the plastic that embodies a new cell phone design. COLORS can also be "specified" over the phone, or in email, just by referring to the number given to each one. A major advantage of computer based graphic design, which radically modified how business art is created, is that this number system is part of the software.

However, even though they make work easier, some teachers feel students may rely too much on COLOR specifiers, and on computer generated COLOR.

There are thousands of more exciting and more inspiring ways to learn about COLOR. As a result, at one point somebody (probably an art teacher) started telling this joke:

> There was a group of art students assigned to
> learn about COLOR by memorizing favorite numbers
> in a specifier. In the school's lunch room, a student
> would stand up and call out a number, and the other
> students would cheer, raise hell and pound the tables.
>
> Then a new student joined the class and was told
> to participate in the game. He was given a specifier
> to learn the numbers. A few days passed, and then the
> new student stood at lunch and screamed out a number.
>
> But this time there was an embarrassing silence
> and then everyone just went on eating. Discouraged,
> he described what happened to a friend, who said,
> "Hey, guy, don't worry. That's just an ugly COLOR."

Where do COLORS come from?

Although they're widely relied on, COLOR specifiers are not usually where we look for COLOR inspirations. One reason is that specifiers don't show COLORS in context, that is, in relation to other COLORS, or in relation with other sources of visual experience. For that reason, experienced artists know it's better to look for COLORS by noticing the ones that appear all around us.

An important habit of visual living is to be alert for COLORS, that is to say, to be constantly "collecting" them. Ideas for COLOR combinations are everywhere and by noticing these as a matter of habit, you can enjoy an ongoing COLOR show and, if you choose, you can easily find more than enough inspiration for a lifetime of rewarding visual expression.

Individual COLORS or combinations of COLORS appear in every interesting scene, and, as you'd imagine, people who work in visual arts are frequently influenced by the COLORS chosen by others who are carrying out the same kind of work. As a result, COLOR groups or trends sometimes seem to appear suddenly throughout all areas of design, and almost like magic, just as they usually do in the world of fashion design (mentioned above).

The result is that systems of COLORS are frequently used by everybody for a short period (usually a year or two) before they are replaced by a new trend. This is more true in business arts (graphic design, let's say) than fine arts (oil painting, for example). In business arts, you can't help notice how the COLOR available for appliances, automobiles, cosmetics and especially fashion changes from year to year to year.

In fact, trends like this are the *backbone* of COLOR selection for fashion, fabrics and cosmetics, industries that work together to choose successful COLORS for every season. There is even a special group of professionals known as COLOR consultants who provide advice, and set trends, for dozens of companies whose products are intended for mass-market appeal, and whose COLORS are chosen to exactly follow these trends.

But COLOR can also be an incredible headache.

One man I know owns a company that designs and sells textiles. He once described several COLOR dyes that were giving him difficulty by reminding me that, "these are *living things* we're talking about."[31] Then consider this: a leading broadcast network made marketing history in the early days of television by broadcasting its best programs, so they said, "in *living* COLOR!"[32] So this idea that COLORS are "alive" is a helpful way to think of them.

COLOR is sometimes the focus of visual energy in an entire area of fine arts also. And COLOR has been the center of interest in the life work of dozens of our most well-known fine artists.

Throughout history, big news in COLORS came when new pigments or dyes were found. Those discoveries made it possible to create new COLORS, ones that were previously unavailable outside of nature. That's why, centuries ago, purple became "the COLOR of kings" because it was originally very expensive to produce purple dye for fabrics.[33] Now, almost every COLOR of ink and paint can be located inexpensively. But even today, some pigments we have are not perfect. That means mixing special COLORS is sometimes still a problem. Even today, there is no perfect blue paint that can be mixed with perfect yellow paint to make perfect green paint.

(More about mixing COLORS is coming up.)

We are all influenced by trends in COLOR which sometimes seem to spring up out of a "life" that COLOR appears to have on its own. But the most common origins of COLOR inspiration for anyone who is living visually are the random impressions of COLOR that fill our daily lives. That's where COLOR may lead you to enjoy a pleasant visual surprise, even in the midst of everyday visual clutter. People who take time to notice may begin to realize that emotionally meaningful COLORS are *everywhere*.

A secret to understanding COLOR as a lesson of light is to pay special attention to it, and equally, to remember the emotional impact that you have sensed from COLORS and COLOR combinations. That's a big part of visual living. Perhaps, even, there's no better preparation for someone planning to brighten up their kitchen or gather a fashionable wardrobe than to become sensitive to COLOR (by collecting it). And, of course, it's also a big part of working in any visually active profession. In all these satisfying ways, COLOR can become an important part of your life.

Where do COLORS live?

There are pleasing and inspiring COLOR combinations seen everywhere. Beautiful fabric patterns or window displays have probably been created from the COLORS seen by a business artist on his way to work. And it wouldn't be surprising for anyone who is visually sensitive to notice the COLORS on a bulletin board where lots of papers come together in spontaneous groups or "collages," or in a garden, where the flowers create an interesting energy. New COLORS for a corporation's logo program may grow from COLORS seen by an art director when he opens a dresser drawer and finds two shirts side by side, or when he notices two food packages next to each other on a supermarket shelf.

Ice cream parlors with a dozen or more open containers are another place to see unusual COLORS in context with each other (that is, side by side). The same is true for parking lots full of brightly COLORED cars, bookcases where dozens of different COLORED book bindings influence each other, or clothing stores. Another good variety of random COLORS is found in the advertisements appearing side by side in any COLOR magazine.

Wherever you are right now, take a moment to look up from reading. No doubt there are exciting COLORS surrounding you this very minute. Ignore everything else, take five right now, and start appreciating COLOR.

Remembering COLOR can be more easy than remembering other information. I have found it is easier to remember the COLORS that attracted me to a poster or a brochure, than it is for me to recall the names of people at a party. COLORS which appeal to you (enough to attract your attention) have a uniqueness about them that sticks in your memory. Later, I can remind myself of what I saw by flipping through a COLOR specifier, looking for swatches.

In business, the swatches that match the COLORS in your mind's eye can be used to communicate with clients and production people. Otherwise, you might use a swatch to show a bakery shop the COLOR of icing you want slathered on a special party cake.

Beyond this organized professional number system for COLORS, manufacturers of many products also distribute other kinds of printed guides that show the available COLORS for items like printing papers, paints, cosmetics, wall and floor materials, appliances, felt-tip markers and home decorating materials. In addition, home centers have computerized paint mixing machines which produce gallon after gallon of precisely matched wall paint. This help, available to anyone, is *free*, so you can be certain the impact of COLOR, no matter where it is, will be exactly as you wish it to be.

But even with all this reference available, many who work in visual arts still have the habit of saving small swatches of COLORS from fabric stores or magazines. This is especially helpful when trying to recreate gray COLORS (there's hundreds of them) which are, contrary to most other COLORS, difficult to recall from memory.

The COLOR of money

We're surrounded by COLOR, but few people are familiar with the effect COLOR has on the appeal of *everything* we see.

For example, most people purchase clothes, appliances and groceries not knowing that in many cases, COLOR is precisely influencing their decision. Imagine you're in a supermarket and you buy a package of frozen vegetables. Suppose the package is red and green. Although you may not realize it, it's possible thirty different shades of red and thirty different shades of green were evaluated for that design. Nevertheless, with up to *sixty* individual COLORS considered, the best description of that package's COLORS in words may still be simply "red and green."

On top of that, perhaps 200 more COLORS other than red and green may have been considered for that package design also. As the process evolved, the designer was no doubt searching for an effect she or he had seen (or "felt") or "collected" before.

* * * *

Chapter four continued
AN INTRODUCTION TO COLOR
The fourth lesson of light
Would you help yourself to a blue banana?

There are four conditions of COLOR:

Appropriateness of COLOR
Side by side variation of COLOR
The additive primary COLORS
The subtractive primary COLORS

Let's look at each one.

Appropriateness of COLOR

Deep inside, we experience emotional responses to COLOR that are tied to our idea of what the appropriate COLOR for something is, and what COLOR is not appropriate. It far outweighs our opinion of what is beautiful and what is ugly. Most people believe that some things are just plain *supposed* to be a certain COLOR.

The feelings we share with one another in these preferences are widespread, especially among people of the same cultural background. Because of that, it's rare, although not impossible, to make a serious mistake in choosing COLORS according to rules of appropriateness. (And we'll soon see how I once made such a mistake.)

Probably the most familiar examples of the strong emotional responses associated with COLOR are found in the foods we eat. No one would buy black sweet potatoes, or green hamburger meat. We have a strong sense that oranges are orange and butter is yellow. You would be correct to say these preferences in food COLOR originated with the natural COLOR of these products. But frequently some additional COLORING is added, even after normal processing, to make food items seem even *more* "natural" in COLOR.

Other widely accepted appropriate COLORS include white wedding dresses and nurse uniforms, black limousines, red and white barber poles, red, white and blue American flags, brown footballs and colas, black type in books (such as this), yellow taxicabs and yellow welcome-home ribbons for your friend or brother who just got out of jail. (You wouldn't tie a *purple* ribbon 'round an old oak tree.) Have you ever seen an orange Santa Clause suit, a green Valentine, a red Saint Patrick's Day necktie or piano keys that were *not* black and white? Have you ever heard of a brown Christmas? I doubt it. (Blue and white, yes, but not brown.)

Furthermore, I'm fairly certain you would never help yourself to a blue banana. Blue isn't an *appropriate* COLOR for bananas.

Some things are acceptable (appropriate) in most COLORS, but not all COLORS. Human hair can be beautiful in hundreds of shades, but purple hair is only partially accepted (and, let's face it, even kings frown upon it). These days, shaving cream is ok if it's white, blue or green, but yellow is not appropriate for this product. Neither is red, unless it is a gel that turns white when it lathers.

In the current era of COLOR, architectural design for homes and buildings usually avoids blue if the material is brick. In other words, these days, blue brick is out. A few years ago I was looking for a house but something seemed to tell me, "Don't live in a house that's blue brick." So I took that advice, and I moved into a house that's white brick. But consider this: in the evening I light it up with blue lights. For reasons that probably can't be put into words, that odd-sounding twist of rules seems ok. The house looks pretty, and the lights get compliments from the neighbors.

Allow me to digress: If your house is already blue brick (and you agree with my COLOR opinion), not to worry! Blue brick can be nicely painted. Whitewashed brick with COLOR showing through it can be beautiful. Paint the brick red first, then white. Allow the red to show through here and there, so the brick looks weathered.

Then there is this: in the world of visual meaning, appropriateness of COLOR often *changes*.

Years ago, white was the only appropriate COLOR for kitchen appliances. Then in the very COLORful 60s practically any COLOR became appropriate. We're back to basics now in kitchen appliance COLORS (or at least back to neutrals), but some of those dreadful avocado kitchens are still around. Many people feel now, in this new millennium, that those kitchens were creepy, but back then everybody loved them. And those old appliances sometimes attract very good bids in online auctions, as do other "mid century" design items, especially lamps and chairs.

Red was once the only appropriate COLOR for fire engines. Then someone pointed out that yellow is more visible, especially at night. Now no one knows what color fire engines should be.

That's how COLOR appropriateness changes.

So where does appropriateness of COLOR fit into our understanding of visual expression? Just here: Since everyone has a broad understanding of appropriateness in COLORS, and since everyone pretty much agrees on what is and is not appropriate (except for fire engines), it's possible to violate that understanding *on purpose*.

When that happens, we see appropriateness of COLOR as a strong source of visual experience. Questions are raised, almost automatically, when the wrong COLOR appears in a frame of reference. But defining just what those questions are, and what an inappropriate COLOR *means*, is a challenge reserved mostly for analysis in the visual language, not in everyday spoken and written words. What does a bright orange apple *mean*?

Nevertheless, artists can (and do) use wrong COLOR choices (that is, *inappropriate* COLOR choices) *on purpose*, to create visual expression that asks questions.

A beautiful shade of pea-green

It's impossible to say if a COLOR is beautiful or ugly unless the situation is known. To see what I mean, consider your reaction to these two sentences:

"She has beautiful blue shoes,"
and
"She has beautiful blue skin."

Where any COLOR appears is much more important in our understanding of beauty than *what* a COLOR is. You can prove this to yourself. Try this experiment: Open your closet and pick one of your own favorite pieces of clothing, something you like because of its solid COLOR. Then imagine the following objects to be the same COLOR. If you're like me, you will discover that imagining one (or more) of these things to be the same COLOR as your favorite shirt or dress is quite unappealing:

Choose a COLOR from your closet,
and imagine it as the COLOR of:

1. A living room rug
2. Your car
3. Your toothpaste
4. The setting sun
5. Your dog
6. A kitchen appliance

Separating your appreciation of COLOR away from the limited language that's available to describe it may be a slow process. However, when you have become familiar with the way appropriateness of COLOR affects our opinion of it, you may find yourself in a confusing situation. You may find a particular COLOR is beautiful in one place, and not at all appealing in another place.

We may even describe a certain COLOR in one situation as "ocean" green (a flattering reference), and in another situation as "slime" green (not an attractive sounding shade). Remember that I'm talking about the exact same COLOR in two different places. We can perceive the same COLOR as both ugly and beautiful, depending on where we find it.

That is what we mean by appropriateness of COLOR.

A hotel avoids untimely demise

Not everyone around the world shares the same sense of appropriateness of COLOR. While working in Asia, I made a mistake using COLOR that was difficult for me to take seriously.

For that reason, in fact, I made the same mistake twice.

Here's what happened: In Taiwan, some individuals have a feeling about the appropriateness of COLOR on printed envelopes. Their belief is this: any white envelope that arrives in the mail with no COLOR on it except black printing (or black writing) indicates a death occurred in the home of the sender. This belief is held strongly even if there's information on the envelope that says it's a regular letter or even junk mail. That is to say, if a white envelope arrives in the mail in Taipei with nothing on it except a name, an address and the words "You're invited to a party" printed in black (in Chinese), the person who receives the mail may believe that he is invited to a funeral. Although this superstition is becoming less widely held, it was once dramatically brought to my attention.

Working in that country as a business artist for a new hotel, I ordered white envelopes with the hotel's name and return address printed in black letters. The envelopes were needed for the formal invitations to the grand opening of the hotel. After they were sealed and addressed in black ink, some red trim had to be added by hand on about 2000 pieces before they were mailed.

Some of the executives at the hotel were terrified of sending out envelopes that were all black and white. Earlier in the day, after spotting them in the mail room, my Chinese bosses came running into the hotel design department yelling, waving the envelopes, and wondering, I suppose, if I understood that the hotel was announcing its opening, and not its closing.

The second time, two years later at a different hotel, but still in Taiwan, I again ordered white envelopes with the hotel name and return address in black letters. (And by the way, I'm not really a moron. That's the *appropriate* COLOR for a formal invitation in the United States, and most other places.) This time, however, I remembered the issue and arranged to have the addresses hand written in blue ink, and this approach took care of the difficulty.[34]

I learned other COLOR preferences Chinese people have. In China, people like red sooooo much they always ask why it's not the principal design COLOR *everywhere*. "Why isn't this brochure red?" or, "Why isn't our company name printed in red ink on the letterheads?" or, "Why not create red uniforms for all the waiters?" Unlike other nationalities, they give the COLOR red a moral meaning. For the Chinese, wherever and whenever it appears, *red always means "good."* Some Chinese business people are very happy (and very successful) when virtually everything is red.

I sometimes learned my western COLOR sensitivity and art training were out of line with local traditions.

Other countries may also assign special meaning to COLOR.

Green is, of course, the national COLOR in Ireland, and it now also stands for concerns about global climate change around the world. In addition, appropriateness of COLOR is important in an abstract way also. Graphic designers are sometimes called on to specify the "correct" COLOR (that is to say, the appropriate COLOR) for things like "health care" or for "financial management."

Decisions like these lead to the COLORS selected for corporate communications including company logos, annual report covers, package designs and even for new products and office interiors. And incidentally, in western countries, and speaking generally, in the current visual era the traditionally appropriate design COLOR for both health care and finance is some shade of blue.

It requires someone with a good feeling for COLOR to sense when it's safe to break from established COLORS used in business. And here's one case: for years nearly all computers were beige. Then one company introduced "candy" COLORS. They were a big success and soon other computer makers followed with additional new COLORS. Now, as I'm sure you know, computers are manufactured in practically every COLOR.

At one time I worked with a company that agreed to market a new product inside a black package. It was the first black package ever in that product category. And beyond that, it was also one of the first black packages in *any* category. It was considered risky, but soon became widely accepted. The package established a uniqueness for the brand (which was otherwise practically identical to others like it), and the black COLOR became a marketing asset.

And speaking of black

In the next chapter we will talk more about black and white. That's because they're important in understanding "opposites," and how opposites relate to CONTRAST. We'll see in addition that black and white have come to stand for bad and good.

In fact black is *often* used to represent evil in the visual language (hence one of the hesitations about using it for a new consumer package). I'm sure you'd agree that Darth Vader in a green camisole would not have worked. And here's a crazy thought. I wonder if black is offended by its negative image? Or by the fact that many people don't even consider black to be a real COLOR.

I have a theory that the second class citizenship endured by black, a visual role it can't shake, is partly because, in the last century, and within older technology, black was forced to represent the other COLORS. This trend began with the invention of photography (which was of course black and white, or dark brown and white, for most of its first one hundred years) and of course black was the standard of photography, printing, motion pictures and even television until the technology for full COLOR film, printing, movies and TV was developed. This substitute role, played by black (and gray) for so many decades, may have robbed it of some vitality. Black is the old way, other COLORS are the new way. Furthermore, no one ever brags about producing anything in *living* black.

You might say black is history if you get the point.

And for additional evidence, remember all the animated discussions that filled entertainment reporting during the 1980s when it became possible for computers to transform movies that were originally produced in black and white into full COLOR versions. Some people were upset that these icons of cinematic art, all magnificently designed and lit *on purpose* for black and white expression, were converted to COLOR. On the other hand (and unfortunately), other people just could not have cared less. For them COLOR is always better than black and white, and that's that. End of discussion.

I'm mentioning this only to let you know that lots of visually sensitive people would not agree that black is somehow damaged goods. Black is actually a vivid, powerfully beautiful and unique COLOR, equal in every way to red or green or blue or yellow.

In fact, one renowned artist admitted, "I've been forty years discovering that the queen of all colors is black." Granted, he didn't say black is the *king* of all COLORS (and he lived long before photography and movies possibly changed our perception of it), but it's nevertheless quite a revealing comment from an individual famous for the breathtaking and subtle use of COLOR in his paintings.[35]

And more recently, Louise Nevelson, the great sculptress mentioned earlier, said on an audio recording that accompanied the catalogue for her 1980 exhibition at New York's Pace Gallery:

> "(Black) is the most aristocratic color in
> the world . . . *You can take almost anything*
> *and once it's black it has another meaning.*"[11]

So, as you begin to live visually, remember there is wonderful magic in this COLOR called black. It's magic that surrounds you everywhere – if you care to look for it. Try this right now: look up from reading to see if there's any "living" black around you.

Side by side variation of COLOR

The second condition of COLOR is side by side variation.

For an important new product introduction, a team of business artists spent four 16 hour days searching for a group of just three COLORS. They were creating the graphic "look" they needed for advertisements, packages, brochures and posters. They evaluated over 1500 individual COLORS (more than the standard specifier contains) and then presented the client with a selection of 42 three-COLOR groups. Eight more sets showed COLORS repeated from the first groups, but arranged in a different order, because that changed the effect each COLOR had on the one next to it.

Each one of the 50 unique combinations was rejected by the client, and the process was repeated again from scratch.[36] That can show you how serious the choice of COLOR is for advertising a new product. There are millions and millions of dollars at risk.

And the wrong COLORS can ruin the whole thing.

By the way, this story is a true one. I know because I helped resolve that COLOR exploration, with 16 hour days included.

COLORS (just like people!) can be dramatically changed by their relationship with each other, and COLORS in combination can significantly increase the impact of a frame of reference. Even emotional and spiritual energy can be modified by the interaction of COLORS. They can become darker, or lighter, or may otherwise significantly change, all depending on the other COLORS near by.

This is very relevant to decision-making in business.

By adding just one more COLOR to a textile or fabric design, or to the pattern within a carpet, the result can be so dramatic that a better selling product comes to life, perhaps even reborn from one that previously failed in the marketplace. For clever marketing executives who are living visually (with business artists at their side) a small change in COLORS can translate into much better sales.

Then consider: How important are the interactions of COLOR in three dimensions? Ask an interior designer.

In any interior design, a last minute change in the COLOR of curtains, for example, can alter the appearance of walls and furniture. The opposite is true also. If you are thinking about changing the COLOR of walls inside your home, better be careful. That will affect the COLORS in the curtains and furniture.

Furthermore, in an unusual way that they affect SPACE, just changing COLORS can make a room look smaller or larger. As a rule, the lighter the COLOR of a room, the larger it will appear. This effect is important in architecture, interior design and in set design for live theater, and it's related to one of the conditions of DEPTH (lightness and darkness of COLOR).

Side by side variations of COLOR can reach out and touch everything. Some smart gallery owners are successful because they judge correctly what COLOR mats to use when framing their prints. Choosing the proper cardboard mat or frame will make each image or painting appear its most attractive. COLORS are so sensitive to the COLORS that surround them, that any picture that is tastefully matted or framed can easily seem to be *twice* as valuable as the same picture matted or framed by someone not sensitive to COLOR. If you are already living visually, you're probably aware how frames and mats can almost miraculously change a picture.

A more complex reaction to side by side effects of COLOR is experienced when a strong COLOR is stared at for a long time, let's say three minutes. If you stare at a solid COLOR for that long, and then look away, your sense of sight is temporarily tinted, not with the original COLOR but, oddly, by a different COLOR.

That COLOR is known as its theoretical complement.

Children's' museums will sometimes apply this secret to create "the American flag trick." Inside a darkened room, on a dark wall, an American flag is displayed next to a white rectangle the same size. The flag has green and black stripes, not the familiar red and white ones. Both the flag and the white rectangle are illuminated by spot lights. Kids are told to stare at the flag for a minute and then look at the empty white rectangle nearby. As a result, since red is the complement of green, for a few seconds their eyes automatically see a normal red and white flag in the blank space.

It's really just the afterimage of the green flag, which lingers on the light sensitive part of our inner eye. You can try this illusion if you search images for "flag illusion." (Bookmark this page.)

In the early days of computers most monitors had green letters on a black background, so this after effect illusion, described above, was sometimes a bother to business artists. I experienced it many times while using my first processor. After sitting at the monitor doing paperwork (this was before we used computers for design), I would take a break and then sometimes notice that some tiny white type on a package sample, for example, would appear to be pink! The reason is, my eyes saw the white type as the complement of the tiny green type I had stared at on the computer screen.

I was aware that I could not judge COLORS for my work for several minutes until the symptoms wore off.

Now let's talk about COLOR theory
and the primary COLORS.

A journalist for a magazine article about men's clothing once wrote that a formal white gentleman's suit he was evaluating had an "absence of COLOR." Normally, you wouldn't expect that a fashion reporter would be criticized for making a casual mistake in COLOR theory, but in this case a reader, who seemingly had too much time on his hands, wrote to the magazine about it.

The magazine published his letter which said in part:

> "Now I know my college education was not a waste.
> While reading your article about men's fashion, I noticed
> it said that white is 'the absence of COLOR.' Thinking back
> to my required art class, *which I loathed*, (my emphasis)
> I remember being taught that white is the presence of all
> COLOR, and black is the absence of all COLOR."

The letter, which was reprinted in the magazine's "letters to the editor" section, was strange for several reasons.

To start with, perhaps the letter writer's college education *was* a waste (and maybe that's why he had the time to write such pointless letters). I say that because, in the casual way it was written, the article was *correct* to say that white fabric represents the absence of COLOR. (As opposed to white light, which, as we will see shortly, represents the *presence* of all COLORS)

Maybe, while loathing his art class, the letter writer got his COLOR lessons wrong. But the fact that the fashion magazine printed the incorrect criticism is a pretty good indication of how confused just about everyone is about COLOR.

COLOR exists outside any real system to classify it fully.

Yet in the interest of standardizing COLOR applications for design related business, including computers, the internet, printing, and for fine artists who mix their own paints, a great deal has been done to explain the interaction of COLORS with one another.

Working artists, especially business artists, need at least a modest understanding of these technical characteristics of COLOR. Probably the most important information, particularly for the thousands of people who work in graphic design, art direction, web page design, textiles and stage lighting, is the interesting way in which primary COLORS work together. So here goes.

Here's an introduction to both sets of primary COLORS.

That's right, both.

It is not commonly understood that there are *two* sets of primary COLORS. These two sets are called the additive primary COLORS and the subtractive primary COLORS. There are two sets of primaries because of two general ways that COLOR exists, that is, as COLORED light itself, and as white light that is then reflected off COLORED pigments.

That's important, so here it is for you to highlight:

COLOR exists two ways: as COLORED light itself,
and as white light reflected off COLORED pigments.

As we'll see, each of these kinds of COLOR really does need its own set of primaries, and also as we will see, in both sets of primary COLORS, all COLORS are represented.

How COLOR arrives in our eyes:	Which primaries control it:
As COLORED light itself.	Additive primaries
As white light reflected off COLORED pigments (surfaces).	Subtractive primaries

I assume you can imagine COLORED light, but let me clarify that a "pigment" is anything used to COLOR something else. For example, ink is a pigment for printing on paper, dye is a pigment for COLORING cloth or hair, and oil paint, acrylic paint and water colors are pigments for fine artists who paint pictures, etc. To make it simple, you could say nail polish is a "pigment" for fingernails.

The additive primary COLORS: red, blue and green

The additive primary COLORS are red, blue and green.

They are important for anyone working with COLORED light such as stage designers, light show artists and web masters.

The additive primary COLORS represent all COLORS in this way: combinations of different amounts of red light, blue light and green light can be "mixed" together in order to produce almost any other desired COLOR. Stage designers can prove this with ease, and they frequently do. They may choose to light a particular scene on a stage (a rock band, let us say) with three different spot lights, one red, one blue and one green, with each of the three spotlights pointed at the lead singer. If you haven't already worked with COLORED light, you might be surprised to hear this: the light that results from the mixture of these three COLORS is *white*.

This means although the lead singer has three spotlights on him, one red, one blue and one green (and NO white spotlight), people in the audience will see him as though he is standing in white light. And that's the reason these three COLORS are called the additive primary COLORS. If you "add" them all together, as COLORED light, you'll arrive at white light, which is, at least in theory, the combination (in equal amounts) of all COLORS of light.

If your home has any ceiling or wall fixture with sockets for three bulbs (often found over bathroom sinks), try an experiment. You'll need three COLORED bulbs of the same strength, perhaps 40 watts. Buy a red one, a blue one and a green one, and put them in the fixture. When you flip on the switch, you'll see, although there are no white lights in the room, a sheet of white paper held in your hand will appear to be lit with a normal 120 watt white bulb.

Three variations can further explain primary COLORS.

First, unscrew the red bulb, so the light in the room is produced only by the green light bulb and the blue light bulb. By holding the sheet of white paper under these two lights, you will see the resulting COLOR produced by the blue and green bulbs together is a kind of light blue. This light blue is one of the rare COLORS that is lucky enough to have an exact name of its own. It's is called *cyan*, and, as we will see in the following pages, cyan is a very important COLOR in its own right.

Next, screw the red bulb back in its socket, and unscrew the green bulb. This time, when white paper is held out beneath these blue and red bulbs, the resulting COLOR on the paper will be a sort of purple, called *magenta*.

Lastly, replace the green bulb and then unscrew the blue bulb. This time, with only the red bulb and the green bulb providing light, you'll discover that the white paper will appear to be yellow! If you are like me, you might feel that making this discovery (that red light added to green light makes yellow light) is one of the most remarkable visual lessons that light has to offer.

To summarize: Blue light and green light together make cyan light. Red light and blue light together make magenta light. Red light and green light together make yellow light. (Highlight this.)

By performing these experiments, you'll learn the basic way COLORED lights work with one another to produce other COLORS, and you'll be giving yourself a useful introduction to the second set of primary COLORS, the subtractive primary COLORS.

The subtractive primary COLORS:
cyan, magenta and yellow

Earlier, we said COLOR exists as COLORED light itself, and as white light reflected off surfaces that have been COLORED with pigments such as inks, dyes and paints. This is important because the way COLORS work with one another is different depending on whether the COLORS are lights or pigments.

However, there is a unifying relationship between these two groups of COLOR. It is simply the way one set of primaries produces the other. We have said the primary COLORS of light (the additive primary COLORS) are red, blue and green. Now we will find that the primary COLORS of pigments are cyan, magenta and yellow. These COLORS, you will recall, are produced in the experiment described above by unscrewing first the red, then the green, and then the blue bulb. What I mean is (and this is another surprise to anyone beginning to learn about COLOR) the combination of any two additive primary COLORS in lights produces one of the primary COLORS of pigments. We call these the subtractive primary COLORS.

The additive primary COLORS (in lights) are used for creating COLORED effects for stage design, light shows, web sites and television images. The subtractive primary COLORS (in pigments), on the other hand, are used for producing the thousands of COLORS needed to recreate photographs, paintings and illustrations in full COLOR printing.

Four COLORS and printing

The subtractive primary COLORS can be seen in action in any full COLOR printed picture.

These are the images you have seen your entire life, starting with the pictures in the first books you looked at as a baby. The subtractive primaries are found in all the advertisements and photographs that appear in all books and magazines.

To learn about this, look at any COLOR ad in a magazine.

Unless you look carefully, all the photographs in magazine ads seem to be made of dozens of individual COLORS, and many of them appear "solid."

If there's a picture in a magazine that shows a woman wearing a green dress, the green COLOR of her dress will appear to be printed from solid green ink. At a glance, that green dress will probably appear to be printed with ink that is separate from another ink used to print, let's say, a blue sofa in the background of the picture.

Even though that is how magazine pictures look, you might be surprised to hear that every COLOR you'll find in any magazine advertisement (with the occasional exception of silver or gold) is created from a combination of only three inks, inks which match the three subtractive primary COLORS, which are, again, cyan (light blue), magenta (light purple) and yellow.

There is no green ink used whatsoever.

How, you might wonder, is the green dress possible?

This apparent miracle is accomplished by a printing method called "four COLOR process."

Four COLOR process is a system of mechanical procedures, using computer analysis and photography, that converts the COLORS of original, paintings and illustrations (for which artists actually *do* use hundreds of individual pigments, including green) into a mix of only the subtractive primary COLORS, cyan, magenta and yellow. These *are* primary COLORS because they can be combined to create a reasonable match for most (but not all) other COLORS.

Three separate printing plates are then prepared which print millions of tiny "dots" of these three primary COLORS, usually no larger than about 1/200th of an inch (3mm) wide. The dots are all printed side by side of each other so they appear to our eye to recreate the COLORS in the original artwork.

Imagine again a green dress.

A green dress in four COLOR printing is produced by printing thousands of tiny cyan (light blue) dots right next to thousands of tiny yellow dots. Since the dots are so tiny, our eyes will automatically mix them together, and as a result, they are "fooled" into seeing a green dress.

This is because cyan ink and yellow ink, if actually mixed in a little glass jar, will make green ink. In four COLOR process, our eyes do the mixing. In fact, some of the dots actually do mix on the paper, either because the ink is wet, or the dots overlap. If you have a magnifying glass, look with it right now at a COLORful picture in a magazine, and you will see the dots we are talking about.

Where do subtractive primary COLORS get their name?

It's because, to arrive at white COLOR, it is necessary to "subtract" them from the white surface they are printed on. Referring to the letter sent to the magazine, that is why we must say a white linen suit represents an absence of COLOR. White linen fabric contains *no* COLORED pigments. (Of course, that is what the fashion journalist wrote in the first place.) This is the opposite of the additive primary COLORS which must be added together to arrive at white light (like the white light on the rock and roll singer).

If you follow this relationship between the additive and subtractive COLORS closely, you may ask two questions.

First, what happens if you "subtract" the additive primaries, and, second, what happens if you "add" the subtractive primaries? In both cases, in theory, the result is black. In COLOR theory, black is the absence of all additive COLORS and the presence of all subtractive COLORS.

In the experiment with three COLORED bulbs in a light fixture, if you can somehow "subtract" these three additive COLORS, that is, if you simply unscrew all three light bulbs (or turn off the switch), the result is black.

That is, there is no COLOR (and no light) in the room.

The room is dark.

The room is *black*.

On the other hand, if you add pigments of the subtractive primaries together, that is, if, inside a small jar, you mix together small quantities of cyan, magenta and yellow inks, in theory, you should get solid black ink. However, as we said earlier, the pigments (inks) that are available today are still not perfect. There is no perfect cyan ink, or perfect magenta dye, or perfect yellow paint, (or perfectly COLORED nail polish, for that matter).

Science has yet to produce these.

This means that any combination in equal amounts of the three subtractive primary COLORS in pigments produces, not black, but instead a muddy brown COLOR. For this reason, in four COLOR printing, a fourth COLOR must be added, which *is* solid black ink. (Solid black ink is produced from chemicals which are already solid black, like the carbon caught on the bottom of a saucer when it is held in a candle flame.)

In four COLOR printing then, black must also be counted as a "COLOR" when analyzing any original artwork like paintings and illustrations. There is a separate photographic (or scanning) process that figures out where (and how much) black is a part of the original image. The correct amount of black is then reproduced within the printing process by an additional "plate" (a fourth plate) of tiny black dots to be printed right next to, or on top of, the cyan, magenta and yellow dots.

So in printed pictures, where black appears to be solid (say it's the black shoes a man is wearing in an advertisement), the black plate basically prints solid black dots. In places where black is missing, say in the pedals of a white rose shown in the advertisement, the black plate prints almost no black dots.

To simplify, think again of the black shoes in an ad.

In theory, a printing press could create those shoes with an equal number of cyan and magenta and yellow dots (since "adding" together these subtractive primary COLORS should produce black). Our eye would do the "adding" and as a result we'd be fooled to believe the shoes are black.

That is the theory.

However, since pigments (inks) aren't perfect, the shoes will instead look dark brown. To overcome this weakness, a fourth ink is also needed, and it *is* solid black. The shoes in the ad are therefore made of equal numbers of cyan, magenta and yellow dots, all of which are practically covered up with a layer of black dots.

Your desktop printer works in much the same way.

There is another simple experiment which shows a different relationship between the additive primary COLORS of light and the subtractive primary COLORS of pigments.

We discovered that mixing two of the additive primary COLORS in lights produces one of the subtractive primary COLORS (of pigments). We'll see now that the reverse is also true.

That is, if we to mix magenta ink and yellow ink, (that is, ink that matches two of the subtractive primaries) the resulting COLOR is red, one of the additive primary COLORS. If we mix magenta ink with cyan ink, the result is blue, another additive primary COLOR. And if we mix yellow ink with cyan ink, the result is green (like the woman's dress), the third additive primary COLOR.

Mixing together any two subtractive primaries will produce one of the additive primaries.

The lazy person's primary COLORS:
red, blue and yellow

Although the additive primary COLORS (red, green and blue) and the subtractive primary COLORS (cyan, magenta and yellow), as described above, are the "official" primary COLORS of light and pigments, let's be honest, this is all pretty confusing.

That's why there is a tendency, even among the most serious artists, to simplify these ideas. As a result (while conveniently ignoring light and focusing only on pigments) it is frequently said that THE primary COLORS are red, blue and yellow.

This is an easy way of saying, that for general purposes (let's say it's water COLOR painting in high school) red paint, blue paint and yellow paint (along with black and white) can probably be combined to make most of the COLORS you'll need to paint a picture of a barn and a cow on a hill next to a pond.

Don't laugh, but that's primary enough for a lot of people.

This is easy to understand, since cyan is really just a shade of blue, and magenta is basically a variation on red. So to save students and beginners all the confusion of COLOR theory, these funny sounding names, magenta and cyan, as well as the terms additive and subtractive are often just ignored.

And in common practice, most advanced fine artists who paint portraits, landscapes, abstract canvases (and even barns with cows next to them), using acrylic, oil and water COLOR pigments, don't mix their COLORS from primary paints anyway. They usually work with as many as thirty or forty separate COLORS of paint which they keep handy in pre-mixed store-bought tubes.

For anyone who is only casually engaged with visual living, the "lazy man's primaries" are all you need to know, if anything. But for graphic design students, some knowledge of both sets of primary COLORS is required. This is true because computer monitors show only COLORED light, meaning that every COLOR on the screen is made from a combination of red light, blue light and green light.

An ongoing problem in graphic art is that these screen COLORS don't translate well into COLOR on printed surfaces. Although computers brought many benefits to graphic designers, overall our daily chore of managing COLOR has become more difficult than it was in the old days, not less. And this is not getting better. Just last week, my printing company had to run a job on press *three times* to get the COLOR right. Extra care and effort is required to control the outcome of COLORS created by modern high-technology processes (whether they are displayed, broadcast, projected, or printed).

Lastly, and speaking of computers, perhaps you have heard your COLOR monitor referred to as an RGB monitor. That means, of course, that all the COLORS on the monitor screen, and also all the COLORS on any standard television screen, are created by a picture tube or plasma technology that creates only three COLORS of light. They are, as you already know, red (R), green (G) and blue (B).

If you inspect the screen of a computer monitor with a powerful magnifying glass you will see the separate COLORED dots of red, green and blue light we are talking about. (On some flat monitors, you'll see COLORED dashes, not dots.)

Seeing white when it's not there

That also means if you inspect a monitor using a magnifying glass (let us say you're watching a DVD of "Titanic") don't be surprised to discover that Rose's beautiful white dress has *no white* in it whatsoever. Instead, it's made of equal numbers of red, green and blue dots of light, which your eye "adds" together. (This really is an alarming thing to explore. While writing this page, I again examined a monitor picture with a magnifying glass and after all my years of working with COLOR, I'm still amazed how the white COLOR simply vanishes when you look at it through the magnifier.)

One last point. Try to imagine what happens to Rose's dress in "Titanic" if you watch this film in a regular movie theater. (Not on

TV.) In that case, the COLORS on the movie screen are created, not with dots, but by shining bright white light through the plastic movie film in the projection room above and behind you. As the white light from the projector passes through the film, it is changed into COLORED light that matches the COLORS in the film. (Of course, the light for a white dress isn't changed very much.)

The light then continues on its way, passing above you from behind, and it hits the movie screen which is white. Then this light, unchanged by the white movie screen, bounces into your eyes.

That means, in this case, if you get close to a movie screen with a big magnifying glass and examine Rose's dress, you will, this time, actually see *nothing but white*. Unlike the technology needed for conventional TVs and computer monitors, inside movie theaters there's no need to create the illusion of white (or the illusion of any other COLORS) on the screen. That's true because the light itself, coming from the projection booth for Rose's dress is already white, and the light coming to the screen for her yellow sweater (having already passed through the yellow film) is already yellow, etc.

Although they do not do it in movie theaters, projecting the three additive primaries onto a white screen is not unheard of.

That's how old projection TVs worked.

Those were the large TVs you sometimes saw in hotel lobbies and in sports bars before flat screen technology was invented. Those TVs didn't use film because unlike a movie theater, for television it's impossible to keep film inside the TV for everything that has to appear on the screen. Instead, a special box was mounted on the ceiling of the room. Inside this box, a standard cable TV picture signal was converted into red, green and blue "spot light" pictures.

These pictures were then aimed at (projected at) the oversized screen located about twelve feet (about four meters) away. At the screen, the light of the separate pictures, made up of the three additive primaries, "mixed" together, and, well, you know the rest. In some cases, the three pictures were projected from behind, and the screen allowed them to shine through it, so you didn't actually see the projector anywhere.

Adjusting to COLOR

One afternoon in Florida, I was channel surfing on a regular TV set and I caught the start of Gilligan's Island. I figured I'd escape reality for while, so I began watching. When the first commercial came on, I decided to tune in the picture better. Faces on the screen were too red, and all of the background COLORS were brighter than natural. I was visiting a friend who had an old TV, and I thought maybe his housekeeper had bumped the set's COLOR buttons while she dusted, since that had happened to my own TV.

I spent two or three minutes with the remote and balanced the picture so close-ups of faces looked natural, and long shots of scenery and landscapes were realistic looking. When Gilligan came back on, the sky over the island had changed from a metallic hard surface into the infinitely layered DEPTH and SPACE it really is. I told myself that my friend was lucky to have someone very knowledgeable about COLOR, like me, to adjust his set.

I watched for a few more minutes and then my friend came in from work. He put down some packages, but said he had to leave again. Then, on his way out, he glanced at the TV and said, "If you fool with the controls, I'm sure you'll get a much better picture."

That made me wonder if he had an eye defect. I looked at the picture again, and all the tropical COLORS on the screen were about as accurate as I had ever seen them. But when my friend came home that night, he worked on the set again until it was back to the way it was before my adjustments. As a result, a few minutes later on Star Trek, Mr. Spock was looking *very* alien.

Then I noticed that a bald anchorman who was speaking on a local news program was badly sunburned, a condition which, when combined with the unusual TV settings, made him look somewhat like an orange Picard.

Then it hit.

It dawned on me that that's how some people in America's "Sunshine State," including my friend, want *everyone* on TV to look, including palefaced starship commanders.

That is, with the kind of radioactive *suntans* that are such a big visual part of Florida.

* * * *

For review, here are the four conditions of COLOR:

> Appropriateness of COLOR
> Side by side variation of COLOR
> The additive primary COLORS
> The subtractive primary COLORS

Before continuing to read, take a moment to look for these conditions of COLOR. You'll find that they're all around, no matter where you are. Try it now. Find a COLOR that is appropriate, or else find a COLOR that is affected by another COLOR nearby.

* * * *

Chapter Five

CONTRAST as a source of visual experience

Dialog

EVERY NOW AND THEN, someone finds a work of art seemingly lost inside a thrift shop. And sometimes it's valuable.

Perhaps it's hanging there, or standing there, undiscovered for a long time before anyone notices it and restores it to a more dignified location. When the news gets out, people may be surprised it took so long to be recognized. Frequently, there's a story about it in the newspapers, and it may be put on display where everyone can see it. Sometimes it ends up appraised on "Antiques Roadshow," or donated to a museum.

The person who found it may even get rich by reselling it.

Something like this happened not long ago.

In California, a woman bought a painting in a thrift store for $5, and was allegedly offered millions for it.[37] What's going on here? How can it be that something that's visually valuable can get lost, and then go unnoticed for a long period of time?

Obviously, there's more than one reason that can happen. For one thing, ever since there's been art, lots of it has been lost simply because of war and natural catastrophes. Hundreds if not thousands of works are, to this day, still missing worldwide after the looting and lawlessness that took place during and after World War II, and more recently, because of the conflicts in Iraq and elsewhere.

When that happens, sometimes the history of a piece of art is *also* lost, or forgotten. And that could mean, even if art reappears, its value may be unknown or unappreciated.

Another part of the puzzle is this: Some art is valuable not because of how it looks, but because of what it represents. Some is valuable not necessarily because it speaks with visual beauty and/

or compelling energy through the nine lessons of light. Rather, it's because *a situation* (part of CONTENT) makes it important.

If you can, remember the *Goddess of Democracy*, the sculpture created by art students during events in Beijing, China, late in the last century. She was a thirty-three foot tall white plaster statue of a woman holding high a torch. If that original sculpture had survived in Tiananmen Square, it would be very valuable today.

The statue represented extraordinary CONTENT (that is, the CONTENT of human values, which we will learn about in the next chapter). Nevertheless, as a work of sculpture (as a FORM) she was not particularly satisfying. She wasn't art like Michelangelo's *David* is art. To see what I mean, search images for "goddess of democracy," then open a second window and search "michelangelo david."

Do this now, before you continue to read. Display the pictures side by side and compare and evaluate their artistic energy.

Even though her organic FORM was not very satisfying, the *Goddess of Democracy* had the potential to rival the American *Statue of Liberty* as a monument to the idea of democracy. In fact, despite its fate (it was eventually destroyed by soldiers), the visual message of CONTENT in that statue was so important that there are replicas of it erected at new locations outside of China.

The *Goddess of Democracy* was born spontaneously during human turmoil. To define it (in words), the *Goddess of Democracy* did not *express* CONTENT as a lesson of light. Rather, she *became* CONTENT as a lesson of light. As an icon for freedom, she (quite literally) *stood for* emotional and heart rending experience. By comparison, Michelangelo's *David* is essentially pure organic FORM.

Goddess' CONTENT was more expressive than her FORM.

David's FORM is more expressive than his CONTENT.

It's not surprising the *Goddess of Democracy* evoked such emotion. But consider this: Do you think it is possible a more visually gifted group of students may have created an even *more* compelling sculpture on an occasion like that? Something more commanding and passionate than the *Goddess of Democracy*? Perhaps a statue whose *FORM* might have actually changed history? Could students have created a sculpture so moving and meaningful that the sight of it standing above the events could have altered history?

Can *any* FORM on *any* occasion carry power to completely mobilize people to achieve *total* (and peaceful?) success?

Of course, we'll never know what might have happened.

But there's clear evidence that this may be possible.

There are historic accounts of heraldry (and even cloud formations) that have had that miraculous effect, rallying soldiers to win unlikely victories during battles where the odds against them seemed overwhelming or even insurmountable. The American and British flags, among many others, have also worked this marvel and likewise, soldiers are usually encouraged to carry pictures of family and loved ones because images that represent cherished ideals are powerful incentives that instill courage and heroism.

Despite the outcome of events (read more on the internet), the *Goddess of Democracy* certainly accomplished that.

Furthermore, if you look again at those days in Tiananmen Square, there was other evidence of the impact visual images can marshal. Who can forget the photograph of a single man who stood in the path of Chinese tanks? You can see that incredible picture by searching images for "chinese tank man." (Bookmark this page.)

The primary three lessons of light within that tank image are CONTENT (the emotional and intellectual message conveyed by a solitary man facing military force); geometric FORM (the strong geometric relationship [composition] between the man and the tanks); and CONTRAST (which we will learn shortly is the appeal of any frame of reference which contains opposites, in this case, the opposites of strength and weakness).

Two powers of
the nine lessons of light

Anyway, perhaps I digressed too much here, because in this book we're learning how the visual language works, not how history works. So, returning to the thrift store, still another reason that art can get "lost" is, you might say, built into the two basic ways the lessons of light work within a frame of reference.

These are the two principal powers that the sources of visual experience bring to visual expression. And again, although these distinctions may help explain the visual language in general, they are not what you would call scientifically valid. No one should consider the following guidelines to be part of the creative process. But still, there's some truth in these thoughts about the basic influences the lessons of light bring to a frame of reference.

Read the brief description of these powers found on the following page, and then highlight them for review.

The two principal powers of the nine lessons of light

- The first power of the lessons of light is that
  they can attract our eye away from the visual clutter
  that surrounds us, and in that way, they help us focus
  on a specific area of interest (a frame of reference).

- Their second basic power is that they can carry the
  emotional message an artist is trying to communicate.

These two powers are shared by all nine lessons of light, but they are really just extensions of two powers of FORM we discussed in the second chapter.

There, we learned that people love the emotional messages hidden in organic FORMS, but are almost powerless to resist *looking at* geometric FORM. Remember, geometric FORM includes composition, and composition is one part of the visual language that is very successful at catching our attention from the corner of the eye.

Of course, not all composition is trying to do that.

But when it is . . . watch out.

Each lesson of light has some amount of these two powers.

Each can grab our attention *or* carry emotional messages.

Either of these two powers can be the foundation of visual expression. But if a painting that is a genuine work of art is found abandoned in the back of a second hand store, or forgotten in your attic, it is probably not using the visual language to grab your attention with strong composition. I say that because, generally speaking, it's that kind of impact within a frame of reference (strong composition) that people who are not living visually will usually react to first. If a frame of reference doesn't have that appeal, many people will just never focus on it.

Although the growing number of collecting programs seen on TV, along with the popularity of ebay, may be changing this, it's still possible for a wonderful and valuable painting to sit inside a closet or out in the barn for years (and years and years).

If a genuine work of visual expression is discovered "lost" in the back of a store, or in some other out of the way place, it is probably using the sources of visual experience primarily to carry an emotional message. That also explains why perhaps half of the work you might find hanging in a museum might go unnoticed if you purposefully displayed it, instead, on a restaurant wall in a bad part of town. People who don't have the habit of looking for visual meaning (i.e., people you might find in a bad part of town) usually need that first power of the visual language, a sort of exaggerated use of the lessons of light, before their attention is captured.

And quite a bit of great visual expression exists far (and I do mean *far*) above that need for simple attention.

Accomplished artists can concentrate less on attracting people's attention, and more on giving their work important visual/emotional meaning. It's possible that artists sense that any people who do look their way may feel the questions they raise are more significant if less energy is devoted to getting attention. This works out fine, since once an artist is well-known, people will want to see what he or she is "saying." People then begin to look for the work of an artist who has earned that kind of status. At that point even less effort is needed in getting attention. That is to say, there are ways of speaking through the sources of visual experience to get people's attention, and other ways to speak through them so the visual message conveyed is spiritually lifting to people who bother to notice.

But there is no rule that either approach is the more likely to anchor meaningful visual expression or represent financial value.

Just because a work of visual expression is subtle or indirect does not mean it is speaking with less authority. And for practical purposes, a frame of reference needs a little of both approaches. It needs some visual trickery to grab our attention out of the corner of our eye (like the diagonal in the whale composition), and it needs a satisfying visual message so that we feel justified spending one of our precious few moments of visual consciousness looking at it (like the FORM of the whale in the same example).

When a painting is discovered in an unlikely place, it often means only that someone with visual curiosity has looked for meaning within its frame of reference; someone who is living visually has found questions that aren't otherwise crying out for attention. They have glanced over and *recognized* emotional meaning carried to the eye by the lessons of light.

And of course, that means you will need to become familiar with these lessons before you make those discoveries (and before you stumble on, recognize and then perhaps pay only $10 for a million dollar painting at a garage sale).

By recognize, I don't mean you remember seeing it in some dusty art book. Instead, it means recognizing the energy expressed by the lessons of light, and realizing this thing everyone is ignoring is visually important. You can learn to recognize this energy even if you have no interest in actually creating visual expression yourself. Again, that's often the skill an art dealer or collector acquires (or a good yard sale shopper). What I mean is, someone living visually, even someone who is *not* an artist, *can* do it.

And you can too. You can enjoy that ability to know when something is art and when something is not art. Although galleries and even museums make mistakes (maybe more often than you'd think), when you finally begin to recognize important visual expression, you will also begin to understand why the artwork you find in galleries and museums is *in* those galleries and museums.

Of course, it doesn't hurt to also remember things you actually see in a book or at an art show. Twice I purchased chairs for $3 that are in the permanent collection of NY's Museum of Modern Art. One was in a thrift store, yet another at a yard sale. Each caught my eye with its visual energy, and I then remembered one from a design book and the other from a furniture exhibition that I once attended. They're valued around $400 each. One was marked down from $10 to $3 late in the afternoon because, apparently, no one in northern New Jersey that day had read "Help Yourself to a Blue Banana" (or visited the Museum of Modern Art). Sometime after those discoveries I found yet *another* well-known chair, this time for only $1 (at another yard sale) and resold it on ebay for $550.[38]

All this "good luck" is really just a perk of visual living.

And by the way, this discovery of lost art in an out-of-the-way place is nothing new. Two hundred years ago in a second hand store, a man in Rome "recognized" a painting glued to the door of a cupboard. His visual curiosity led him to discover it was part of a much larger Leonardo da Vinci masterpiece, and believe it or not, he eventually found the remainder of the same painting nailed to a shoemaker's workbench.[39] Of course, da Vinci is one of history's greatest artists whose work includes the *Mona Lisa*, which is generally accepted as the world's finest painting. So keep looking!

The last few paragraphs refer to serious art and design, and in particular to paintings and chairs that are ignored in out-of-the-way places. But there's probably a more practical reason to separate the power hidden in the lessons of light into two categories as suggested above. That's because in business art and design, this ability to grab attention, especially with striking composition, is a primary and driving force in just about every commercial effort.

In advertisements, poster design, fashion photography, web page layout, and for the design of signs, brochures, trade show displays, point of sale material and direct mail pieces, there's no need to redefine the meaning of art. A primary and urgent requirement is simply to get people's attention. The bowling ball/beach ball billboard mentioned earlier did not have deep emotional meaning (and it certainly is not art). It just used ANATOMY to get my attention.

For that reason, as we said in chapter two, geometric FORM, expressed as strong composition, is the workhorse of the lessons of light in business art. It's a generality, but you'd probably agree that a display for a hair color product, designed for drugstores (or a billboard that's promoting beer), is probably going to be more eye-catching than a Rembrandt painting. The store display and the billboard will use the lessons of light to grab your attention so you read about the hair coloring (or the beer) and *buy it.*

But a Rembrandt painting will have a far higher goal.

The painting uses lessons of light to carry emotional meaning and to ask questions about the human condition.

The greatest shows on earth

Since a frame of reference is almost always smaller than the entire area of our field of vision, that means there are almost always areas of visible activity that are outside any frame of reference we're interested in. It follows that even when we think we're fully aware of seeing, there are still things well within our field of vision we completely ignore. Like watching a circus, our eye concentrates on the center ring, and misses less interesting events elsewhere in the tent.

Also ignored in our daily visual life are thousands of scenes which *do* appear directly in front of our eyes, but don't have any frame of reference interesting enough, or startling enough, to bring our vision into consciousness. This part of our visual life, a sort of visual sleeping time between frames of reference, accounts for probably 95% of the time our eyes are open. All these ignored scenes are the clutter we talked about in the third chapter.

However, since visual experiences are created not only by artists and by individuals who are living visually, but also by Mother Nature and chance, how can we be sure they will all have only one, two or generally speaking (at the most) only three strong sources of visual experience, with others only supporting these (or neutral)? To put it differently, and referring back to the introduction: Why do I keep saying visual experiences, even in nature, have only three (or less) strong lessons of light (the one, two, three rule)?

The reason is, even in nature, this is the only kind of frame of reference that's strong enough to jolt our visual attention into consciousness. It takes a frame of reference such as this to alert us that something worth looking at, something worth seeing, is taking place, . . . is appearing before us. That precious 5% of time that our eyes are fully aware is dominated by visual experiences that express only one, two or three strong lessons of light.

So, frames of reference that include more than three strong lessons of light, even in nature, are simply too confusing to keep our attention. And those which don't present *any* strong lessons of light are usually never noticed.

Imagine that a living room is designed by a committee of four people. The finished frame of reference (the room) might have dozens of competing areas of visual interest. If the room is filled with one person's favorite COLORS (walls and carpets), along with one other person's favorite FORMS (furniture), a third person's expression of SPACE, and somebody else's selection of TEXTURES (wallpapers, carpets and upholstery), chances are that a fifth person (let's say it's you) will find it uncomfortable. The reason is, you will not find a single strong source to anchor your emotional response.

When it's someone's job to create, or to re-create, a frame of reference, whether it's a serious professional responsibility or simply some weekend project to brighten up a bathroom or create a party poster, he must control all of the visual activity within it. It doesn't matter how many isolated parts it has, it must still have an overall visual unity when experienced as a whole.

When it's finished, the work should have one primary lesson of light or, generally speaking, at the most, only three.

When done correctly, people will say, "Wow, look at that!"

Controlling a frame of reference
like this isn't as difficult as it sounds.

A web page can have CONTENT as it's primary lesson of light if the page is dominated by an image that reflects the conditions of CONTENT (which we'll learn in the next chapter), and a prom dress can certainly have FORM as its primary lesson of light, when it gently brings some additional excitement to the already interesting shape of a human female body.

A library room filled with 35 pieces of furniture can have COLOR as its single strongest lesson of light if the furniture (and everything else in the room) is selected with this goal in mind. That doesn't mean everything in the room has to be the *same* COLOR. It more likely means that a combination of COLORS has been called into service to create that unified and pleasing sensation. The furniture must be selected carefully so when it is brought together, the effect is an overall satisfying sensation of COLOR. If you are the person choosing the COLORS, no doubt you've acquired that skill by "collecting" COLORS earlier in your mind's eye.

However, lastly, although rare, there are exceptions to the one, two, three rule. There are sometimes successful frames of reference, whether a room, a painting or a package of detergent that have more than three strong lessons of light. Creating a cluttered frame of reference like this (one our eyes are willing to look at even though it has more than three strong sources of visual experience) requires the effort of a talented and visually alert person.

But even so, a frame of reference like that is not usually as strong, or as engaging, as other frames of reference with three or less sources of visual impact.

In the visual language, as in written language, simple is usually better. Successful-but-cluttered frames of reference are sometimes called "eclectic."

* * * *

Chapter five continued
AN INTRODUCTION TO CONTRAST
The fifth lesson of light
The proof that opposites attract

You often hear it said that "opposites attract."

What that usually means is that people with opposite character are often romantically attracted to one another, and of course, the opposite ends of a magnet (the "plus" end and the "minus" end) also attract each other. However when someone living visually says opposites attract, he or she may mean this: he or she may mean when any "opposites" appear together in a frame of reference, they have the unusual ability to "attract" our visual attention.

Since that is basically the definition of a lesson of light, this makes opposites a powerful tool for conveying visual meaning.

We call that tool CONTRAST.

Frames of reference that have CONTRAST as a source of visual experience fall into two categories. First, there are frames of reference which actually do contain opposites, and secondly, there are frames of reference which contain conflicts. As a general rule, opposites are sets of ideas or objects which are intellectually different, while conflicts are comparisons of visual characteristics.

The two conditions of CONTRAST:

Opposites
Conflicts

Visual opposites - The first condition of CONTRAST
Why is that bad guy wearing a white hat?

Our willingness to accept that two things are the opposite of each other is one way to understand the world in its simplest terms. Ancient accounts of history, beginning with the Bible, teach us the difference between goodness and evil, and between lightness and darkness. These opposites are so basic they have become, in a way, related to each other. Lightness, or white, usually means good; and darkness, or black, has come to mean bad or evil.

To some degree, even the opposites of day and night share this relationship with good and bad. Although these relationships between good and bad and white and black are learned ideas (intellectual ideas), they are known and accepted by practically everyone everywhere.

Here's how they are related:

White	Black
Good	Bad
Day	Night

The ideas in each column are visually related
to one another. In addition, at least at the
most basic level, anything in the first column
is the opposite of anything in
the second column.

These opposites are so established that you can ask anyone, of any age, in any language, and in any country what the opposite of white is and they will all say "black." Similarly ask anyone what the opposite of good is and a universally understood answer around the world is bad or "evil."

How many other strong sets of opposites are there?

One day I asked a class and several good answers were offered including: young and old, happy and sad, living and dead, beautiful and ugly, fat and skinny, and short and tall.

Each of these sets of opposites is a valuable visual tool.

It's possible to speak through them to build visual meaning because everyone accepts these pairs as being in CONTRAST to each other. And CONTRAST, like the other lessons of light, is one of the basic conditions out of which visual impact can be created and visual questions can be asked. Our eye is naturally drawn toward, and interested in, a frame of reference that brings to our attention the fact that one thing is the opposite of another.

For proof, try to imagine these photographs (or sketch these scenes on your paper):

A smiling baby next to a crying baby
A skinny fashion model sitting next to a circus fat lady.
A little person standing next to a basketball champ.

These images may or may not be important works of visual expression. But even in the simplest execution (including your own efforts on your blank paper) these sets of things are always (let me repeat always, always, always) visually interesting.

This is an important, basic observation about visual living.

So before you continue to read, try to create one or two of these situations on your paper right now. Even if you can't draw, and I assume you can't, try this anyway.

Almost any effort here will probably make the point.

Take a moment to draw one or two of the images suggested above. When you are done, draw a box around your sketch so the frame of reference is clearly defined.

Look at your finished sketch(es) and you will see the CONTRAST in opposites. But, even so, there is something here that is easily overlooked. To see what it is, imagine that, rather than drawing a crying baby next to a smiling baby, you are assigned to draw a picture of "good" next to a picture of "bad." A quick, simple image of good and bad standing there, or sitting there side by side.

Try it now on your paper.

Draw a picture of good and bad.

If you can succeed in this, I would be interested in seeing your drawing. Likewise, I would be surprised if you or anyone could produce a convincing picture of fat next to skinny, young next to old, or life next to death (or even crying next to smiling).

The reason is that these opposites aren't possible to express visually until they are placed in context of some sort, as in crying and smiling *babies*. Life and death mean nothing visually until we are referring to living and dead *apple trees*, or living and dead chickens. In the same way, a picture of fat and skinny is impossible to draw until we know what is fat and what is skinny. The same is true for young and old. Or good and bad. That is to say, these widely understood opposites have no visual life until they are matched with additional information which *is* capable of being expressed visually. That's why it is said above that opposites are, for the most part, intellectual ideas, *not* visual ideas.

Imagine a photograph of an old man sitting on a bench in a park. If there's no other visually interesting detail within the photograph, the lesson of the picture is probably CONTENT. We'll learn very shortly (in chapter 6) that CONTENT is our intellectual curiosity about the old man's age, clothes and facial expressions, etc. And, in case you are wondering, on its own, this variety of CONTENT (a photograph of an old man sitting on a park bench) does not necessarily sound very interesting.

However, now imagine the same photograph, but this time the man holds an infant baby. Without seeing this picture (although again, I suggest that you try a sketch here), you can probably imagine how visual curiosity is increased by the addition of CONTRAST to the picture. There is visual interest generated by the CONTRAST of the *old* man compared to the *young* baby. Each time a frame of reference clearly shows something very old next to something that is very young, or very new, there is an almost automatic increase in visual interest, and visual meaning.

What does this visual meaning in the CONTRAST of a baby and an elderly man (in other words, the CONTRAST between the opposites young and old) communicate to us? What questions does this ask? Is the question, "Does life always go on?" or does it say,

"Does time catch up with everyone?" or does it imply, "Does age create wisdom?" The fact that these questions cannot be simply answered (if they can be answered at all) is why we sometimes feel we can't "understand" what visual artists are saying in their work. And, of course, keep in mind, whatever questions we may actually put into words are dwarfed by other questions that can be stated only in the visual language.

They are questions that words simply cannot ask.

A famous painter once said, "I don't think artists like myself have the faintest idea what we're doing, but we try to put it in words that sound logical."[40] Perhaps that can be said about this entire book also. It's trying to put the visual language into words that sound logical, while all along I am very aware that this cannot ever be completely accomplished.

Nevertheless, successful visual expression must ask questions. And truthfully, some may be observations we *can* put into words. But again, many will be questions reserved for asking only in the visual language. Visual meaning is powerful, inspiring and influential precisely because it cannot be easily "translated." Visual experience is important because it expands our understanding of life in thousands of directions that written and spoken languages cannot ever duplicate.

Therefore, the message of this book is: to understand visual meaning, become familiar with the language artists speak. It's a language used by every artist, but it is not composed of words. Rather, it's the lessons of light. Fortunately, there are only nine of these lessons, and they are the ideas you are reading about.

Although there are only nine lessons of light, there are billions of different meanings to visual information. The reason is that, within each lesson there are thousands of variations. Then, when the interaction of all nine within a frame of reference is considered, each one in some way modifying or influencing every one of the others, it explains the infinite number of possibilities that exist.

For an example, imagine the change in meaning that would occur in the photograph showing the old man in the park with the baby if the old man was dead. The meaning might change from the CONTRAST of young and old to the CONTRAST of living and dead. Can words explain the change in meaning this represents? No, actually I don't think they can. And, after all the attempts are made to explain this change of meaning, in words, perhaps the only certainty is this: if the old man is dead, the meaning of the photograph does dramatically change. How and why this happens, or what it means, is probably not a message words can describe. Instead, it's an emotional message reserved for understanding only within the special language of visual meaning.

Imagine the same photograph, but now the baby is dead.

What if both the old man *and* the baby are dead?

You must agree, these are significant changes in meaning, but they are impossible to put into words.

In these pictures, in order to express CONTRAST with living against dead, the two people would not have to be different ages. A living 30 year woman can easily be CONTRASTED with a dead 30 year old woman.

And imagine this: a photograph that shows a living 100 year old man next to an 18 year old dead man (when of course, we would expect the opposite). All we can say in words is that the CONTRAST in a photograph such as this is significant. But it is significant only in a way we can understand visually.

> *Here are some other*
> *CONTRASTS that might appear*
> *together in a frame of reference:*

A human male and a human female
A beautiful woman and an ugly woman
A smiling clown and a crying clown
A strong man and a weak man

These are CONTRASTS that come to life because the objects of the CONTRAST are identified. In this short list above, the CONTRASTS are all identified as characteristics of people. We are especially sensitive to CONTRASTS in people, but for the second one, instead of two women, visual meaning could also, easily, emerge from a photograph of a beautiful lamp next to an ugly lamp. The requirement for visual meaning is only that the object of these CONTRASTS be identified.

Beauty does not CONTRAST with ugly until beautiful and ugly things are identified. But the objects do not have to be the same type of objects. So consider this: a photograph of a beautiful woman holding an ugly dog. This frame of reference would also express the CONTRAST between beauty and ugliness, even though women and dogs are not similar things.

Non-visual opposites

Each CONTRASTING set of opposites discussed above (big, little; happy, sad; beautiful, ugly, etc.) is a learned set of opposites. Each conveys visual meaning based on information we first needed to learn through our sense of vision. Babies don't know who is ugly or who is beautiful (although there is evidence that infants are more attracted to a pleasant face than an unpleasant face).

However, after years of observing the world, people eventually begin to agree, at least more or less, on what is pretty and what is ugly, although there is certainly room for discussion about it, even among visually sensitive people.

Other types of opposites, though, require that we evaluate the world from a non-visual point of view. These include all of the opposites from our other senses. That is to say, there are opposites in touch, smell, taste and hearing also, and once learned (as they are in childhood), they can be represented with visual meaning in a frame of reference.

These non-visual CONTRASTS include loud and quiet (from our sense of hearing), hot and cold, and heavy and light (from our sense of touch), and sweet and sour (from our sense of taste). Also, it's not difficult to imagine two opposite smells, like perhaps the smell of a rose compared to bad eggs. Like the concepts above, each of these opposites must be associated with objects before they are expressed visually. There is no such thing as a picture of heavy and light. Before we see the CONTRAST between heavy and light, we must know *what* is heavy and *what* is light.

A photograph of a canon ball next to a feather is a frame of reference which has as (one) source the non-visual CONTRAST of heavy and light. That is, we know heavy is the opposite of light, but our eyes did not teach us this. Nevertheless, if you sketch this idea on your paper (or on the blank page at the end of this chapter), you can see there is visual interest in an image like this. Sketch a picture of a canon ball next to a feather. Draw a box around your drawing to define the frame of reference. Then *look at* your sketch.

Learn from the CONTRAST of heavy and light.

On the other hand, our eyes *do* teach us that fat is the opposite of skinny. That is why we refer to those opposites, and the others mentioned with them above (big and small, short and tall, etc.), as *visual* opposites.

False opposites (and words fail again)

Another category of opposites that can be expressed within a frame of reference are false opposites. Although often called opposites, these things are not really associated with any of our five senses. For example, an artist is sometimes thought of as the opposite of a scientist, and in the U.S., a republican is often thought of as the opposite of a democrat. Likewise, north is the "opposite" of south.

I think, therefore I am
not visually sensitive

Once again, if you're an intellectual, you might wonder how important it is to understand some of these thoughts.

How can this talking about visual perception help you learn the visual language? Is it really necessary? I'm certain some readers are wondering about that. An answer once again is that words are by far the most common and most widely understood form of communication, even among people who are visually sensitive, including all the best fine artists and the best business artists.

But no matter how good an artist is, no matter what mastery he or she has of this inspiring method of communication, he or she will still use words to help accomplish simple tasks and communicate everyday messages.

So consider this. Suppose the greatest writer who ever lived (let's go with Shakespeare) walks in a restaurant one morning. He's hungry and wants to have breakfast. When the waiter comes over, of course Shakespeare needs to tell the waiter in the best way possible what he has in mind. But no problem. Shakespeare, the greatest writer in the world, quickly decides to use words to order his breakfast. Shakespeare believes that words will be the very best way to communicate with the waiter.

So, in his mind, Shakespeare prepares the words to achieve his goal. He thinks for a moment, then says to the waiter, "I'll have a bagel with a smear of cream cheese." Mission accomplished. The waiter understands perfectly what Shakespeare wants, and a few minutes later, he brings over the bagel.

Now imagine that the greatest artist who ever lived (let's go with Michelangelo) also goes into this restaurant for breakfast. He sees Shakespeare and says hello. Michelangelo is also hungry and also needs to communicate to the waiter, again in the best way possible, what he wants for breakfast. So Michelangelo, the world's greatest user of pictures for communicating, thinks about how best to communicate to the waiter exactly what he wants to order.

What do you imagine he does?

Michelangelo thinks for a moment and then motions for the waiter to come. He pulls out a drawing pad, evaluates his options once again and then, after reviewing in his mind the possible ways he could place his order, he puts the drawing pad away and instead he says to the waiter, *in words*, "I'll have a bagel with a smear of cream cheese." How interesting and important that is!

How interesting and important when you consider this: even though he is the greatest user of pictures to communicate, in this situation, Michelangelo realizes he will be more successful using the spoken language, instead of the visual language, to order breakfast.

Of course my point is that no matter how well you learn the visual language, it will never fully replace the usefulness of the spoken language, especially in everyday situations like ordering breakfast. Both Shakespeare and Michelangelo understood, in a restaurant, the best way to communicate with the waiter is with the assistance of words, even though Michelangelo knows he is the world's leading expert at communicating with visual expression.

Shakespeare did fine with words

In fact, *everyone* is and always will be much more familiar with words than with the nine lessons of light. So once again, you may ask why we even bother to learn the visual language in the first place? Again the answer is even though words are useful in expressing thoughts and feelings, including all the thoughts and feelings of writers *and* artists, there are still some things words cannot express. When a person feels the need to express *those* thoughts and ideas, he or she will turn to the visual language.

We may say, generally speaking, Shakespeare never felt the need to communicate emotions that words could not express. What that means is, he did just fine with words, thank you very much.

But Michelangelo did feel a need to express beyond words. Although Michelangelo used words effectively in his everyday life, as we all do, he also mastered the nine lessons of light. Shakespeare nailed the language of words. By comparison, Michelangelo, like all visual artists, nailed the visual language, even while he also continued to use the language of words.

Because words are so widely understood by everyone, that's why we're using them here, as best we can, to help explain the visual language and, just as important, to raise your visual curiosity.

Then, if your curiosity *is* raised, you will teach yourself the visual language. If your curiosity leads you to look for examples of the things we are describing in the real world, the world you actually live in and see, your progress will be amazing. We're doing this even though we know we're going to discover limits. Wonderful as words are. Wonderful as words can be. They're often simply of little value in explaining visual expression.

So, here is still another approach to explaining this difficult idea. The following paragraph is an example of the limits we may encounter when we try to use words to explain art. This is an example of how senseless words can sometimes become when they try to capture visual meaning with logical analysis.

See if you can follow the perfectly normal verbal (word) logic presented here as these two paragraphs try to make a point, a point that slowly deteriorates into aimless nonsense:

Here goes:

Visually speaking, you would probably agree with me that in some ways a white man can be thought of as the opposite of a black man (again *visually* speaking). And as we said above, an artist is sometimes thought of as the opposite of a scientist. But, if that's true, is a white artist, then, the opposite of a black artist, or of a white scientist? Or is a white artist, more than anything else, the opposite of a person who is both black *and* a scientist?

What if the artist is a woman, and the scientist is a man? What then? Is a white female artist, more than anything else, the opposite of a man who is also a black scientist? Does that make them even *more* opposite? Then what if the scientist is fat and the woman is skinny, or the black man is tall, and the artist is short, what then?

To put it simply, any opposites can be expressed in a frame of reference to add visual interest. But trying to analyze them outside the visual language is probably ridiculous.

And these two paragraphs (above) probably prove it.

Opposite, or just different?
Black and white, the only non-intellectual opposites

With only one exception, every set of opposites mentioned so far has required some context to be understood. As we shall see below, that one exception enjoys a unique place in visual expression. The exception that I'm referring to is the set of opposites called black and white.

To help you see how special black and white are as opposites, let's first review some of the ideas about CONTRAST we have already discussed.

We said that sets of opposites require that we know what is opposite before they can appear in a frame of reference. We need to know what is skinny and what is fat before the ideas of *skinny* and *fat* can be understood. Although we learn about skinniness and fatness, and tallness and shortness, etc., with our eyes, it's necessary for us to recognize these visual ideas with our intellect also, as characteristics of things.

Otherwise, "opposite" means nothing.

Again, although we accept that an angel is good and a devil is bad, using our two eyes to recognize this, it is impossible for this CONTRAST of good and bad to work visually until we learn what a devil is, and what an angel is.

An infant doesn't see CONTRAST in a drawing of angels and devils. First, he has to learn they are opposite. From that point, and for the remainder of his life, they are useful visual images he will react to as CONTRAST if they appear together in a frame of reference. And, because everyone eventually learns that angels are good and devils are bad, we can, and do, constantly use these images to stand for good and bad.

In the same way, all the other opposites we accept as being in CONTRAST to each other rely on our intellectual understanding of the world. That is to say, goodness, badness, northness, southness, happiness and sadness, etc., are all learned ideas, ideas that have visible characteristics (such as tears for sadness, for example) that are also learned.

Black and white,
the only truly visual opposites

There's only one exception. There's only one set of opposites we don't need to learn about. It is the only set of opposites that does not rely on an intellectual understanding of the world.

These are the only truly visual opposites, black and white.

To see what I mean, imagine you are asked to draw a picture of "black." This time, if you take a black crayon and scribble a mass of black on your paper, I'd agree it's fair to call that a picture of "black." The same is true for white. In this way, black and white are different from other opposites. Black and white do not require a context in order to be CONTRASTED in a frame of reference.

We can recognize black and we can recognize white, and we can react to their "opposite-ness," without knowing what is black and what is white.

Although just everyone understands what *opposite* means, if we don't count false opposites, there are actually very few sets of things or ideas that *are* opposite. So far in this chapter we have referred to less than ten, counting fat and skinny as one, and black and white as two, etc. If we lump them all together, it is likely the total is less than two dozen. That is to say, there may be less than two dozen sets of opposites we identify with our five senses.

That means if CONTRAST as a lesson of light relied strictly on opposites, it would be easy to define. But that isn't the case. Frames of reference can have strong CONTRAST even when there are no sets of opposites to recognize.

That is to say, CONTRAST can also exist in a frame of reference that contains *conflict*.

Conflict, the second condition of CONTRAST
Visual information fighting itself

A frame of reference with strong *conflict* presents a comparison that is so interesting, or so full of tension, our eye can't ignore it. As we describe these comparisons, we'll see that they are always examples of one lesson of light in conflict with itself.

For example, no one ever suggested that red is the opposite of blue, but if red and blue (which are, of course, COLORS) appear side by side in a frame of reference, one easily sees how they conflict with one another.

A TEXTURE like the surface of a coconut is not the opposite of a TEXTURE like corduroy fabric, but if they appear side by side in a frame of reference (or just laying on a table) it is easy to see how these conflict with one another as well. And for a third example a FORM in the shape of a pyramid will conflict with a FORM in the shape of a sphere. They're not opposites. They just *conflict*.

To see an expression of a strong conflict like this, in action, search internet images for "Trylon and Perisphere" to discover pictures of the famous 610 foot tall theme building at the 1939 World's Fair in New York City (which was unfortunately demolished long ago). It was a tall, tall pyramid standing next to a big sphere (that is, a big ball). The visual appeal of the Trylon and Perisphere is that they conflict with each other. (Bookmark this page.)

In fact, any of the nine lessons of light will conflict with itself if two examples of it exist side by side. However, in a typical frame of reference, these conflicts are meaningless, and therefore go unnoticed. That is to say, if a photograph shows a man wearing a brown cashmere sweater and blue wool pants, we are not usually aware of the conflict between these two TEXTURES (cashmere and wool) and these two COLORS (brown and blue).

That's true because neither wool and cashmere, nor brown and blue conflict *very strongly*. If there are no additional remarkable sources of visual experience in a photograph like this, chances are we will simply ignore it. There is nothing strong enough in the CONTRAST of blue and brown, or in the CONTRAST of cashmere and wool, to grab our interest and cause this frame of reference to be one of the few we bring into conscious attention.

As your visual life broadens, you'll understand that all COLORS CONTRAST with each other, and all TEXTURES CONTRAST with each other. And this is equally true for all FORMS, SPACES, DEPTHS and each of the other lessons of light.

To say it again, how very unique this makes the CONTRAST we experience between black and white! Black and white are COLORS which CONTRAST sharply with each other, and they're also universally accepted as opposites. This is interesting because none of the other sources of visual experience contains pairs of opposites. Every set of things we agree are "opposite," with the exception of black and white, are intellectual concepts we learn as children.

Furthermore, we accept them as opposites in visual experience only when a frame of reference shows us things we can identify, things that put oppositeness in context of some sort.

It's true that other lessons of light can be in conflict without needing "things" to identify them. For an example, TEXTURES can conflict without our knowing what they are, and likewise, COLORS can conflict, SPACES can conflict, and in fact each of the nine lessons of light can conflict within itself. But none of the sources of visual experience contains a set of genuine opposites within itself, with the exception of COLOR. That unique distinction belongs to the pair of opposites we call black and white.

The blues are cool

I wrote earlier that even though we can agree that red and blue conflict sharply, no one ever suggested that red is the *opposite* of blue. Actually, though, a student once did suggest that red and blue are opposites.

He reminded us that red and blue have come to represent the opposites of hot and cold when they appear on water faucets. Of course (unlike black and white) by themselves, or even when associated with other things, these two COLORS don't have that opposite meaning. For example, although a red water faucet (hot) might be thought of as the opposite of a blue water faucet (cold), that's where it ends. A red car is not the opposite of a blue car. And a communist soldier is not the opposite of a non-communist soldier who is not happy.

Again, that makes black and white seem special.

Black and white are opposites everywhere they appear, and no matter where they appear.

Red sometimes stands for "hot" in places other than faucets. It got that meaning because wave lengths of red light produce more heat than those of other (visible) COLORS. That's why the lights on top of the French fries in a restaurant are red. On the other hand, wave lengths of blue light produce less heat. The result is that, in a limited way, red has come to stand for hot and blue stands for cold, or cool. And by the way, for that same reason, people sometimes refer to COLORS which contain some reddish tint as warm COLORS. And COLORS which tend toward blue are cool COLORS.

And, speaking of blue light (I digress even more) here is a rule of thumb about sign making: it's usually a bad idea to make a sign using blue light. The reason is, especially from a distance, the long wave lengths that make up blue light do not focus well on the retina of the human eye.

As a result, blue neon, when seen from a distance will usually appear blurry and out of focus. Red neon, on the other hand, creates shorter wave lengths of light which *do* focus well on human retinas. Therefore, red neon letters will nearly always appear sharp and crisp. You can generally assume that the name of a store spelled in blue light will be less effective than the same sign made from red light. On the other hand, outdoor signs created for night clubs and bars sometimes use blue lights on purpose, because they actually *want* to look sort of dreamy.

Who cares if CONTRAST
can be in CONTRAST with itself?

It's understandable to wonder if some things you are reading are important. Does anyone care if black and white are opposites, or if there are such and such conditions of DEPTH, or if CONTRAST can CONTRAST with itself? People who have no experience with the visual language, and no clue what the fuss is all about, can fall back on schoolbook logic. When these examples are too odd, they can be ignored. Life can easily go on.

In fact, life does go on for most people without this extra visual dimension. But if you have the curiosity, you won't regret following instincts until visual understanding becomes a daily experience. You'll think of new ways to be creative. It's likely, when you're living visually, you may get compliments on your manner of dress, or the way you plant a garden, or decorate for parties, or sign your name, or style your hair, or arrange baskets (TEXTURE and FORM) on top of kitchen cabinets.

But, even so, you may still find that some things you're reading are a bit unusual. Again, one trouble is we're talking about them in English when they are intended for the visual language.

We're losing fun (and gaining confusion) in the translation.

So here's something else that may sound odd. I wrote above that CONTRAST can CONTRAST with itself, and I pray you didn't open the book here for the first time. If you did, your enthusiasm might stop. If you came to this page early in your experience with this book, you might say, "Wow, I'll never understand *that*."

But understanding these things in words is only a brief substitute for understanding them visually. As a result, yet again, here's perhaps another unusual statement: Nobody (including me) *cares* if CONTRAST can CONTRAST with itself.

I could not care less.

So why should you read it here?

It's because, sometimes, when people *see* CONTRAST in CON-TRAST with itself, . . . *they like it.* Do you get it? How can I explain to you why a person might find something pleasing about a photo-graph of two different and COLORful Scottish kilts (plaid skirts) that are draped, side by side, across a chair?

Suppose I say, "Hey, I like how that looks. I really, really like the way those two kilts look together as they lay across that chair."

And then suppose you say, "Why do you like that?"

You may expect me to respond with a comment like, "I don't know, *they just look cool.*" That's the kind of thing you often hear when people try to explain visual expression. But let's be honest, a comment like that is essentially meaningless.

By comparison, the only *accurate* and *meaningful* thing I can tell you (in words) is that I like how the CONTRAST within the plaid pattern of one of the kilts is CONTRASTING (conflicting) with the CONTRAST in the plaid pattern of the other kilt.

The words are a mouthful. *They sound like blather.*

However, what I'm experiencing, the visual experience of what I'm *seeing*, is actually pretty simple and pretty pleasant. What I'm seeing is easy to look at, and, most of all, pleasing to my eyes.

When I look at the kilts, I'm not thinking about anything.

I'm not thinking about lessons of light, or *"Help Yourself to a Blue Banana,"* art theory, or even kilts. But suddenly, for *visual rea-sons only,* the CONTRAST between those kilts may jump out and be satisfying to look at.

Without analyzing it, someone may just like how it looks.

He may like the feeling of it.

He may simply think, ". . . wow, far out! Two kilts hanging on a chair. Who would have thunk that could be so cool."

The sight of kilts draped across a chair (or some other conflict-ing CONTRASTS) may start asking visual questions. When that happens, you're starting to get it. And you will know what it means to enjoy seeing CONTRAST that's in CONTRAST with itself.

You'll begin to know what is nice about living visually.

There are, of course, many people who enjoy art and design who achieved their visual skills without this help from words. But if you're not one of them how will you learn? You know now you can do it by becoming familiar with these nine tools, the lessons of light.

You can use that understanding to start living visually.

How flexible are the lessons of light
in describing serious visual expression?

How good are the lessons of light in helping us understand visual meaning, to genuinely *see* masterpieces of visual expression? Do these rules apply only to bicycle parts and Scottish kilts?

The answer is no. Not to worry. The lessons of light are the keys for understanding any visual expression. They are embedded within all serious works, even in the most important visual expression in great museums.

In describing those plaid kilts above, it says CONTRAST can CONTRAST with itself. A frame of reference that has conflict (one of the conditions of CONTRAST) is showing us two examples of a lesson of light that are CONTRASTING *with each other.*

So here are more examples related to CONTRAST.

Here are two additional places where CONTRAST is inspiring to look at.

I am referring to two pictures by the artist Claude Monet, a French painter who lived about 100 years ago. Both of these paintings exhibit CONTRAST (conflict) that's easy to see. You don't need to look at these paintings right now, but I will give you key words to search for them after you have finished reading.

The first is one from a series of twenty five paintings called *Haystacks.* (He painted this scene repeatedly, capturing different values of light.) One is called *Haystacks at the end of Summer.* It is a simple painting that shows two haystacks side by side and it's surprising how engaging this picture is. One reason is that the image presents our eye with the CONTRAST of two conflicting FORMS. The CONTRAST is found in the strong FORM of the two haystacks themselves. (The painting essentially shows just two haystacks.)

Like the *Trylon and Perisphere,* any two FORMS, including similar FORMS like two haystacks, will provide some visual interest as they CONTRAST. However, demonstrating the powers of visual expression marshaled by a great artist, in *Haystacks at the end of Summer* two FORMS deliver a virtual *ton* of visual interest, inspired by real haystacks Monet saw as he went about living visually.

The second painting is called *Poppies.*

In this picture, Monet captured a field of poppies, and in the foreground, a woman and her child are strolling through the flowers. (Actually it's Monet's own wife and son.) But there's a satisfying second detail in this painting: in the background, yet another woman and *another* child are also strolling through the poppies. (I believe he added his wife and son a second time to the same painting.)

To my eye, this painting is interesting and engaging in part because the second mother and child CONTRAST (conflict) with the first mother and child. In this case, the lessons of light are showing us CONTENT conflicting with itself. It's the CONTENT of the first mother and child that is CONTRASTING with the CONTENT of the second mother and child. (We'll see why that's CONTENT in the next chapter.) Once again that sounds complex, but you don't need to know anything about *"Help Yourself to a Blue Banana,"* or the lessons of light to enjoy these Monet paintings. But should you ever hope to explain *in words* why these paintings are appealing, these observations are among the things that can be said.

Of course, when Monet started work on *Poppies*, he did not say to himself, "I'm going to paint a picture that uses CONTENT in CONTRAST with itself." In fact I'm sure it never crossed his mind. He just painted a thoughtful picture that had meaning for him, and then left it up to us to discover our own feelings for it.

What is the meaning we find in two conflicting haystacks or in two conflicting women and their children strolling through poppies? Of course, that's for you to decide. The answers (if any) will come in the visual language, not in everyday words.

If you're curious, and I bet you are, you can see these paintings by searching images for "haystacks at the end of summer" and "monet poppies." (Bookmark this page and come back to it once you've finished reading.)

Applying what you've read
to an everyday situation

Even if you're rarely in museums or galleries, living visually is still an everyday experience. It can become part of every thought. But if you are just now beginning to explore your visual world, you may wonder how the process works. I'll try to explain.

First, try bringing to mind these exciting visual situations:

Imagine gazing up at dazzling holiday fireworks, or studying any of those mysterious "alien" designs called crop circles, or enjoying Hokusai's amazing Japanese print called *The Great Wave* (bookmark here, and search this image later), or looking at just about *anything* in Las Vegas. In these unusual environments, or marveling at iconic works of art, it's easy to understand what the excitement is.

But that same process of seeing can be part of every day.

So instead, now imagine that you're riding on a crowded city bus, traveling a busy road. Let's say your eyes are "asleep." Visually speaking, nothing on the street or inside the bus has a frame of reference that has snapped your vision into consciousness.

You daydream about *"Help Yourself to a Blue Banana."*

What comes to mind at first are frames of reference, and you remember that they are a sort of stage where interesting things take place. Because nothing interesting appears around you right now, you figure you must not be around any frames of reference at all.

That sounds logical, but it doesn't take into consideration this important fact: Not all frames of reference *are* interesting.

It's true that a frame of reference is a stage for visual activity, and when the lessons of light are expressed there effectively, people usually notice it. That's the formula for creating a visual message most people will react to. But just because there are no frames of reference around grabbing your attention does *not* mean there are no frames of reference around at all.

Frames of reference are everywhere, even when they are not visually attractive. And here's my point: It's not unusual for someone living visually to notice them even if they *aren't* eye catching.

For example, imagine that the bus turns into a shopping district. Outside, the sky becomes dusk and the bus stops at a light. On the nearest street corner, there's a bright department store window with all its lights turned on. The display behind the glass has hundreds of loose pieces of thick rope dangling down from the ceiling.

The ropes are long enough to touch the floor.

There are several plastic models inside the display including a woman and some gorillas. At the far end of the window, the plastic woman, who is wearing a red business suit, is looking toward the bus from inside the ropes.

She separates the ropes with parted arms just like someone who is winding her way through high weeds, and her wrists are decorated with a watch and several bracelets.

At the other end of the store window, out of her sight, there's a clearing in the dangling ropes. Standing in the clearing is a plastic family of scary looking gorillas, with shiny black noses.

The gorillas are admiring some pre-washed designer blue jeans they are wearing. They are looking at themselves in a mirror that's propped up against a big coconut tree. Instead of coconuts, the tree is blooming with volleyballs, beach balls and basketballs.

It's a COLORFUL and interesting window display, designed to sell red business suits, watches, jewelry, sports equipment and blue jeans. The display window is a strong frame of reference that primarily uses COLOR, TEXTURE, FORM and CONTENT to catch our attention, and increase our interest in the merchandise.

But now consider this: next door to the department store is a government welfare office. The welfare office window has three government posters taped onto the glass from the inside. Only one is straight, and two are faded by sunlight so their printing is difficult to read. The newer one is printed in black ink. A brown see-through curtain is hanging behind the glass window. A desk lamp is visible through the curtain, although the office is closed. The curtain is torn here and there. One corner of the glass window has a crack. The office name appears on the window in gold letters. The typeface is Caslon. Half of the letters are peeling.

Here's the point: *Both* windows are frames of reference.

But only the department store window uses the lessons of light effectively to attract our attention (by calling on the COLOR of the clothing, the TEXTURE of the ropes, the FORM of the woman and the apes, and the CONTENT [humor] of the situation).

The welfare office window is a frame of reference that has no interesting lessons of light to attract us.

Everyone riding on the bus now turns to see the department store window. But no one (except you) notices the welfare office.

You decide to study it. You're living visually, and you're curious about *all* visual experiences, not just those with strong frames of reference. You're enjoying your eyes, and thankful you've learned how satisfying visual living can be.

The CONTRAST between
natural and man-made

I once had a chance to express CONTRAST in the design of a brochure. It was created to help raise money for the Central Park Conservancy, a group that cares for the big park in New York City. The park's managers wanted something they could mail to people, asking for donations to help with the maintenance of the park.

It was a small brochure, and on the inside cover, I suggested that we reprint a famous photograph that shows some decorated stonework on a large outdoor staircase in the park. The stairs lead down to a central fountain, and they are both well-known landmarks in the park. The stonework on the staircase is carved to look like trees and leaves, etc. In the background of the photo, behind the staircase, the *real* trees and flowers of the park are visible.

To make the design special, I told the printing company to make an opening in the paper along the top of the staircase in the photo. When the brochure was assembled, this slot became a sort of pocket where we placed the cards that asked people to donate money. The slot separated the *natural* part of the park (the trees, etc.) from the *manmade* part of the park (the stone staircase, etc.). And the cards sticking up from the slot seem to say "Your donated money will help the park managers take care of *both*."[41]

This design expressed the CONTRAST between the park's natural features and it's manmade features. It was even recognized in a contest for fund raising brochures.

You can see a picture of this brochure by visiting my web site, behindthescenesmarketing.com. On the home page, click on "our work," then click #64. (Bookmark this page.)

* * * *

For review, here are the conditions of CONTRAST:

    Opposites
    Conflicts

Before continuing to read, take a moment to look for examples of these two conditions of CONTRAST. You'll find they are all around, no matter where you are.

Chapter Six

CONTENT as a source of visual experience

Dialog

> ONE AFTERNOON, I ASKED some young people,
> "Why are you attending art school?"
> One of them replied,
> "Because art school is better than real school."

That probably sounds funny to you, but he was right.

Art school is *not* real school.

That's true because one goal of art school is to help students *un*learn the traditional habits of analyzing the world that we are all taught in regular (real) schools.

That day I suggested a different answer to the same question, but not so funny. "Why are you attending art school?"

"The answer is easy," I said, "You are here to learn to see."

At the time I felt that the simplicity of this statement seemed impressive. But now I know it is not a very good answer.

First, it sounds ridiculous to someone who has already been using his or her eyes (seeing) for years. Second, it seems more helpful to tell students they are attending art school to learn to "unsee."

And what we have to unsee is CONTENT.

CONTENT is just simply the biggest obstacle we face when a goal is to start experiencing the visual language, and specifically the eight other lessons of light. In this chapter we'll read about how unseeing CONTENT is a big part of everyday life for anyone who is enjoying their eyes and living visually.

And, hopefully, we'll learn how to do it.

This is going to take some time and explaining.

So I'm axing the dialog right here.

Chapter six continued
AN INTRODUCTION TO CONTENT
The sixth lesson of light
Overcoming your addiction to the
visual drug called CONTENT

In our mind's eye, we each have a collection of images that can excite us or upset us.

Is it your country's flag waving? Pictures of homeless people? An image of Christ? Two men getting married? Barack Obama speaking? A photograph of your family? The Boston Patriots loosing the Super Bowl (after achieving an otherwise perfect season)? Janet Jackson's breast? Prince Harry dressed as a Nazi? A newborn baby?

O.J. Simpson on trial *again?*

Each of these images expresses strong CONTENT.

Any one of these might be powerful, satisfying or even painful when seen by one person yet, at the same time, remain meaningless to someone else. Frames of reference with images such as these are filled with the strong emotional meanings we recognize and relate to from previous experiences. This personal collection of memories is a huge resource that everyone uses to judge everything.

This "collection" represents a large part of the sixth lesson of light called CONTENT, and everyone searches for connections to it in every piece of information that comes into view. We all rely on these opinions over and over (and over and over and over) to help us judge what we see. These stored up opinions serve as the backbone for judgments we all make about the CONTENT of virtually everything we see.

As a general rule our reaction to CONTENT can be classified, at least in part, on our feeling about three categories of values. They are called human values, civil values and self values, and they are among the six conditions of CONTENT.

These are the six conditions of CONTENT:

> Human values
> Civil values
> Self values
> Typography
> Humor
> It's of something

Human values

Human values are the most widely held ideas about life.

They are the opinions shared among people of all countries and races. People everywhere live by them, and for the most part, these values have been principles of human nature for as long as there have been humans. They include all of the commonly held human emotions including the desire for love, success, health, freedom and happiness, and the fears of death, pain and failure.

Because these ideas are widely recognized and understood, we could say they are the strongest statements of CONTENT as a lesson of light. They are the most influential images of CONTENT to the widest international audience. You could say they are universal. For a particular individual, you or I for example, more personalized civic or self values may at one time or another surpass human values as an issue, or even obscure them. But human values still fuel the emotional experiences that the largest part of the human population can respond to at one time in a unified emotional way. A child is trapped in an underground well somewhere in Texas, and for three days the *whole world* watches the rescue on TV.

Because human values are so widely shared, they also have the greatest potential to anger people when circumstances divide an issue among two or three of these principles. That's when the difference between right and wrong becomes hard to define. That's when people bring their individual point of view strongly into focus.

For example, now and then news stories will appear on TV, in newspapers and across web sites about fur hunters who trap and kill baby seals for their skin. The skins are processed for clothing and fur coats. Many people feel killing seals for this reason is morally wrong. It's a controversial international issue, with strong arguments on both sides. But even if you are sympathetic to the economic rights of seal hunters (they have earned a living this way for hundreds of years), you are likely to agree that news photographs of seal murders show scenes that are difficult to feel good about.

The photographs of seal hunts show hunters standing over dead seals with spiked clubs in their hands. The scene is snow covered, and the blood of the animals is bright red against the snow covered ground. It is clear seals of all ages have been clubbed.

Most people find the pictures so alarming they forget about the economic condition of the hunters, and focus on what seems like mindless violence.

Photographs such as these can have a strong influence on people. The emotional involvement people feel affects their judgment. Something seems wrong. A deeply felt value system is being abused. The pictures seem to say: Do something to stop this. Photos of seal hunts are filled with "human value" CONTENT.

Other more troubling representations of human value CONTENT include images of violence during World War II and pictures of victims following nuclear attacks. More than a half century later, these pictures still strengthen the determination among most people to avoid war and eliminate human prejudice. They keep alive our belief that we must prevent any recurrence of such events and evils. Most people around the world have a similar reaction to these human value images.

And more examples: Pictures of the American successes on the moon and on Mars are awe inspiring to people of all countries, and, despite problems within England's royal family (or, more likely, because of them), almost everyone loves to see pictures of British royalty in and out of trouble. Similarly, images of school shootings are always penetrating examples of human value CONTENT. Most of the world agreed that newspaper photographs of the 2004 school bombing inside Russia, when hundreds of *children* were massacred, were examples of almost unspeakable CONTENT.

It takes less than an instant for the CONTENT of these types of events to grab our attention, to influence our opinion, and prove their strength as the most intellectually powerful source of visual experience. Human value CONTENT is the most profoundly universal lesson of light. (Let me suggest that you highlight this.)

Civil values and self values

Civil values, on the other hand, are not necessarily shared by all people. They are the rules which make a society or organization operate smoothly. Among other things, they are feelings about nationalism, culture, politics and religion. Photographs filled with the CONTENT of civil values might be reacted to with different, possibly opposite, emotions, depending on the society or belief group to which a person belongs.

Pictures of victory celebrations for Wimbledon, World Cup and Olympic games are looked at with different emotions, depending on where they appear, and who sees them. Fans of the winning teams are happy, while people who supported the losers are filled with regret. And pictures of the Pope saying mass in St. Peter's have an emotional meaning for Catholics all over the world, but may have no impact on their non-Christian countrymen.

The third group of CONTENT values are self values.

These are opinions everyone is likely to recognize, but reactions to these kinds of messages vary from one individual to another, even within the same society or belief group. Self values are the ideas that we rely on to judge people on an individual basis. They include value judgments about others such as how handsome, rich, happy, good or friendly a person seems to be, to name only several of perhaps thousands of self value judgments we recognize.

I say she looks sexy, you say she looks cheap.

For another example, try to recall the first trial of O.J. Simpson in 1995 (when the football star may have gotten away with killing his ex wife and her friend). Some people could look at his picture and still sense the emotional respect and admiration he earned as a star athlete. Others saw his image and sensed a deceitful and insincere side of his personality.

When a frame of reference catches our attention, before we are consciously aware of *any other* sources of visual experience, we have already (virtually *instantly*) processed the CONTENT of the image for possible emotional meaning. In most cases, we do, in fact, find some emotional CONTENT. At that point in comprehending the world, only the most visually active individuals continue to analyze what they see, . . . looking beyond CONTENT.

It is a fact of life that few people bother to look beyond the death, love, terror, kindness, eroticism, hatred or the patriotism of an image. Few people look for additional sources of visual expression in the same scene. To summarize, although everyone responds to all nine sources of visual experience, only individuals who are living visually are ordinarily concerned with seeking out any serious visual meaning beyond CONTENT.

That is why I say CONTENT is the source of visual experience most likely to cripple our ability to master the other building blocks of visual understanding.

On the list that follows, the images described contain strong amounts of CONTENT. Try to imagine these scenes in this manner: Imagine that you are reading a news magazine. You turn a page and come on a double page COLOR photograph of each scene. Picture at least five of these scenes to yourself as vividly as possible. Make up any necessary details to complete your mind's eye images.

Some strong examples of CONTENT values.

With your pencil, check off at least five scenes you are familiar with.
Then imagine each as a double page COLOR photograph in a magazine.

Picture a high school shooting.

Picture A-Rod hitting his 500th home run in Yankee Stadium,
August 4, 2007. (By the way, I was there that day.)

Picture Lord Carnarvon opening the pharaoh
Tutankhamun's ancient tomb in Egypt in 1923.

Picture a newborn baby with his mother in a delivery room.

Picture Space Ship One landing after its first flight.

Picture Iraqi dictator Saddam Hussein hanged.

Picture naked children running down a Vietnamese
highway with napalm burns covering their bodies.

Picture Martin Luther King, the American civil rights
leader, assassinated in April of 1968.

Picture Martha Stewart in jail a few years ago.

Picture U.S. President Bush speaking aboard a Navy carrier
in front of his "Mission Accomplished" banner in 2003.

Picture Mike Tyson biting Evander Holyfield's ear a few years ago.

Picture Charles Lindbergh, the first person to fly solo
across the Atlantic Ocean, landing in Paris in 1927.

Picture a brown man and a pinkish-white man holding hands.

Picture fur hunters, clubs in hand, standing over
bleeding and dead baby seals, whose skin and
the surrounding snow are bright red with blood.

Picture the explosion of the Hindenburg airship in 1937.

Picture Mussolini, the fascist dictator of Italy, hanged
up-side-down after World War II in Milan in 1945.

Picture a UFO hovering over a farmhouse today.

Picture Princess Diana helping third world children

Picture the 2004 asian tsunami crashing over a beachfront.

Picture the American Space Shuttle lifting off
its launch pad for the first time in 1981.

Picture Bill Clinton hugging Monica Lewinsky.

Picture Hurricane Katrina devastating New Orleans, Louisiana.

Picture terrorists bombing a day care center.

Picture the autopsy of an alien creature.

Picture David Paterson, the first blind/black man to govern
a U.S. state, delivering his 2008 inaugural address.

Picture Neil Armstrong standing on the moon.

A role for language in CONTENT

As we've said over and over again, words are frequently an obstacle to gaining an understanding of visual ideas. So this may sound surprising to you: using words to describe CONTENT is not a problem. Words are the most intellectual tools we have for communicating, so perhaps maybe it is *not* surprising to find they serve perfectly as an aid to understanding the most visually intellectual idea, namely CONTENT.

As proof, there are many words that can describe the emotions represented in the scenes listed above. They are words that define the most exciting, frightening and thought-provoking ideas. In some cases, there are two or three words which can describe the impact of those images, as the revised list (shown on the following page) suggests. On the new list, possible words are included that might describe each of the scenes.

In any example of CONTENT, thousands of details are in play. So, in addition to the ones suggested on this revised list, other words could describe those details. In the case of school violence, perhaps you know one of the victims, or maybe you live near the crime scene. CONTENT is the total of all these impressions, and obviously, that may change from one individual to another.

These types of events attract the complete attention of people. They make great newspaper headlines and are the subjects of best selling books and blockbuster movies. It would be unusual to find anyone who does not have an emotional opinion about them, although those opinions may vary greatly from person to person.

As a result, when two words are listed below as descriptions of a scene, the words may not be similar. That is, two people can see pictures of the same event but have different, even opposite reactions. The descriptions provided cover many possibilities. But there may be other words that also suit the situations described.

For example, if you are a fur hunter, you may think the seal issue is an act of survival (for the hunters). Or you may look at a picture of the Space Shuttle, and describe it as wasteful.

For that reason, on the new list, blank space is provided for you to write your own description of the scenes. So turn the page, and with your pencil, check the words that you find appropriate as a description for each scene, cross out any that you may disagree with, and then add new words (at least five) that you believe could be suitable to describe what is taking place.

Here's one example of how to do it:

Space Shuttle launching . . . Progress, adventure, *wasteful*

In addition, also include words that describe details that are particularly meaningful to you. For example, you can't watch a TV show about an alien autopsy without considering the possibility of fraud. So I might also amend the list like this:

Alien autopsy . . . . Disbelief, curiosity, *fraud.*

A scene filled with strong CONTENT	The word(s) that describe this scene (add at least five of your own words)
A high school shooting	Senselessness, _____
A-Rod's 500th homer	Excitement, history, _____
King Tut's tomb	Adventure, suspense, _____
A baby just after birth	Life, hope, _____
Space Ship One	Progress, inspiration, _____
Saddam hanged	Justice, lawlessness, _____
Burned children	Terror, horror, _____
Martin Luther King killed	Murder, intolerance, _____
Martha Stewart in jail	Justice, injustice, _____
Mission accomplished	Shortsightedness, _____
Tyson biting Holyfield	Violence, _____
Lindbergh in France	Success, triumph, _____
Two men together	Love, commitment, _____
Baby seal murders	Death, violence, _____
Hindenburg exploding	Disaster, sabotage, _____
Mussolini hanged	Revenge, justice, _____
A UFO sighting	Fear, opportunity, fraud, _____
Princess Diana helping	Love, charity, _____
Tsunami disaster	Disbelief, panic, _____
The shuttle launching	Progress, adventure, _____
Clinton hugging Monica	Affection, betrayal, lust, _____
Hurricane Katrina	Tragedy, disbelief, _____
Terrorist bombing	Horror, senselessness, _____
Alien autopsy	Disbelief, curiosity, _____
Governor David Paterson	Pride, hope, _____
Man on the moon	Wonder, adventure, _____

The fact that we have so many words to understand these scenes indicates how widely influential CONTENT is as a source of visual experience. Just think how human visual experience would change if we had this many words to name COLOR.

If you have not filled in the spaces on the list above, take time now to add new words as shown.

CONTENT as visual expression in man-made art

So now we must ask: can situations like those on the list be re-born in art with the impact (the CONTENT) of the real event?

Is it even *possible* to create such strong visual expression?

Can that be done?

A superficial "yes" might explain how someone could use the nine lessons of light to help recreate CONTENT. For example, to paint or photograph the inhumanity of seal murders, an artist or photographer could use CONTRAST and COLOR (bright red blood against white snow, etc.). But this answer doesn't do justice to the honesty that visual expression requires. Artists are dedicated to honestly experiencing the emotional CONTENT of the things they see. We could say, in successful examples, artists allow the joy or pain of an experience to become visual expression *all by itself.*

That is to say, after experiencing an event rich in CONTENT (like those on the list) an artist may carry around with him, some-where in his subconscious mind (or barely conscious mind), a work of visual expression ready to happen. He may feel this inspiration almost as a physical sensation. Whether he decides to take action because of this feeling (that is, to try to make art of it), or to merely store it in his memory as part of his repertoire, doesn't change the fact that, in this process, he has collected an example of CONTENT.

Someone may experience inspirations like this as often as every day, each time aware that these are the seeds of visual expres-sion. But, it is important to point out, inspirations like this come only through the visual language. That is to say, for example, a per-son with these skills may see a young well-dressed couple calmly sitting inside the steamy kitchen of a cheap restaurant, and realize immediately that they are, for some reason, visually meaningful. He won't care that he can't explain in words why he knows this. He is satisfied to let the CONTENT speak on it's own, in visual terms.

In fact, noticing the visual language in such random circumstances might confirm to an artist, somewhere deep inside, that he *is* an artist. You may have had that sensation yourself.

Whether someone takes action on an inspiration like this (by starting a painting, let's say, or pulling out his camera) or simply accepts it as part of living visually, does not alter the fact that inspiration for visual expression has occurred.

He'll know the seed for visual expression has presented itself.

Art can 'happen' like this hundreds of times in anyone's lifetime, perhaps thousands of times. For a working artist it happens many times more often than you would know by just counting the pieces in his or her life's work. That's because, when someone is collecting CONTENT, or even entire works of visual expression, in his mind's eye, he will usually decide to make real pieces of art from only the most exciting, troubling or meaningful examples. If he is concerned about people's reactions to this work (and he may not be) it is only to hope we agree the results *are* exciting, troubling or meaningful. *Why* this is true is usually not important to an artist.

Sometimes, an artist may be more interested in simply experiencing an event, live, as it happens, than he is with transferring it to canvas, stone, print, film or monitor. Artists have lives away from work too, like everyone else. On the other hand, a work of art often results when an inspiration from CONTENT (or another lesson of light) motivates an artist so strongly that *not* to express it right away seems unusual or even unthinkable. That leads to the proverbial artist running back to his studio to capture what he has seen or experienced before it fades away.

Almost everyone has experienced at least the beginnings of that sensation. If you've ever wished you had a camera to preserve some moment, I mean if you have ever said, "Get a camera!," well that's the start of the feeling we are talking about. Some things just need to be saved, or retold, or expressed, to be re-lived for others to experience. When you feel that way, you're no doubt being inspired by something out of the ordinary. That's how a person might feel when he decides to turn that "something out of the ordinary" into a work of visual expression.

Some artists see themselves as having no choice about this. As a result of certain experiences, some artists feel they must create art. Why this is true is a mystery. In other words, the lessons of light are how people see. But they are far away from being *why* they see.

This process of being inspired and then taking action can happen either consciously or subconsciously. There are people who feel on a subconscious level that certain experiences must be turned into visual expression and there are others who may go through the entire process from experience to finished artwork completely conscious of their decision to make art from one experience, and not from another. Somewhere between these extremes are artists who collect inspirations, and at a future date combine several (or many) of these to create art. They may do this with no conscious awareness of where and when the original inspirations took place.

In fact one famous painter said, "You never know how influences come in. If they come with me, they come in casually. I'm certainly never conscious of them, if I am truly interested in what I am doing. Knowledge of the works of certain others is, of course, important. But that doesn't mean that you should think about it. These things should go into your bloodstream and disappear."[42]

In most cases, the process of being inspired happens in that way. But an exception is when someone creates visual expression directly from life. What that means is, it's possible to express inspirations at the same moment they're collected. That happens when an artist paints a still life composition as she evaluates a batch of fruit on a table, or paints a landscape as she actually gazes at it from a hillside. Most photography is likewise inspired directly from life.

Avoiding the tendency
to preconceive CONTENT values

Maybe it sounds like visual talent is nothing more than an ability to mimic the emotions of life, and capture them in a frame of reference. For example, joy at birth, sorrow at death, sadness at failure, etc. But that is not really how we measure the success of visual expression, or its value.

Instead, when evaluating visual expression, we must judge, most of all, whether or not an artist has *preconceived* his emotional response to something. We need to ask, "Does this 'work of art' preconceive the emotional message that it's delivering?" This is critical because that is something visual expression must never, *never* do.

Imagine this. Suppose you are an artist and your cell phone rings. It is a friend calling who is a police detective inviting you to visit the crime scene of a mass murder, and you agree to go. This is something you have never seen before. But here's the point: It is not enough for you, an artist, to expect to feel horror at the scene (which is what most of us would expect to feel), to then see the scene, and then hurry back to your studio and "express" horror in some visual work using the nine lessons of light.

Instead, an artist (you) must convince us in the work that horror *was felt* at the moment a gruesome event is seen, and also that horror was felt *because* it was seen. Visual expression requires this honesty before it seems meaningful. I suppose the biggest mystery of visual expression is the question of how people detect this honesty in a work of art. How is it that we know, just at a glance, that some visual expressions spring from an addiction to the truth, while others are simply reheated preconceptions? If we walk into a gallery and see two paintings side by side, how do we know that one speaks to us in this honest way, and the other wastes our time?

Although there are not any easy answers, we will explore this question more in the following pages and chapters. However, one thing is certain. A person who has few emotional responses to life, or who only pretends to feel his or her emotions, cannot create art.

Consider this: Suppose another phone rings and a different artist gets an invitation to view yet another scene of mass murder. This time, the artist looks at the grotesque sight and feels something other than horror. To make a point, let's say it's humor. For whatever reason, let's say the whole thing just seems funny to this artist. Then he returns to his studio and creates art from *that* inspiration. This time, however, to be valid, the resulting visual expression must convey this different genuine emotion.

It may seem revolting, but visual expression that conveys a genuine sense of humor about mass murder is, as a rule, more valid (and probably more valuable) than visual expression that conveys a preconceived sense of horror about the same scene. If you're following me, you can no doubt imagine how this "honesty" can get an artist in trouble.

The destructive role that preconception can play is always a potential obstacle to overcome during the creative process in visual expression.

That's important, so let's repeat it to highlight:

The destructive role that preconception plays
is always a potential obstacle to overcome
during the creative process in visual expression.

The insulting kind of preconceptions

For yet another example, and perhaps unfortunate, consider this disturbing fact: visual expression that genuinely shows us an honest disdain, disrespect, or even hatred for political, religious or patriotic ideals is always going to be more valid and, once again, probably more valuable, than expression that shows reverence for that ideal in a preconceived way.

In other words, in his or her "reverent" artwork, did the artist honestly revere what it represents? Or is the work merely a restatement of widely held, preconceived reverence? Alternatively, when he or she creates a hateful, disrespectful expression, does the artist honestly hate what it represents?

In visual, artistic and financial terms, the answers to these questions make all the difference in the world.

The exercise at the beginning of this chapter, and the one that follows, will remind you, and perhaps *teach* you, that each of us has the power to feel emotionally any way we wish.

Because most people feel one way about an event is not reason for you or I to feel that way. If we are living visually, it is important that all the opinions we choose are tied to the emotional CONTENT of our experiences. Our opinions must ring true to the pictures of the world our emotions deliver to our eyes.

We can't learn opinions. We have to feel them.

These last few paragraphs speak about the genuineness that visual expression needs. We know it is a difficult process. It is just plain hard to honestly express what you feel. Nevertheless, being able to express what you feel is also a talent that most (but certainly not all) societies throughout history have admired and rewarded.

But one problem is this:

If the ability to create successful visual expression deserves our respect, how is it that some of that expression is so *dis*-respectful? Are we supposed to admire a frame of reference that expresses with genuine, bonafide and unpreconceived visual power and truth, but also ridicules or insults something we admire?

Again, a common example is when religion is insulted.

This issue is often argued between government and people who support art. It's a lightning rod for controversy, especially when a government subsidizes visual expression and, as a result, the tax money ends up paying for work that insults some of the things that the government and taxpayers care about.

The reason government support is important is, like everyone else, even artists have to eat. And, although the best artists are often very rich, there are many (fine) artists, even good (fine) artists, who barely earn a living. Without some help, it's possible that society would produce less art. And to speak generally, that probably means we would have less understanding of the emotional significance of being humans. To speak generally, that probably means we would have less understanding of the emotional significance *being alive*. And that is probably a bad thing.

But there is no way for government to support visual expression and also restrict it. The government can't say, "We'll only support work that isn't disrespectful of things we believe in. We'll only support work," (for example), "that doesn't insult religion or democracy." There is just no way that can ever work.

As a result, the discussion is still open. On one side is the argument, "We will always need our government to subsidize visual expression and help it flourish." And then from the other side, the logical rebuttal, "It's foolish to pay to be insulted."

What's the answer?

Both sides are sincere. And they will never be totally compatible. But there is a way to relate them to each other. It doesn't change anything. The government is still needed, and visual expression can still go where it wants. But it's a way to frame the issues.

Here's what I think:

If an artist *is* an artist, and if he creates work that is offensive (to some people), we cannot deny either his right to do it, or his right to enjoy the credit (or the money) we give to people who know how to do it. We can't deny credit or money to people who have that talent. After all, it is the ability to create honest expression that we value. The work itself is just the proof that a person has the ability.

(If you doubt that, remember there is lots of crummy art that is valuable only because that person has, in some *other* work, at a previous time, demonstrated his or her better talent.)

So suppose that we are feeling good about art, and suddenly comes along something that offends us. Suppose also that no one denies this work is a genuinely felt, unpreconceived expression of emotion. Nevertheless, it's insulting some people.

Artwork like that teaches us several things.

To start with, if the work is genuine (based on the value system we have been discussing), that would prove *at least* this: It proves at least that there is, at the minimum, one honest human way (the way of that artist) to understand life in the manner suggested by the work. In other words, it defines a way (possibly an extreme way, or even an extremely negative way) of looking at something. But it is, nevertheless, an honest way to look at it.

Real visual expression is honest, and of course, that's going to hurt if it insults one of your beliefs.

But the achievement of visual expression is not only in what it expresses. It is also a sort of celebration that a person was able to honestly express *anything at all*. (Keep in mind, for most people this is hard to do.) To put it another way, if we don't like art that offends us, the answer isn't to forbid certain kinds of art. Instead, if we don't like art that offends us, the answer must be to forbid certain kinds of people from becoming artists, a silly idea.

The reason is that (some) artists have only one concern: to express what they are able to express. Like any variety of people, including non-artists, some artists just couldn't care less about the greater good of mankind. For that kind of person, fulfilling a need to express truthfully is the only reward he or she seeks. That means if someone has successfully gone through the effort of expressing himself truthfully, the last thing that matters (to some of them) is that the result offends anyone.

You could say a person who has that outlook, artist or non-artist, is hardly an outstanding citizen of planet earth. But it in no way reflects on whether he is able to create visual expression. He may still be a good artist. Perhaps even a great artist. And it in no way means his work is inferior. A great singer is no less a great singer because he beat up his wife.

A great person? No. A great singer? Yes.

Look at it this way, reduced to basic motivation:

Let's say that, by crawling through manure (or let's be honest and just call it shit) on your hands and knees, you can somehow earn the money that you need for an operation, an operation that will allow you to walk again. You are probably going to do it. (I don't mean that's a kind of art. I mean suppose you actually could earn money that way.) When you are finally walking again, you simply won't care if someone says, "I can't believe you crawled through shit on your hands and knees." You won't care what they think. You knew you had to crawl through it to reach your goal of walking again. For you it was a no brainer.

And by the way, there's no need to be hypothetical about this kind of severe decision making. In real life, in 2003 an incredible man actually amputated his *own hand* in order to escape death after he was trapped in a ravine. Imagine how ridiculous it would sound to say, "I can't believe you cut off your own hand."

He *had* to cut off his hand to reach his goal of staying alive.[43]

In much a similar way, some individuals know they have to explore certain kinds of visual expression to reach their goal of creating honestly. They just have to do it. No doubt in their mind.

Returning to the example, someone else may be able to earn the money they need for their operation (to restore their ability to walk) by working as a musician. And I'm sure you'd rather do that musician's work too. But what if you're tone deaf and have no other skills? What if, for you, the manure thing is the only way you can earn the money you need. You'd probably do it.

In fact, I'm almost sure you'd do it. I know I'd do it.

But here's the point: however the money is earned, in both of these cases, several months later both people (meaning you after the unpleasant work, and the other person after earning money as a musician) are walking again. See the point? One person may create art that offends us. Another may create art that uplifts us. But in both cases, several months later they are both satisfied they made honest art. They both achieved their goal.

And neither may care what anyone thinks about any of it.

Some artists simply do not worry about, or even consider, what anyone thinks of their effort. In fact, when someone asked him if his work would last, one extraordinary artist responded, "I tell them I don't give a damn. I'm painting for myself. If my paintings are worth anything – if they have quality – that quality will find a way to preserve itself. I paint for myself within the tenets of my own upbringing and my standards." Point made. Case closed.[44]

Fortunately for us, that man's work is uplifting.

But in a free society, regardless of how appealing the possibility sounds, there can simply be no law that says visual expression has to be uplifting. It just will not work at any level.

Visual expression that offends us, like all visual expression, is the result of a process. Sometimes it's a long process, one that takes some struggling. So the artist is probably glad when it's over, and successful. He or she may not care at all what anyone thinks of the process or the outcome. The artist just does what artists do. They make art. They do what allows them to express honestly. If this results in work we can all feel good about (as it usually does) that's reason to rejoice at our human condition.

If not, well . . . it's hard to disagree that suffering through a few offensive paintings or statues is a small price to pay for also having centuries of other paintings and statues that honestly celebrate life.

But it's a price we have to pay.

Then there is this: I might believe that someone who creates offensive art doesn't care about the greater good of mankind. I may believe she isn't sensitive to people's feelings. I might think she isn't even sensitive to *my own* cherished beliefs. But in fairness, the artist probably doesn't agree. An artist may honestly believe that the best way she can contribute to the greater good is to create as honestly as possible. She may believe this is the gift she can give, regardless of what her work is, who it offends, or who objects to it.

In fact she *probably* believes this.

I suspect that anyone who is living visually, supporting art, perhaps after thinking very hard about it, will finally agree. You will probably finally agree that allowing art to explore where it may is the best way of keeping our society moral, ethical, spiritual and free.

You will probably agree that it's a price we have to pay.

So, to summarize, we can't forbid certain people from becoming artists (or at least that sounds like a silly idea to me). And if they do become artists, and if they're good, we can't forbid the work they show us. (That is not so much silly as it is unworkable, or even illegal in a free society.) What we *can* do is not look at it, or better still, ask yourself, "Is there some way I can personally influence life so it becomes a human experience about which this statement (this visual expression) is no longer valid?"

Of course, if the premise or foundation of "art" is not valid, if the honesty is not there, the work is no longer art, and the "artist" is not entitled to any of the creative liberties we are discussing.

That's a questioning process that is open for anyone. It is a reason to support artists in their freedom to create anything. You don't have to be an artist to understand this and you don't have to be living visually (although it helps). You just have to be alive.

As we said earlier, if you don't know the visual language, you won't understand most of the visual expression and design you see. And it's almost certain you'll never understand it the way the artist intends for you to understand it (if he or she intends for you to understand it, which, again, isn't always the case).

So more advice, then, about dealing with offensive images: *learn the visual language.* You can then effectively take part in the discussion that evaluates visual work, even work that insults you.

You may haply discover that some of it *isn't art after all.*

And, when you're evaluating something that offends you, that's the sweetest discovery there is. I know because I've had the pleasure many times of dismissing, if only to myself, some banal visual clutter that tries to stake artistic ground alien to my own beliefs.

The reason that's so satisfying is this:

If something (even something offensive) is not art, then, as I said above, the "artist" and the work lose all these rights we are discussing. And believe me, if you progress in your understanding of the visual language, the day will come when you'll know if something is . . . or *isn't* . . . art.

Back to the exercise
Associating the emotions of CONTENT with reality

Earlier, we imagined that each scene on the previous list was brought to our attention by a double page photograph in a magazine. Now we'll approach CONTENT more realistically.

To do this, reread the list, but this time you are *on the scene* of these events. Experience each in a vivid state of awareness, live, as it takes place. Take the required journeys through time or SPACE to be present at the moment these events occur.

Make up details to complete your "experience" of the scene.

There are ways to do this. You can imagine pinching yourself at each location to magnify a sense of being there. Or pretend you are questioned by a reporter for your thoughts, or you're asked by someone to take action. For the UFO incident, picture yourself running to call the police, or the army.

So now try to imagine witnessing five events on the list.

The purpose here is to emphasize that seeing events live is different from seeing magazine pictures of them. That matters because it's probably only several times *during your entire life* that you will experience emotionally charged events as a live witness.

These aren't everyday situations.

So appreciate the difficulty of putting the emotional strength of live CONTENT into *any* visual expression.

Imagine capturing the emotional strength of real CONTENT for a work of sculpture, or for an important mural, or for full page photographs in a popular magazine. (Then realize that's the problem a photo journalist attempts to solve perhaps every day.)

A new way of thinking about everyday experience

Visually sensitive people feel emotionally moved by what they see, and that is the first step in producing a frame of reference that moves others. The list exercises (beginning on page 202) are a way to help understand the process. That's why, if you are reading "Help Yourself to a Blue Banana" to learn about the power of images, and where it comes from, it's important to understand the list.

But this type of thinking is no doubt new to you, so it's possible you still don't see where it's taking you. So, if you haven't yet returned to the list and revisited these events "live" in your mind's eye (as described above), take a moment anyway right now and follow these shorter instructions:

A shorter version of the (combined) exercises:

1. Select *one* event from the list on page 202, the one that is most familiar to you.

2. Imagine that you see a photo of this event in a magazine. Imagine this photo in COLOR as clearly as possible, making up details if necessary.

3. Look on the second list (page 204) to see if you agree with the one or two word descriptions of the emotions this scene represents. Cross off any description you disagree with, and add any new ones that occur to you.

4. OK, now "experience" your event more realistically. Pretend you are actually *at* the scene of this live event. Imagine you are personally involved, witnessing it. Suppose you are asked your opinion of the event as it is happening.

5. Then reread the one word descriptions of the event as you updated them on the second list. Try to imagine how these feelings will change in intensity if you're *live* on the scene. The goal is to make yourself realize how much more dramatic CONTENT is when experienced as it unfolds before you in real life.

Make yourself aware of the difference in the level of your imagined emotional response between seeing this event in a photo, and actually being there.

In its visual life, CONTENT can lie, cheat, steal, persuade and amuse. It can overjoy its viewers, or overpower them. It is the source for (visually) understanding and recreating our basic emotions. It is the visual source for what we feel in life, including for life itself. CONTENT is success, fear, love, victory, hatred, death, and regret, to name just several of the thousands of typical CONTENT emotions. That's why throughout all media (newspapers, television, movies, on YouTube, in magazines and video games) the size of the disasters, the violence of the deaths and the intensity of romances are at the center of our interest.

Six dogs in sun visors

CONTENT is such a big part of life that it affects our opinion of the other lessons of light in an unusual way. That is to say, our normal everyday life is so full of CONTENT that an unusual kind of originality often appears within a frame of reference that is *not* dominated by CONTENT.

Suppose that there's a piece of lumber at a construction site. Suppose it's covered with smears of paint and plaster and has a half dozen old nails hammered in it. If this hunk of wood is put in an art gallery, it's alarming how many people will accept it as abstract art.

And all the attention would be for one reason:

A piece of wood like that has no effective CONTENT.

As we'll see, it's common for people, by mistake, to believe that any frame of reference that is missing CONTENT is automatically abstract art, even good abstract art. But people who use that test to evaluate art can easily be fooled. They are the same people who look at things that are mostly meaningless from a visual point, like pictures painted by monkeys, most accidental spillings of paint on a canvas, and most pieces of old lumber, and mistake these things for meaningful visual expression.

The danger is how this approach to evaluating art automatically lumps simple visual clutter into the same category as genuine abstract art. Unfortunately, someone who makes this mistake might then glance at a genuinely electrifying abstract painting and stop looking when it's apparent there is practically no CONTENT in it.

He'll simply apply the convenient (but of course incorrect) formula "no CONTENT = abstract expression," and decide that this work is, in fact, abstract expression. In that case he'd be correct.

However, by only glancing at the painting, the satisfaction of experiencing its real abstract energy, and the questions it asks, is regrettably lost. The questions it asks are completely missed.

Later that same day, that same person might mistake the work of a monkey as art. He sees only that in both cases (in the real abstract painting and in the picture created by the monkey), there is no easily identifiable CONTENT. Although it is a common misunderstanding, a simple lack of CONTENT does not make something abstract art. There is much more to abstract art than that, and we'll explore it (along with abstract balance) in much greater detail when we discuss SCALE (in chapter eight).

The flip side of that mistake is equally bad. Suppose there is a portrait of a beautiful woman, full of CONTENT (and the other lessons of light). And suppose, like the abstract painting mentioned above, it is also a genuine work of honest visual expression, whose primary source of visual interest is, in fact, the CONTENT of the young woman. But someone whose visual perception is dominated by CONTENT may not appreciate the other important parts of this work (perhaps the COLORS of her dress or her eyes or the FORM of her image as it occupies the frame of reference).

He may then wonder, "Why isn't a picture of six dogs wearing sun visors and playing poker not *also* great visual expression?" His logical thought might be, "If one painting rich in CONTENT (the woman) is genuine art, then why isn't another painting that's also rich in CONTENT (the six dogs) also genuine art?"

Of course one answer is this: Although there are exceptions, visual expression only rarely grows out of a strong presentation of a single lesson of light. Generally speaking, whether it is six dogs in sun visors (all CONTENT), or a giant canvas painted solid green (all COLOR), neither one is likely to be meaningful art. Everything we see is a blending of all nine lessons of light. For someone to create work that uplifts (or upsets) us, he or she must usually find a "rightness" in all of them, or in most of them, or at least in *some* of them, all working together to ask questions. Again there's more about this in chapter eight, but for the moment, we should ask: what questions are raised by a picture of poker playing dogs or by a single solid COLOR, compared to questions asked by a canvas that carries the image of a beautifully and thoughtfully painted woman?

It's the questions themselves that should move us.

Generally, visually sensitive people will understand, perhaps unconsciously, that only two or three lessons of light can be the focus of our attention (as we said on pages 30 and 174). Otherwise, the image is too confusing. But a sensitivity to all nine, even those that are neutral, can be evident in a meaningful image. That's what we don't expect to find in portraits of card-playing dogs.

But what about paintings
made on black velvet?

Nevertheless, a discussion like this needs to avoid reaching a conclusion. When discussing visual expression, it's a mistake to say never. Despite these "rules of thumb," you should know they can't guarantee that pictures of dogs playing cards, or paintings of Elvis created on black velvet (another often ridiculed artform), can never be art. Almost any conventional (preconceived) idea about what is *not* good visual expression may eventually invite circumstances where it is shown to be wrong. You can't make any rules about these things and guarantee they will remain true forever. After all, it is the ability to discover new ways to ask visual questions in unique places, places that no one has previously explored, that may make a person a great artist.

So, although I've yet to see it, someone *at this moment* may be finishing up an image of six dogs playing poker *with* Elvis, all painted on black velvet, and it may revolutionize our visual world. She may have simply discovered (collected), all by herself, the circumstances where such an effort asks important visual questions.

Stranger things have happened. A half century ago, one man began to see visual questions within the pages of comic books. They inspired his imagination, and today his paintings are recognized among the most important (and valuable) of the twentieth century.[45]

Actually, the success of that comic-book-inspired artist at one time annoyed me because, when I was young, and years before those paintings shook the foundations of art, my father forbade me from reading comic books.

Lastly this: I wrote several times that good art rarely grows from any single lesson of light. There are exceptions. When a lesson of light, all by itself, prevails within a frame of reference and carries extraordinary impact, it is often FORM. FORM sometimes stands nearly alone as a remarkable visual experience. Or, as we will read later, it's possibly SPACE, which may be the most unique and singularly powerful (non-intellectual) lesson of light *of all*. And, as we said (in the last chapter), uncommon examples of CONTENT can sometimes meet this test. (For example *The Goddess of Democracy*.)

And then there is TEXTURE.

TEXTURE has a very important place in the history of visual experience, and is dominant in many exceptional abstract expressions. With some help from COLOR and SCALE, TEXTURE *defines* Jackson Pollock's *One*, sometimes considered the world's most electrifying abstract painting.[46] So, as your visual curiosity grows, you may begin to recognize these possibilities. When you do, perhaps you'll say, "I get it now. That's what the fuss is all about."

You can see Pollock's *One* at The Museum of Modern Art in New York City, or search images for "one pollock." (Bookmark this page and come back to it later.)

Imagine the image that, at a glance,
moves people to . . . take action!

CONTENT can trigger the instinct to *do something*.

Each time I see disturbing photographs of slaughtered seals, I think that I should do something to disapprove. But I have got to admit, after many years, I have never done anything. Most people are lazy, even about supporting important causes. So for eight of every ten images I find objectionable, I do nothing to respond.

It is possible my apathy is 999 times out of 1000.

As a society, we judge many thousands of images every day as good or bad, right or wrong, then react by doing nothing. People are passive, and trying to get us to do anything can be a big job. So, imagine how powerful any image is that can motivate individuals to overcome their tolerance for events they disagree with. Imagine the image that, at a glance, moves men and women to speak out, to resist, to organize, to . . . take action! It is a rare image that carries this power, and it is invariably an image filled with CONTENT.

Perhaps, again, unspeakable CONTENT.

Our willingness to feel an emotional response to CONTENT comes partly from sensing that should we choose to, we *can* take action. Odd as it sounds, simply knowing that taking action is possible is enough to increase our emotional response to something. It doesn't seem to matter that usually we don't actually do anything.

To see a current news photo of a serious plane crash is food for thought. We are sorrowful for victims and angry at any mistakes made by the pilots, controllers or mechanics. We are hateful of ter-rorists who may be responsible. We're interested in the old discus-sions about how this can be avoided in the future.

We tell ourselves we are going to do something.

Write to our political representatives, call the airline, etc.

(Of course, again, we usually end up doing nothing.)

But try to remember your reaction on first seeing pictures of the explosion of the great Hindenburg, the giant hydrogen filled airship which flew in the 1930s. If you are familiar with pictures of this catastrophe, you probably discovered them inside an encyclopedia or magazine or on the History Channel.

The ship was moored. Passengers were unloading.

All was safe. The ocean crossing was over. Then, unprecedent-ed disaster. But for all the horror of that tragedy, it is not possible to get emotionally upset about it now. It was too long ago.

By comparison, however, consider how you feel now, on this very day, when you hear a small plane has gone down. If you can, remember how you felt when John Kennedy JR's small plane tum-bled into the ocean in 1999.

I have taken flying lessons, and I can still recall the Kennedy plane sorrow, and also the crash several years earlier that killed a seven year old pilot as she tried to set a record. I remember the out-cry about regulating the age of pilots, etc. I was personally and emo-tionally moved as I followed both of those stories.

My point is that a small plane is insignificant compared to the Hindenburg, and the loss of passengers on a tiny plane hardly com-pares to those dozens lost in the airship explosion. But I knew if I chose to, I *could* do something so maybe that little girl, or even John Kennedy JR, would not be dead in vain. I could contact the govern-ment, or write to the airplane manufacturer or call the airport.

(I live only a mile [2 km] from where John took off that day.)

Of course I *didn't*.

But just knowing we *can* do something increases our willing-ness to have emotional reactions to present-day CONTENT. The Hindenburg disaster was even before we were alive. That was *then*. But JFK JR died as I watched TV, and this is *now*. (Bookmark this page and search internet images later for "Hindenburg.")

Still another example: no matter how alarmed Americans were in 1996 over the O.J. Simpson murders, everyone *already* sees those images as history. There is nothing we can to do about those events.

We see it this way: A trial was held. Simpson was judged.

Society has completely changed. We no longer feel the anger (even rage) or the totally overwhelming urge to take action, as many people did when the Simpson case was unfolding. If you are too young (or too old) to remember it, trust me, it was *unbelievable*.

Then consider this more serious related concern:

Despite the horror of the well-known images (and now complicated by immoral individuals who claim it never occurred) Jewish leaders are understandably apprehensive that the WWII holocaust is slowly turning more *historic* as years pass, so, less tragic and dire.

Similarly, there are citizens of Cambodia, Kosovo, Bosnia, Iraq and Darfur who are unable to look at photos of killing fields there, where massacres of loved ones occurred in brutal civil wars. Other people can't bear pictures of the epic destruction of Hurricane Mitch or, most tragic, the 2004 tsunami, Hurricane Katrina in 2005, which destroyed New Orleans, or the catastrophes of 2008 including the Myanmar cyclone and the Chinese Sichuan earthquake.

Images of other deadly storms like Andrew, Floyd and Ivan can likewise be mind-numbing to victims and their relatives. And for any thinking human, aftermath photographs that show scenes from the WWII Hiroshima and Nagasaki atomic bomb attacks on Japan, and even the earlier conventional bombings over Tokyo still, to this day, remain among the most troubling images ever seen.

Yet in one hundred years, people will see vintage news coverage of all these terrible events, and they will consider it only history. They will have little emotional response.

That is why Jewish leaders are justifiably concerned.

This is now, that will be then.

The potential for
personal action matters

When there's little we can do, our response to CONTENT is considerably less emotional. But when earth-shaking events are current, with images that are fresh to our eyes and thought provoking, regardless of whether or not we actually do take action, the likelihood that we become emotionally engaged is much higher.

> *The potential for personal action contributes*
> *to our willingness to have a strong emotional*
> *response to the lesson of light called CONTENT.*

The era before 9/11

As I planned this book several years ago, I made notes, and during that time I wrote this paragraph:

> "And speaking about catastrophes, there have been few events of CONTENT in my lifetime (so far) more emotional than our American space shuttle Challenger exploding in 1986. For me it was devastating. I did not see the explosion on live television, and in the many years that have passed, I have never allowed myself to watch a tape of the explosion. For several years I could not look at magazine photographs of the tragedy. The sense of regret in me was simply too overwhelming."

Even though for me (as an American) the death of President Kennedy (in 1962) and the American moon landing (six years later) were close seconds, at the time I wrote about the Challenger explosion (above) it represented the most stunning experience of visual CONTENT that I could personally recall.

Of course, there's since been a second shuttle catastrophe, the Columbia tragedy, but even though that was also numbing and tragic, I did not feel the same horrible sense of loss.

Here is why I say that. Like many people, I followed all the preparations for the 1986 launch of Challenger, including the preliminary planning, and the selection of "real people" to ride as civilian observers. You will recall the crew included the young school teacher Sharon Christa McAuliffe. That flight was to be a turning point for the American space program, introducing a new *safer* era, an era when everyday citizens might become frequent passengers.

It would be a new era in which ordinary people, like Sharon Christa McAuliffe, began to participate in routine missions. It suggested, in my lifetime, ordinary people might travel in space.

In my lifetime, people like *me* might orbit the earth.

Then such inexpressible irony. The maiden voyage of this heralded new era came to an unbearably abrupt and almost incomprehensibly sad conclusion. I was shattered by the incredible symbolism of destroyed hope, and the death of innocents and innocence. I sobbed at the news. And to this day, I have yet to watch a tape of that brief flight, averting my eyes these many years whenever those several seconds are re-played on TV. Normally I'd refer you here to a search of "Challenger" images but I am not willing, even now, to re-visit those pictures or ask you to look at them.

What struck me that day was the great loss of ideals, where, in a heartbeat, America's sense of pride and accomplishment for 25 relatively problem-free years of space adventure vanished in just an instant. The utter abyss between the lofty goal of Challenger and its bitter outcome stays with me as a sort of wound. It seems to warn me to never be so hopeful again. Such a terrible tragedy.

I realize there are now new opportunities dawning for ordinary citizens (citizens like me) to travel beyond earth's atmosphere (most specifically with the spectacular birth of Space Ship Two).

But that terrible day we lost Challenger still stays with me.

By encompassing an inspiring, admirable American goal followed by a heart breaking national catastrophe, the Challenger mission was, on a smaller scale, a rending precursor to the devastating emotional tragedy of our *new* most CONTENT-filled visual experience, known everywhere as simply 9/11.

9/11 and how it redefined CONTENT

It's sobering for me to read that "(so far)" in my earlier notes about Challenger, reprinted above. Those words were obviously first written before the World Trade Center terror attacks of 2001. I mention that because, plain and simply, on the day they occurred, the 9/11 treacheries and their related visual images, instantly replaced every American's previous opinion of the worst thing to see.

More horrific new attacks, with more loss of life and property than 9/11, and even attacks incorporating more sinister weapons and greater evil, probably can't replace 9/11 in our impression of the most vivid of possible images. I say that because the totality of the surprise on 9/11, the defenselessness of the victims, the uniqueness of the method and the location and significance of the targets in Pennsylvania, Washington and New York, have probably assured that that day will stay etched forever at the top of visual memory.

As a lesson in CONTENT, that day was comprehensive and definitive. 9/11 taught us all how CONTENT expresses itself in visual experience. At the time, it was the "most" in almost every superlative. The most evil, the most unbelievable, the most unexpected, the most unique, the most vengeful, the most unforgivable, the most memorable, the most violent, the most sorrowful and the most cowardly. Pick out any word in the dictionary that means treachery, and that day, September 11, 2001, represented the *most* of it.

In the visual language, 9/11 is a synonym for CONTENT.

We saw thousands of TV images from New York that day. In those pictures, and until they fell, the SCALE of the towers remained awesome, the COLOR of the flames breathtaking, and the SPACE of the clear blue sky above lower Manhattan provided a suitable and majestic frame of reference. Each of the lessons of light played its supporting role. But none of these impressive visual characteristics, even added together and multiplied thousands of times, begins to register in visual consciousness or visual importance when weighed against the calamity of the CONTENT.

God bless America and the victims of 9/11.

Human FORM and CONTENT

You're aware from the second chapter that the human body plays a special role in an artist's understanding of FORM. We *are* FORMS, and it is therefore difficult for humans to see ourselves in the same dispassionate way that we might survey a chimney stack or a pile of magazines.

We experience human FORM quite differently than all other FORMS. Even the FORM of animals similar to us, such as apes and monkeys, is much less interesting than our own bodies.

One reason is that human FORM has more CONTENT than any other object we will ever see, living or nonliving. Most of us are just unable to look at another human without making value judgments (CONTENT judgments).

Does he look rich, or does he look unhappy, does she look healthy and does she seem to like me are among the early questions we may ask ourselves on meeting a new person. If we have time to spare, the questions can go on practically forever. It doesn't even matter if we know the person being evaluated. Our need and willingness to judge people who are complete strangers keep gossip magazines popular and profitable.

Humans constantly look at each other.

Men and women steal glances on street corners, film directors zoom in on movie stars, and there may be no more effective marketing than a single human face talking to us from a full page advertisement. We look at each other continuously, but as we said in the second chapter, people rarely take time to see each other as simple

FORMS. In everyday situations, we are more interested in the intellectual character of each other's appearance (CONTENT) than in the COLORS, TEXTURES, SCALE and FORM of our bodies.

People are just too busy with CONTENT to see each other as sources of additional visual information. That's why I say sculptors, fashion designers and photographers spend their lives telling us what we look like.

Anyone who is living visually works to overcome this tendency, this *bad habit* of letting CONTENT dominate their visual life.

Start your own anti-CONTENT campaign

> Everyone is addicted to CONTENT.
> Artists and designers are addicted to CONTENT.
> Non-artists and non-designers are
>   addicted to CONTENT.
> Your mother is addicted to CONTENT.
> And take my word for it, you (and I)
>   are totally addicted to CONTENT.

Seeking visual satisfaction from CONTENT is so widespread among people of every age, in every social class and every income group, that symptoms of it are customary, and therefore practically invisible. Our preoccupation with CONTENT is the great obstacle in learning how to see the other extraordinary lessons of light.

For example, among friends and relatives, we fail to see the TEXTURE of each other's skin when we concentrate on the CONTENT of facial expressions. In museums, we fail to see the COLOR in oil paintings when the CONTENT of the scene steals our attention. We miss the COLORS on a pretty package when we're disappointed by the CONTENT we find in the price. In a cathedral, we miss the impact of three dimensional SPACE when distracted by the CONTENT of the statues and murals. When reading, we miss the TEXTURE of a printed page, such as this one, when we are drawn to the CONTENT of the words which appear there.

And then consider this: When visiting the Lincoln Memorial in Washington, D.C., many people don't genuinely see the incredible FORMS, SCALES and SPACES that this majestic building presents. Instead, we are distracted by the CONTENT of that big statue of the revered American president, sitting in his big chair. Or by the CONTENT of his speeches engraved into the marble nearby.

I know that can happen.

While visiting on a vacation there last month, I began reading the Gettysburg Address, carved in giant letters on an inside wall of the memorial. A few moments later, as I scanned the words, I felt a dampness on my cheek and discovered I was *crying*. Even for a visually sensitive American, the eight other lessons of light seen at the Lincoln Memorial, however spectacular, are no match for the profound and poetic CONTENT of Abe's powerful words.

(Living visually can be an emotional thing.)

We are blinded by CONTENT.

Yet, if you are interested in visual living, perhaps you sense there's something to do with your eyes beyond opening beer bottles or reading TV magazines. This "something" is to unsee CONTENT, and start seeing the remaining eight sources of visual experience.

That may sound terribly abstract.

How can you simply decide to stop looking at CONTENT?

There is no easy answer, but taking action is called for.

To start, be ready to accept this: learning to overcome CONTENT means overcoming bad habits. They are your tendencies to think and to see intellectually instead of visually. But, just finding any way to begin is an accomplishment. Deciding to take action, to stop the influence of CONTENT, is a step in the right direction.

How?

Well, one powerful way to begin unseeing CONTENT is to start a collection of COLOR. You can move away from CONTENT by deciding to be interested in COLOR from now on. So no matter where you find it, start collecting COLOR. Make your move toward visual living by deciding to collect the COLOR that surrounds you. Remembering to notice COLOR can become a new good habit.

What does it mean to notice (collect) COLOR?

Here are some examples:

When an unwanted letter or unexpected bill arrives in your mailbox, notice the COLOR of the envelope. If your car stops at a red light, notice the COLOR of the car that's next to you. Notice the COLOR of a yellow rose in a printed scarf. Notice the COLOR inside a cereal box or notice the COLOR of a luxurious bathroom. Notice the COLOR of a ceramic elephant or the COLOR of your neighbor's shoes. Try noticing the COLOR of a drugstore logo or the COLOR of rotten tomatoes, an anchorperson's hair or a cellular telephone.

Notice the COLOR of a nasty bruise.

Notice the COLOR of dish detergent.

When some person you like strolls by, ignore romance and notice the COLOR of his or her shirt. Notice the COLOR of movie tickets. Notice the COLOR of a four barrel carburetor, or the handles of a plastic jump rope. Notice the color of someone's eyes.

In fact, from now on, when you meet a new person, notice their exact eye COLOR. Keep a diary that lists the eye COLOR of everyone you know. Make up a name for each of these COLORS, a name that captures the way you feel about it.

Then do this.

Start a collection of all the COLORS you find that are green (or red, or orange, or whatever). Make it yours. Teach yourself how many different visual expressions are simply called "green." You'll find thousands, every one carrying a slightly different visual message. Each ready to help you experience COLOR (or express it).

Make it a five year mission.

Go where you've never gone. Discover COLOR where no one has discovered it before. You can store this collection of COLORS in your mind's eye, write down descriptions of your COLORS in a diary, snap digital pictures or keep scraps of paper that match them. But, however you choose to manage a collection of COLOR, this is one way to start seeing beyond CONTENT.

Taking responsibility for the lessons of light

No place is safe from CONTENT.

Sometimes, even at art school, students are not taught how to overcome it. I have seen assignments sadly ruined by CONTENT, only to hear students told (by teachers) that their work is not *creative* enough, or not *imaginative*.

Meaningless comments such as these are spoken too often in classes and even in everyday evaluation of professional business art. Criticism of visual expression can be more specific and, more importantly, more helpful. Lots of students don't catch on because they don't understand they are responsible for all nine lessons of light. (I certainly didn't realize it when I was starting out.)

Now it's part of every class I teach.

I constantly remind students they have nine responsibilities when they create any visual statement. It's their job to be sure the lessons of light are each carefully considered and controlled. No visual expression can be at its best until this effort has been made.

There is no way to avoid that responsibility.

Teachers need to tell students,

> " . . . the SCALE of your hotel elevation is not effective."
> or, " . . . the SPACES in your ad layout are ruining it."
> or, " . . . try adding greater DEPTH to this stage set idea."
> or, " . . . the ANATOMY in your trumpet drawing is wrong."
> or, " . . . the COLORS for this dress design are not working.
> or, " . . . your guitar concept needs more satisfying FORM."

Maybe it sounds too simple to be mentioned, but students of visual expression need to be told and to be taught how to recognize and express with the visual language.

Grasping this idea is difficult for non-artists and for students alike. Resistance to learning it can be strong. And CONTENT can sneak into an idea even when a goal is to overcome it.

CONTENT just frequently screws up everything.

The typeface name rule
How many letters are there in the alphabet?

For example, keep in mind the typeface name rule.

It means graphic designers have to be careful they are not influenced by the name of a typeface.

The typeface name rule can really mess things up.

This true story will demonstrate what I mean: When I was a design student, a teacher instructed us to pick an actress and then imagine that a magazine is writing an article about her. We were assigned to design a two-page layout for the article. Of course, each student had to decide how all the pictures and words, etc. would be arranged on the pages. We went to work. Most of us played with the visual language to create layouts with a sense of life and energy so readers would be tempted to stop and read the article.

That's the right approach, and, that's what an art director for a magazine is supposed to do.

My actress, in real life, died under mysterious circumstances, and so I used CONTRAST to suggest this. I placed a small black and white photograph of her in the center of the left hand page, and a negative version of the same photo in the center of the right hand page. You could say I expressed the unexplained nature of her death by calling on the CONTRAST of positive and negative images. This was nothing to write MOMA about, but not too bad for a beginner. However, one other student in that class stumbled over the typeface name rule.

In type books and computer software, typefaces are identified by a name which can be almost anything, perhaps the name of the person who designed it, or practically anything else. But, unfortunately, not many typefaces have names that accurately describe what they genuinely look like. (An exception would be something like "Fatface" which actually is a "fat" typeface.)

Also, some typefaces, called "initial typefaces," are designed to be the first letter of a word. They are very fancy capitals and, for readability, the remaining letters of each word should be less fancy.

For the magazine assignment, however, one student in that class chose typefaces for his layout by noticing that their names had some intellectual connection to the actress in his article.

Let's say that one of the typefaces was called "Broadway."

Unfortunately, neither typeface he chose had any appropriate visual meaning or strength for the story. And one typeface was an initial typeface used for all the letters in several headlines. This student didn't make an effort to create visual interest on the pages. Instead, he was satisfied his solution was logical and he thought the assignment was solved. Unfortunately, he was unaware that the layout was not appealing to the eye of a reader.

Selecting typefaces by name is a CONTENT decision, one that may at first seem reasonable, but which simply has no visual value. Designing with type is a skill that requires a feel for the way type is shaped. It is important, therefore, for students and business artists to ignore the clever names typefaces sometimes have, and instead to look directly at each letter in the alphabet (all 52 of them) to decide what is best for a design.

A hunk of burning typography

In class that day, the teacher let that student have it, and we all learned the lesson. That afternoon, I made a promise to myself I would never be influenced by the names of typefaces.

So I went on with my life, but several years later, in a book about Elvis Presley, I saw the typeface name rule broken in an interesting, but seemingly very harmless way. After browsing through the book, I noticed a footnote on the last page.

The footnote said:

> "In honor of Elvis Presley's hometown, this
> book is set in the typeface called "Memphis."

Of course, Elvis was born in Tupelo, Mississippi, but lived as a teenager and thereafter in Memphis, Tennessee, which is where Graceland is. When I saw the footnote, I smiled and thought of the typeface name rule. But as I said, fortunately no harm was done. Memphis is a typeface that is ok for the text of a rock and roll book. I was pleasantly amused. The fact that the book's designer made this nice intellectual (CONTENT) connection without harming the visual impact of the design was a pleasurable discovery.

I put the book back on a shelf, and it slipped my mind until a few weeks later. Then one day my impression of the whole thing changed drastically. I was speaking with a friend and I happened to mention that the Elvis book was set in the typeface called *Memphis* in honor of his hometown.

My friend, who is a type designer, grinned and said, "That's too bad, because Memphis (the typeface) is named after Memphis, Egypt, *not* Memphis, Tennessee. That name was chosen," he continued, "because Memphis (the typeface) is similar to another typeface called Cairo. Memphis was the ancient capital of Egypt and, of course, Cairo is the present capital of Egypt."

I was more amused than ever. Unless I'm wrong, Elvis never set foot in Africa, let alone in Memphis, Egypt. Since then, I'm more determined than ever to never (*never*) break the rule.[47]

Nevertheless, a good exercise for anyone who wants to work as an art director (responsible for things like ads, brochures, books and web pages) is this: invent a better name for perhaps 50 of the most common typefaces. If young designers relate these new names to an emotional feeling about the design of the letters, well that's a start to using type faces in a meaningful visual way. (You can find lists of typefaces to evaluate by searching web sites for "type fonts." Bookmark this page.)

Then, when the process of understanding type is underway, other discoveries follow, starting with the realization that a page of text is more than several hundred words.

It is, in fact, a visual experience of TEXTURE.

This problem of clever names influencing visual opinions is not limited to typefaces. Several nights ago, on a home renovation TV show, the helpful designer suggested re-painting the front door of a house to increase its "curb appeal." To demonstrate the COLOR she had in mind, she held up a large swatch next to the door.

"This one is called *primitive rose*," she said.

The homeowner looked at the door, squinted her eye, studied the swatch for a moment, smiled at the designer and then said, "OK, sounds good to me!"

See my point?

Her answer implied her approval was based on the *name* of the COLOR, *not* how it spoke to her through the visual language. If the homeowner was living visually, and assuming she actually liked that COLOR, she would have said, instead, "OK, *looks* good to me!"

Of course, people who will see the door have no idea what the name of the paint is.

Why typography (in other words, English)
is the fourth condition of CONTENT

Referring again to text and written messages (in other words, words) within visual expression: Although letters are FORMS, generally speaking, any writing within a frame of reference is primarily CONTENT. It's CONTENT because writing is mostly *abstract code* that requires our intellectual attention. We must learn what letters, numbers and words mean before we can understand them. And we have to understand them before they can communicate to us.

Writing is a system of preconceptions in the same way that CONTENT values (human, civil and self) are a system of preconceptions. If we agree on what these preconceptions on paper mean (i.e., these strange little marks we call the alphabet), we can accept their meanings throughout our life. Or, of course, as someone who is living visually, you are also free to ignore them.

Not only is writing, first of all, a preconception. Actually, it may be (along with numbers) the biggest preconception.

And once again, you are free to accept or reject preconceptions. Just because other people may believe snow looks cold doesn't mean you have to believe that snow looks cold. And likewise the letters s-n-o-w written on a paper don't have to mean anything until you allow them to mean it, despite what they mean to someone else. Even after you have "learned" something, you can still reject it.

To further clarify what this has to do with visual expression and visual living, allow me tell you about an interesting oil painting that might help explain it.

Many years ago another French artist painted a picture of a simple tobacco pipe, a smoker's pipe. It is a plain image of a normal pipe on a plain background. In fact, there is nothing unusual or particularly creative about the pipe or the painting. Nevertheless, this is one of the most famous works of visual expression known.

How can that be?

The explanation for this strange sounding reality is simple: Within the painting, beneath the image of the pipe, the artist wrote in French, "Ceci n'est pas une pipe." These few hand-written marks, just eighteen letters, transformed a small piece of white canvas into a world-renowned masterpiece. A few scribbles captured the power of CONTENT (as words) and were marshaled to create an astounding image that has electrified visual understanding ever since.

What he wrote is: "This is not a pipe."

On seeing his painting, you are left to wonder, "What does this mean?" And there are so many possibilities! Does it mean the painting is not a pipe? Of course we can agree on that.

That's easy. The painting is definitely not a pipe.

It's a painting.

Or instead does it mean that a picture of a pipe is not a pipe. That's more touchy, because everyday language doesn't allow for that distinction. Or, does it mean in actual fact that a pipe is not a pipe? In other words, must we assume that a pipe is a pipe? Or are we free to judge for ourselves if a pipe is a pipe? Well we already know the answer. We *are* free to judge if a pipe is a pipe. I guess. At least I think so. Aren't we? Or are we? This wonderful painting simply asks these questions. And uses CONTENT (in this case, the CONTENT of five words) to ask them.[48]

What's your opinion? Is a pipe a pipe? Or for that matter, is a chair a chair, or is a web site a web site or is a view a view?

Wherever you are right now, before continuing to read, look around and, using these thoughts, question something you see.

When he created the pipe painting, that artist probably didn't understand the CONTENT value of writing (in words) any better than you understand it, right now, after simply reading the last few paragraphs. But he decided to question it anyway. He questioned it by adding some writing to the bottom of his picture. Just like that, a masterpiece was born; not because the artist knew any remarkable secrets about visual expression, or had extraordinary drawing skills. Not by reading "Help Yourself to a Blue Banana," or any other art or design book. Instead, this masterpiece came to life just by questioning something. It was born just by asking a visual question.

And remember, this man did not even answer the question. He only asked it. In fact, I am sure it's fair to suggest that he didn't even *know* the answer. As we said in the second chapter, that's usually how artists see their role. Art doesn't have to answer questions. It only has to ask them. Sometimes all you have to do is try.

This wonderful picture accomplished the separation trick.

You can see the painting by searching images for "pas une pipe." (Bookmark this page.)

By the way, although letters and words are primarily CONTENT, they have other lessons as well. As we said above, letters and words can also be TEXTURE, but in addition, letters and words are always, and obviously, FORMS. The FORM of letters and words is a strong source of visual experience. Usually, that expression comes to us by way of art directors and graphic designers who choose an existing typeface for a design. These artists have thousands of typefaces to choose from when they are designing books, maps, menus, signs, logos or advertisements.

But in other cases, someone creating visual expression will design his or her *own* letters. That's often what happens when a new company needs a logo. Many beautiful logos prove how engaging the FORM of a letter can be, separate from (and in addition to) its CONTENT. I'm pretty sure you will agree that the letter "B" logo at the front of this book, which I designed, is successful at this.

The meaning of humor,
the fifth condition of CONTENT

Much of what is written here suggests there is nothing good about CONTENT. It is true that visually sensitive people, and artists who work in visual jobs, often struggle to control it, but CONTENT is not all bad. It just has a way of interfering with other important things. Namely *eight* other important things. However, there are good sides to CONTENT as well, and people who are living visually, just like everyone else, need to keep at least one of these in our thoughts. That's the side of CONTENT that makes things funny.

There once was a popular book describing how a man cured himself of disease by trying to laugh and be happy constantly for a long period of time. He had funny movies and books and TV shows delivered to his sick room continuously, and eventually he made a full recovery. It seems he proved being happy is good for you.[49]

Images that make us laugh, for example cartoons and funny pictures, are made of the same lessons of light that all visual images are made from. Lots of cartoons are funny because of the way someone has compared the ANATOMY of objects.

One that I liked was a drawing of the outside of a residential building with balconies attached to the side of each apartment. On two or three of the balconies people are going about usual "balcony" activities, like sunbathing or barbecuing. But one balcony is drawn to show that its basic proportion is similar to an office desk. So that balcony is drawn to look like a desk that's stuck to the side of the building, with a little man sitting in the doorway wearing a suit, with a phone and note pad, etc.

("Hey, look at this! A balcony can look like a desk!")

To me it was very funny.

But CONTENT, not ANATOMY, is usually the root of humor in simple snapshots. And non-artists, especially people who are *not* living visually, often enjoy funny snapshots hundreds of times more than photographs that have special visual meaning in their COLORS, FORMS, DEPTH, SPACE or SCALE.

I once vacationed in England with a friend. We both had cameras and I was taking pictures of pretty architecture, beautiful landscapes, foggy hillsides and cobblestone streets, hoping the TEXTURES, etc. would come out as I saw them. I was having a great time living visually.

I assumed my friend was shooting the same sorts of things.

The vacation ended and we returned to the United States. Then, after he made some prints, my friend called to say he had the best photograph of our trip anyone could possibly take.

I knew from the sound of his voice that he really believed this, so I guessed it was a brilliant shot of an English castle, or a picture of the queen with an amazing COLOR or FORM that he was very excited about.

But when he brought it out after drinks several nights later, we couldn't stop laughing.

Forget about the queen.

It was *me*, fertilizing the forest next to our rental car.

Explaining the sixth condition
of CONTENT called "at least it's of something."

That vacation picture is a funny snapshot.

It is easy to enjoy simply because, like many examples of good CONTENT, it's a representation "of something." I.e., it's a representation of me, or to be even more specific, it represents me fertilizing the forest. There is nothing abstract about it, nothing mysterious and nothing confusing. It would be silly to suggest it had any hidden or secret meaning. It's just a snapshot of a funny situation.

When my travel buddy and I looked at it that evening, it was even more amusing because of our friendship and because of memories we shared of our trip together to England.

For us, it was a picture full of the CONTENT of humor.

CONTENT is the most far-reaching and influential lesson of light. CONTENT represents millions of emotions and billions of situations and, of course, finding common characteristics among all those possibilities is obviously a challenge. Already in this chapter, we have outlined five different ways to organize at least parts of the visual power that we find in CONTENT. But there are still countless other scenes of CONTENT that present themselves to our eye, scenes that are not characterized by human, civil or self values, or typography (words and numbers) or humor. These are the life experiences that can be grouped into one final condition of CONTENT.

This final condition is called "at least it's of something."

What if, instead of the forest scene, the snapshot mentioned above showed me loading suitcases into the trunk of the rental car. That's hardly a funny picture. But it's still CONTENT. *At least it's of something.* (Again it's "of" me, or more specifically, it's of me loading the suitcases.)

The sixth condition of CONTENT defines all those circumstances when the visual language is doing nothing more than just reporting on the things and/or activities we find in routine life.

The sixth condition of CONTENT isn't terror, it's not happiness, it's not irony, it's not typography and it's not funny. It's not any of those highly charged situations or other conditions we have spoken about earlier in this chapter.

Instead it's the condition of CONTENT that represents the plain vanilla side of human experience. It's the bad prints you throw away at the drugstore photo counter. It's the drawings in an auto parts catalog. It's the pictures you never notice inside a news magazine. It's the statues of the prophets in someone else's religion. And to be truthful, it's even, often, the snapshots taken of other people's vacations. (And sometimes it's even the ones they think are funny.)

Un-hearing CONTENT

As this chapter comes to an end, consider this last important characteristic of CONTENT in visual expression: Visual expression must overcome the fact that visual expression is silent.

Although eyesight is our most important sense, it works with other senses. To see photographs of 9/11, or of Vietnamese children burned with napalm, or pictures of the tragic Oklahoma City bombing is not nearly as terrifying as experiencing these events live as the tragedies unfold. In real life, the sounds of explosions and screams of victims dramatize the emotional nightmare of the moment.

To stand near a launch pad and watch a space vehicle blast off is an experience that is more dramatic because of the rumble of the ground. (I know, again, from having experienced it.) And pictures of delicious food cannot match the same scene in reality when the smell of cooking is filling the air.

Yet visual art attempts to convey all these non-visible parts of what we see without the help of other senses. Visual art is generally soundless, motionless, and without smell or touch.

Consequently, artists often speak with CONTENT in ways that are over-dramatized, trying to capture the emotional impact of real life as realistically as possible.

A final defense of CONTENT
It's not my hated enemy

After finishing this book, a student once wrote, "Content is this man's hated enemy." That really made me smile, but I knew I needed to clarify the reason I emphasize the distracting nature of CONTENT. Hating it is not why. I just regret how CONTENT interferes with our natural curiosity about the other lessons of light.

CONTENT gets some of its worn out reputation for an obvious reason. Although the nine lessons of light have been the building blocks of visual expression since light began, until recently there was very little visual expression, outside of nature, that wasn't completely dominated by CONTENT. Throughout history, most flat art, beginning with pre-historic cave drawings, was created primarily for record keeping and story telling. That means CONTENT has traditionally been one of its primary sources of visual experience.

You'll understand this better if you remember that, until perhaps 500 years ago, most art was created, not for "artistic" reasons, or to soothe the tormented soul of the artist, but rather to record the history or teachings of religious and political power.

Then about 150 years ago a new idea came to visual expression called "impressionism." This was followed by "abstract impressionism." These were the beginnings of abstract art, where obvious CONTENT is purposefully diminished or eliminated. Beginning at that time, and then for about a century thereafter, abstract expression dominated the work of many successful artists.

But in recent history the movement has swung back at least somewhat. The change is led partly by an explosion of CONTENT influencing post modern art and contemporary photography. Unlike painting, photography can far more easily represent or recreate the stark, immediate and un-processed CONTENT we see in reality. In fact, some modern photography is even *more* stark, immediate and un-processed than reality. That has attracted artists' interest.

And as a practical matter, photography is faster than most other visual procedures, including painting. For example, one very respected photographer who moved from paint brushes to cameras said, " . . . there was nothing more to say [through painting]. I was meticulously copying other art and then I realized I could just use a camera and put my time into an idea instead."[50] Her work is a fantastic collection of brilliant CONTENT images in which she often photographs herself as a character caught in a cultural cliché.

McCONTENT

Because we live in a CONTENT world, as our interest in the visual language grows, like a gourmet chef who leaves hamburgers behind, we need to explore beyond CONTENT.

As you move forward, it's exciting to look for the efforts of others who have done the same. When you begin living visually, and experiencing life without CONTENT, you'll discover wondrous things. And it's likely you'll come back from those adventures eager to tell everyone (or to show everyone) what you found.

* * * *

For review, here are the six conditions of CONTENT:

        Human values
        Civil values
        Self values
        Typography
        Humor
        It's of something

Remember: choose one lesson of light, other than CONTENT, and begin a serious collection of it. Pick COLOR, or TEXTURE or FORM. Start a collection that helps you recognize the visual power that lies in visual expression outside of CONTENT.

Chapter Seven

TEXTURE as a source of visual experience

Dialog

A POPULAR IDEA in psychology says that some people need "permission" to improve their life.

It suggests that people who had a strict upbringing get a bad habit. They learn to not feel emotion, good or bad, until they have permission from their parents. Then, the theory goes, as adults they still need that permission before experiencing emotions. Apparently there are lots of psychiatrists who spend their days (and earn good money) giving that "permission" to patients.

I suspect there may be a similar problem that prevents some people from living visually, an obstacle that keeps some individuals from experiencing the visual language. The similarity is this: Being interested in a lifestyle called visual living, or wanting to be, makes a person a little unique from everyone else. You might say it makes you an individual. Accepting the responsibility to be an individual is sometimes a big change in life, and it is normal to subconsciously wish for "permission" to make the change.

But there's a difference between the permission psychiatrists offer and the permission I'm talking about here.

To start with, there is nothing crazy about living visually, so psychiatrists have nothing to do with it. But people who are curious about visual expression are not just looking for a smile, a pat on the back and a friendly go ahead to make the change. Instead, and this is unfortunate, you are looking for these things in a language that you do not understand. You are probably looking for a *reason* to enjoy a visual life, some reason that makes sense. Something logical. And for many people, that's a problem. The "sense" and the "logic" of visual living are not very related to the sense and logic we learn about in grade school or high school, or the logic we learn when using a written and spoken language.

It's ok to say, as I do, that to learn about visual expression you don't need books full of examples of famous artwork. Instead, all you need is the inspiration that surrounds you everywhere. To see what I mean, look around yourself right now. The nine lessons of light are right in front of you . . . in all the visual information you receive through your eyes every moment of every day.

Look up from reading and you will perhaps instantly notice a FORM somewhere near that you never focused on before.

Or a COLOR that is only now beginning to speak to you.

But until you understand what all that information is saying, you may feel you do not have permission to recognize it. You might think, "I'm not familiar with the visual language, so I don't understand." In fact, that's such a common point of view that most people live their life without knowing there is, after all, a funny sort of *visual* logic to all this.

It's a special kind of logic and the foundation for it isn't intellectual. It's not like math class or social studies. Instead, it's the nine lessons of light themselves. What you need to hear is: "OK, from now on it's *all right* to take these things seriously." Although being told something like that rarely happens, hoping that it will happen is a natural part of learning about the lessons of light.

One reason I say this is natural is that I went through all this myself. No one else within my family is an artist, and no one in my childhood understood that working with the visual language is a way to enjoy life, and a way to earn money doing what you like.

As a result, I realize now that during my teenage years I, too, was looking for this kind of permission. Most of what I've written here are things I questioned then, when I was young, and what I've learned since then about visual expression. As a student, I remember hoping someone would tell me how to invent visual information. And tell me it was ok to do it. I wanted to simply ask questions and become aware of the visual language. I hoped to hear answers to those questions in English, but I have to report it never happened.

As a struggling art student, I attended three different schools and many classes. I'm happy to say that, eventually, like thousands of people before "Help Yourself to a Blue Banana," I did learn most of what I needed to know. In fact, many of those classes, and several of my teachers were excellent. But in the end, it seemed that no one really agreed on how to talk about these things. And that's a void I hope this book will help fill.

We're doing our best here to talk about visual expression in simple English, and I think it is probably beginning to work for you. Hopefully there have been moments as you read previous chapters when a light lit in your eye as you glanced around your real world. Hopefully, once or twice, you found yourself seeing (or unseeing) for the first time. Perhaps now you're ready to look at your environment with a new excitement and understanding.

And, hopefully, you will grow in that understanding.

If you do, as you progress, regular logic will release its grip.

No matter how difficult it seems, you can learn new visual skills. The information here is written as part of the support you'll need. These chapters offer "permission" to move away from relying on words and CONTENT, alone, as meaningful ways to express emotions. In other words, if I can do it, you can do it.

When I was young, although no one put into easy words what I needed to know, I did nevertheless continue to learn. But I didn't approach self-study as you would normally approach, let's say, European history.

Instead, I found myself noticing what was interesting about anything that caught my eye. As I collected visual experiences, I noticed they might easily be classified. If a dozen scenes attracted my attention, I would recognize that five were exciting in most part because of COLOR. Perhaps three also relied on SCALE, four had the energy of CONTRAST and two or three found strength in TEXTURE. Perhaps some called on FORM with DEPTH for their visual truth. And of course, there were always many things that were dominated by CONTENT.

As I thought about these observations, I could see there are only nine basic visual powers, and I named them the nine lessons of light, since light is what makes them all visible. (This approach explains why I said in the foreword that the nine lessons of light are, in some ways, like a databased version of visual education. That is, you collect nine classes of visual data and then evaluate them.)

So that's where we are now.

Even though words can't explain everything, there are many things they *can* reveal. Words can serve as a guide into the visual language, and they can be very helpful even if you are just casually interested in visual expression. Words can help lead to the everyday fun and satisfaction of visual living.

In addition, the words that describe the nine lessons of light can also be used to talk about visual problem solving. For students, they are a system to talk about visual expression in an understandable way. Students may be lazy, absent or unprepared for class, but when they *are* interested, they can get criticism in a language they very easily understand.

Words can now fill the silence until visual senses awaken.

But what good is visual communication
if words can't completely explain it?

I said earlier that practically everyone in the world is more familiar with writing and with the spoken languages (in other words, words) than they are with the visual language. So a fair question is, why does anyone bother to use the visual language at all?

Again the answer is, although the visual language is not universally understood, it has power to express things that words can't express. When a person discovers a need to express those kinds of feelings, he or she becomes an artist, and uses the visual language. People use the visual language in this way, even though we know not everyone understands it.

Consider this: although most citizens of China can't understand Spanish, Spanish writers continue to write books in Spanish anyway. It's the only language they know that expresses what they need to express.

In the same way, artists express within the *visual* language, even though this is also a language that many people in China (and everywhere else) don't understand. But, like Spanish writers, visual artists keep using that language anyway.

Artists continue to use the visual language because it is the only language they know that can adequately express the messages they need to communicate. Once you accept there's no words to completely explain the visual language, you can start living visually, and move toward *genuinely* experiencing visual expression. You may even be ready to be responsible for how things look.

You may be prepared to say, "I am an artist."

At that point, whether you've created a dress, a canvas, an ad, a building or a symphony of garden flowers arrayed around a backyard water fall, you will finally be enlightened. You'll be free to accept an inevitable rule of non-verbal communication, a rule that's at the center of understanding and creating art and design:

The simple truth:

It will be impossible for you to completely explain your
visual decisions using any written or spoken language.
This is true even when you create the *most* accurate
and *most* meaningful visual statements possible.

Nevertheless, just as people in China can use their Chinese
language to help them to begin learning about Spanish, you can use
English to help you begin understanding the lessons of light. It's an
approach that offers everyone permission to grow visually, without
leaving everyday logic, everyday words and the everyday written
and spoken languages, completely behind.

Eventually, you'll unsee

But no matter how comforting it is to find a place for words in
explaining visual matters, there is a real limit to any non-visual
approach to understanding visual impact, including everything you
are reading here. If you're just beginning to learn, that may be a long
time away. But if you continue to progress, the moment will come
when you'll separate from this support. At that moment, you may
throw away virtually everything I've told you, and the visual language will become complete and separate from words.

When that moment comes, when you have practiced and practiced visual lessons, when you no longer need to find intellectual
meaning (CONTENT) in everything you see, you will arrive at the
place where breathtaking visual expression begins.

* * * *

Chapter seven continued
AN INTRODUCTION TO TEXTURE
The seventh lesson of light
Reach out and touch some art

Recently, a restaurant I sometimes visit was renovated.
The new interiors are done using a southwestern-American
style, and the interior designer included lots of tiles and exposed
surfaces normally found in that part of the United States.
When I went there after it reopened, I noticed how pleasant

the environment felt. It's sort of breezy and open, even though it's in a big city. This was especially impressive because, at the time, it was the middle of winter. On some walls, the designer applied sun burnt tile on concrete. In random areas, the walls are partly untiled. As a result, the TEXTURED concrete CONTRASTS with the smooth tile.

There are some other areas also left unfinished, as if all the work was simply halted in midstream. For example, woodwork over the bar does not seem to be completed, but the spontaneous look contributes to the relaxing atmosphere. I admired the designer for understanding how the unfinished look would help make the interiors calm and unstructured. The place does not take itself seriously, and that's a nice characteristic brought to the SPACE by the designer. I admired her for using visual sense to decide when the work was finished, instead of worrying over details.

But my point of view changed the next time I went in.

A new sign read: "Excuse our appearance while renovations continue." My visual curiosity was triggered and I wondered, "Is the interior really 'finished,' and is the sign only there in case someone is uncomfortable with its casual look? Or will I go there soon to find the tile work 'completed' and the bar finished off?"

Whatever happens to the restaurant, it reminded me about how we should rely on our eyes to tell us things. Some people might look at a wall that's partly covered with tile and call it "unfinished." On the other hand, my visual sense told me the renovation *was* finished, even though some tiles are missing. To reach that conclusion, I relied on visual, not intellectual, instincts. The satisfying appearance of exposed concrete told me that someone decided to create a feeling with TEXTURE. When I sensed it was successful, I accepted that the job was done, and by a visually sensitive designer.

Predicting TEXTURE and other
sources of visual experience

A comedian once said that the weather forecast called for continuing dark tonight, then turning to widely scattered light in the morning. The humor in this joke is in the obvious and it strikes us as funny because we are frequently unaware of even the *most common* visual circumstances.

Of course, if you think about it, the weather forecast *every* day is for continuing dark tonight turning to light in the morning.[51]

But until a comedian points it out, it doesn't register.

That's probably the funniest weather forecast there is, but it doesn't suggest some other visual developments that take place as weather changes. A forecast that takes into account additional visual details of weather might sound something like this:

> We'll see three dimensional SPACE tonight with some tiny bright CONTRASTS, and a larger CONTRAST with some ANATOMY. Conditions turning to gray, grayish red and sky blue COLORS in the morning, accompanied by a bright display of circumstantial DEPTH, dazzling CONTRAST and shadows everywhere. There will be continued blue sky and CONTRAST until gathering afternoon FORMS and gray COLOR, north and west. Followed by dark gray COLOR, TEXTURE, and flashes of CONTRAST. Tomorrow night, we're expecting a return to black three dimensional SPACE and tiny CONTRASTS.

Using your visual imagination, I'm sure you can understand this forecast. It describes how seven lessons of light are contributing to the appearance of common weather conditions, including the night sky filled with stars and the moon (and ANATOMY of a face in the moon), followed by dawn, sunrise, overcast skies, rain, and lightning (flashes of CONTRAST).

Remember to see TEXTURE

Noticing the visual environment is as easy as remembering to bring your vision into consciousness, even without a strong frame of reference grabbing your attention. Practicing this conscious effort to look at things is a shortcut to unseeing CONTENT.

Imagine these examples of TEXTURE that you might find in a rainstorm (these are TEXTURES that might appear with no easily defined frame of reference to catch your attention): First, there's the TEXTURE of the clouds in the sky, then more TEXTURE when rain fills the sky. Then there's TEXTURE on the ground where raindrops burst. Especially bring to mind the TEXTURE of rain falling on the surface of lakes and rivers.

TEXTURE decorates thousands of everyday objects, bringing with it a satisfying visual energy. It's frequently part of the visual appeal that attracts our attention to a new product, or any new frame of reference. But just as often, TEXTURE, much like FORM, is closely associated with the usefulness of objects. That is to say, TEXTURE has both visual unique-ness and surprising and appreci-ated visual useful-ness.

Here are two lists: TEXTURES that are
useful and TEXTURES that are decorative

Things whose TEXTURE is useful:

1. cheese graters
2. nail files
3. tire treads
4. a printed page
5. a window screen
6. steel wool
7. sandpaper
8. saw blades
9. welcome mats
10. the surface of drawing papers
11. an LP record or CD
12. leaves on a tree

Look for examples of other things
whose TEXTURE is useful, and list them here:

13. _____

14. _____

15. _____

16. _____

17. _____

18. _____

Things whose TEXTURE is decorative:

1. a cane chair
2. a man's beard or
3. 2 days' growth
4. wall paper
5. rattan
6. rippled glass
7. oil paintings
8. leaves on a tree
9. carpeting
10. fabric
11. stucco or brick walls
12. laid paper
    (paper used by designers)
13. plaster ceilings
14. seer sucker suits
15. wicker

See if you can add to the above list
of things whose TEXTURE is decorative:

16. _____

17. _____

18. _____

19. _____

20. _____

21. _____

Connecting the senses

> First man: "I heard it was hot in Cleveland."
> Second man: "Really? How loud was it?"
> First man: "How loud was what?"
> Second man: "How loud was the heat
>   you heard in Cleveland?"

Of course, no matter how good your hearing is, you'll never be able to tell the temperature in Cleveland with it. Heat and cold are not sensations we can evaluate with our ears. Likewise, imagine trying to hear COLOR, taste FORM or smell CONTRAST between black and white. Although these questions are sometimes thought-provoking, and especially so for visually sensitive people, expecting our brain to make these kinds of mismatched sensory judgements is a waste of time.

Or is it?

Regardless of your opinion about this, it points out a unique characteristic of TEXTURE. It's a characteristic of this lesson of light with no equal in the remaining eight sources. I'm talking about the intriguing relationship that TEXTURE shares between our sense of sight and our sense of touch. That is to say, TEXTURE, unlike any other visual characteristic, can be both seen *and felt.*

Exactly how significant that is is hard to say.

But to realize, among our five senses (that is, sight, touch, smell, taste and hearing), and the nine lessons of light, there is only one place that overlaps seems somehow important. The point is, except for TEXTURE, there are not any sources of visual experience we can sense through touching, hearing, smelling or tasting. And it is only in seeing and touching that TEXTURE shares itself.

It's true that some other things we can feel, like hot and cold, can be expressed visually (for example, by photographing fire or a piece of ice). But these types of comparisons between the senses do not share the uncanny similarities that exist between seeing a TEXTURE, such as the front of a suede jacket, and then reaching out with closed eyes to actually touch it and feel the TEXTURE. The point is, you can see *and feel* the TEXTURE of a suede jacket.

By comparison, if you see a red tomato, then reach out with closed eyes and touch it, you can't tell that it's red. Again, what that means is that COLOR is *not* a sensation shared with our sense of touch, as TEXTURE is.

Imagining TEXTURE

Each time that TEXTURE appears within a frame of reference, it has visual characteristics and power to be imagined as something you can touch. An extreme example would be a photo of a yogi's bed of nails. As a visual experience, the TEXTURE of the points of the nails creates a strong impact. But who can see this picture without also wondering how it would feel to lay down on it?

*One might say that *FORM* can also be seen and felt. However, in 3D visual expression, TEXTURE is often just tiny FORM(s) anyway, which means words don't adequately allow for this exception.

And, if you've begun to understand the power of CONTENT, you will also agree that our intellectual curiosity (that is, our curiosity about why anyone would *want* to lay on a bed of nails) is also a strong source of visual experience in a photograph that shows a bed made out of nails.

This relationship between seeing and feeling TEXTURE was once the inspiration for an advertising campaign for a liquor company. The headlines said "Feel the texture" with a photograph of an attractive woman wearing a velvet dress as she sips the liquor. For better or worse, this brought to mind everyone's ability to imagine the sensation of touching velvet on a woman's body. Of course, the smooth TEXTURE of the liquor was also implied. From an advertising point of view, that is a strong visual message of TEXTURE.

The SCALE of TEXTURE

Although every TEXTURE that we can touch can also be seen, the reverse is not true. That is to say, there are TEXTURES we can see, but we cannot feel. The explanation for this odd sounding possibility is fairly simple, but I discovered one day that one student couldn't understand it.

The confusion came when I held up a series of photographs and asked a class to identify the visual strengths in each one. In this kind of exercise, pictures are shown quickly, one after another, as the class decides what is attractive about each image, that is, which lesson(s) of light are attractive.

Once students have gained the habit of noticing every detail in every picture, the genuine visual impact of an image is hard (or at least harder) to overlook.

One picture in my series that day showed the beginning of a marathon race, just as athletes began moving across a bridge. The photographer took the picture from a helicopter above the bridge, and zoomed in so the athletes filled the frame of reference. The picture was a bird's eye view of thousands of tightly packed runners, as they moved across the bridge.

In that photograph, some students easily identified the TEXTURE of the thousands of athletes' heads seen from the shoulders up, supported by the bright COLORS of their running clothes. But one student said, "I can't see any TEXTURE in the picture."

Admittedly, the image showed a TEXTURE that could never be touched the way the TEXTURE of let's say a carpet or a velvet dress can be touched. That is, you can't just casually pat 2,000 runners on the head all at once. Your hand simply isn't big enough. As we continued to discuss the picture, it became clear that this characteristic of all giant TEXTURES is an obstacle for some people.

After a few minutes of misunderstanding, the student asked, "Is the TEXTURE you are referring to the surface of the cloth of the running suits?" Practically immediately the origin of the problem crystallized. Apparently he couldn't see TEXTURE that he could not *also* imagine touching. Since the TEXTURE in the photo was many times too big to touch, he did not understand it to be TEXTURE.

That is to say, the fabric TEXTURE of their running clothes was *not* the TEXTURE we were talking about. The TEXTURE of the fabric was, for practical visual purposes, *in*visible. The runners were far too tiny for us to see details of their running suits, let alone the TEXTURE of the cloth or thread used to make them. Nevertheless, as he searched his mind for a way to see the TEXTURE, he came up with that possibility.

When that student saw the picture for the first time, he knew it showed the start of a race. For him, this was the important power of the picture. But for an artist, when a photo is of something, that is only one part (the CONTENT part) of its visual impact. The other possibilities, as you know, are the other eight sources of visual experience. And as we've said before, even if a picture is of something, there are often other more powerful, and more thought provoking, visual circumstances at play.

What does TEXTURE say?

This photograph was one example of an image whose CONTENT (the marathon race) was less interesting than the TEXTURE which shared its frame of reference. Speaking visually, the TEXTURE within the image was more exciting than its CONTENT. In the same way, you will recall that COLOR was more exciting in that print found in a closet. In that case, CONTENT within that old print was a less strong lesson of visual energy than COLOR. (Page 133.)

Although this race picture might have been a news photo of the event, the meaning captured by TEXTURE was, for myself and for most of the class, more interesting and more thought-provoking than the intellectual fact that it showed the start of a marathon.

What does TEXTURE in a marathon picture bring to mind?

What visual questions does it ask?

The following are some possibilities.
(These are questions that TEXTURE might ask):

What makes thousands of people crowd together?
or

Isn't it interesting how everyone on earth
is pretty much the same size?
or

When you see so many tiny people together,
doesn't it make the problems of individuals seem
less important, considering the size of the universe?
or

Isn't life basically a rat race?
or

Aren't we all just brothers and sisters
searching for the same answers?

And of course, as we have said before, there are also many, (many, many) visual questions found in TEXTURE, including this one, that cannot be expressed in words. Let your visual sense read meanings, like these, into things you see. You'll start to understand the emotional messages fine artists and business artists are sending.

My student erred when he relied on his CONTENT habit to imagine how TEXTURE feels. He believed that, since there was no touchable TEXTURE in that photo (except the cloth in the athlete's clothes), then there was no TEXTURE there at all.

The class that day explained to him that when thousands of heads and shoulders fill a frame of reference, that's a visible TEX-TURE just like a picture that shows a close up of a carpet, with its thousands of details. It is interesting to realize we can touch the carpet and feel its TEXTURE as well as see it. But, visually speaking, there is little difference between TEXTURES we can feel and those like the marathon picture that are simply too big to feel.

You can see similar helicopter views of a marathon race by searching internet images for "verrazano runners." (Do not carry out this search now. Instead, bookmark this page and come back to it when you have finished reading.)

Big TEXTURES

Our world is filled with TEXTURES that are too big to feel.
Here are some of them:

1. The surface of oceans, rivers and lakes
2. An airplane view of forests, farms, cities, or mountains
3. A cloud filled sky, seen from the ground
4. A cloud filled sky seen from an airplane above it
5. A field of wheat or corn (or any planted or plowed field)
6. A star-filled sky
7. Empty seats at a stadium, or sold out seats at a stadium
8. A division of marching soldiers
9. A shopping mall parking lot on the day before Christmas

Think about your own environment, about other places you
have visited, or about photographs you have seen. Then try
to add to the above list of TEXTURES that are too big to feel:

10. _____

11. _____

12. _____

*The rain catchments at Gibraltar
and photographing a big TEXTURE*

Several years ago I had an opportunity to photograph a very
big TEXTURE. I found it in an unusual place.

As perhaps you know, the Rock of Gibraltar is a huge stone
island in Europe, connected to Spain by a narrow land bridge about
half a mile wide (less than a kilometer). There are about 30,000 people who live on the island, but, because it's solid rock, there aren't
any wells for drinking water. Because Gibraltar belongs to England,
which has difficult (you might say *rocky*) political ties to Spain, the
English government needed a way to provide drinking water for res-
idents during those times that Spain might refuse to supply it.

The solution was a huge engineering project that smoothed a
thirty-four acre (14 hectares) slope on the eastern face of Gibraltar,

and covered it with TEXTURED concrete tiles. Rain water (drinking water) falls against this slanted surface, runs down the tiles, and is collected in storage tanks at the bottom.

The photograph I made is a picture of that vast concrete surface, focusing down on it as I stood high above. The picture is composed so the frame of reference is filled with the patchwork of concrete tiles (like the marathon image is filled with runners). A sea gull flys over the TEXTURED surface below where I stood. It's a photograph with several interesting areas to experience visually, and they are all nicely presented inside the picture's frame of reference.

People who see it are engaged, and they bring their attention to full consciousness. It's a picture that people enjoy, and it captures TEXTURE, CONTENT and FORM.

TEXTURE is strong because the tiles, which make a sort of checkerboard pattern, fill the whole background of the scene. CONTENT is strong because it's difficult to understand how the picture was taken. (What is it a picture of?) Although the camera was pointed down, the sea gull soars through the picture as though the photo may be looking up, and the pattern of tiles appears to replace the sky. Lastly, the (organic) FORM of the gull represents life, and this is always important.

Other sources are neutral in the photograph, but here is how I would describe them: Circumstantial DEPTH is there because the sea gull appears in front of the big tiles. But it provides no visual interest strong enough to draw our attention to the picture.

For that reason, DEPTH is neutral.

ANATOMY is present because the TEXTURE appears to be the sky, but really isn't. That is, the TEXTURED background shares the ANATOMY of sky because it's in the right place, and even the COLOR of the concrete is a blue-gray range like some skies. But by itself, this ANATOMY is not strong enough to attract our attention.

For that reason, ANATOMY is neutral.

The COLOR of the sea gull CONTRASTS (conflicts) with the background COLOR of the tiles. (Remember, like a man wearing a blue sweater and brown pants, COLOR will conflict with itself inside a frame of reference.) But neither the COLOR in the picture nor the CONTRAST is impressive.

For that reason, COLOR and CONTRAST are neutral.

The SCALE of this picture is life-size, and as we'll see in the next chapter, that means SCALE contributes very little to the visual interest of the scene. And although three dimensional SPACE fills the area between the camera's point of view and the concrete background, it is also unremarkable as a source of visual experience.

For those reasons, SCALE and SPACE are neutral.

That's how lessons of light can be a summary of the visual impact of a photograph.

However, with a description like this one, we are not necessarily describing emotional impact. And we are not summarizing the visual questions it may ask. What we *are* doing, is being certain that we've actually seen the picture. We're being certain that no visual detail escapes attention. After you have the habit of noticing details, visual curiosity will automatically assign meaning to what you see.

How to be your own teacher

Life always moves on so, in 2001, after 100 years, the water tiles at Gibraltar were removed and the terrain there was returned to vegetation. However, you can still locate pictures if you search internet images for "gibraltar catchments." (Bookmark this page.)

Nevertheless, you may be wondering why I don't just *show you* this actual Gibraltar TEXTURE photograph, the photo I made.

Again, why doesn't this book illustrate what the words say?

After all, practically every art book does it that way.

But, as we said before, there's a drawback in looking at visual information before you're prepared to understand it, and also in looking at visual information believing you already understand it. There's even a drawback in looking at images while someone tells you what to notice. It reduces your own visual curiosity.

If an artist (in this case me) successfully expresses in a photograph certain ideas he has discovered, he is probably using all the sources of visual experience in a sort of harmony, with one, two or three of them of primary interest. That means if you begin looking at sophisticated art, or photographs, before you're familiar with all nine parts of the visual language you may be confused.

It is somewhat like reading a book in which you understand only half the words. Or perhaps it is like reading a book in which you *see* only half the words.

On the other hand, if you examine a frame of reference, the sea gull photograph for example, *after* you are told what to look for (a learning process found in other art books) there's less hope you will challenge your own visual ability and less likelihood you'll use your own visual c-u-r-i-o-s-i-t-y.

I mean, if you have answers to a test, why struggle with the questions? That is why I hope that you don't carry out the suggested internet searches here until you have finished this book.

However, if you're anxious to start, here is what you *can* do.

If the description of the sea gull photograph makes you curious (and I bet it does), and if you wonder if you can identify the lessons of light in other images (and I bet you do), take time to follow the short exercise below. (You can do this now.)

1. Look through a COLOR magazine in your home and choose three pictures. Find pictures that fill a whole page.

2. Analyze these with the approach I used to describe the sea gull photo. Try to find some pictures where the COLOR knocks you out or the TEXTURE fascinates you. Look for unusual shadows and DEPTH. Look for a clever expression of ANATOMY (like missiles turning into eyes and lashes). Find a sculpture, or a building whose FORM is outstanding (or has a nose). Keep a list of the lessons of light handy (write the list from memory on your paper, or refer to page 330), then look for all of them in each picture you choose. In other words, investigate the pictures you find with your own visual curiosity.

3. If none of your pictures seems visually interesting, you may need to look in other places, for example in books or publications about photography or that feature photography. Nature books often have photography that shows the FORM of animals. Calendars show landscapes or portraits or still life scenes. A typical photograph of farm country may reveal the TEXTURE of a field of wheat, or look for DEPTH represented by advancing and receding COLOR in a mountain scene. In fact, many calendars reprint well-known art, including paintings and sculptures. At some point, you'll be ready to begin evaluating these important images using what you have learned so far.

4. Remind yourself of the lessons of light as you look at each. See for yourself that most interesting images have no more than three lessons of light actively attracting attention. (Read the next page before you begin.)

For example, suppose you find a photograph of a horse with a cast on his leg, standing on a trim, and well-cared-for green lawn. Make a record of which lessons are strong in this picture. The horse would be FORM, the lawn would be TEXTURE, and the interesting question, "Why does this horse have a cast on his leg, since it is customary to shoot horses with broken legs?," is the CONTENT of the image. ("It's of something." A horse with a broken leg, etc.)

Make a summary for each of your three pictures like this:

Horse picture: . . . . . . FORM, TEXTURE, CONTENT

If you're ready to try, take a break from reading.
Find three pictures to evaluate.
After you realize that everything you see can be analyzed in this way, you'll be able to teach yourself the visual language.

Also, before continuing to read, bring to mind the first exercise from the preface of the book. Recall whatever it was that caught your attention as you looked up from reading.
(You wrote it down in the blank provided on page 17.)
Try to define it using the lessons of light.
That should help you to understand what you've learned so far. It should help you appreciate that you now have a new way of thinking about visual information.
Do these things before you continue to read.

When you have finished "Help Yourself to a Blue Banana," try these exercises again. See if you can quickly bring to mind each lesson of light as you analyze three pictures.
Then, as soon as you can, apply your skill to more thoughtful images or artwork. What I mean is, it may be time to begin *seriously* evaluating what artists have decided to bring to your attention. Perhaps you are ready to start identifying the visual questions artists ask through their work.
So try it now – first with pictures from your home.
Or if you think you're ready, perhaps you are even prepared now to put the book down and head for a museum or gallery.
(But bookmark this page so you can find your place, and finish reading when you get back.)

Winning expressions

Let me suggest another plan you can make.

Decide to watch for art contests announced in newspapers or on the radio. Sometimes, museums, schools, magazines and similar organizations sponsor contests to create designs for posters and other things. You'll find competitions for stamp designs, sculpture and cake decorating. Plus, if you look, there's photography contests open to anyone with a camera, and competitions for flower arranging for people who have gardens. (You can search "art contest" or similar words on the internet to find others.)

When a contest is announced, or you find one online, *enter* it. But here's what I'd like you to try. Plan ahead of time that you'll let one of the lessons of light *win the contest for you.*

If you find a poster contest, decide that COLOR will be the winner. Then make a poster that really expresses with COLOR. Add a few words (CONTENT) plus the other lessons of light (or maybe not), but keep in mind that it's COLOR you're counting on.

If you find a stamp design contest, skip COLOR and instead try ANATOMY. Then add CANADA or U-S-A or GREAT BRITAIN wherever it seems to fit. Or give perspective (DEPTH) a chance, as I did for that contest I entered (and won) about bicycle safety.

For a sculpture contest, you're going to deal with FORM.

So really nail it. Put together a FORM that is incredible.

Do something that asks you (and us) a visual question.

For a serious photography contest, a possible approach is to capture DEPTH in an exciting full color composition. Try using the perspective of train tracks (a typical photo contest winner), or else photograph something that's very old next to something very new.

In other words, let CONTRAST take first place for you.

In addition, here's another hint about photography contests. Unless it's sponsored by a photo magazine or a museum, the winner of a photo contest is usually going to be CONTENT. So look for the most adorable baby you have ever seen, doing something that is just disgustingly cute.

Then just snap the picture.

In many photo contests, that's the winner.

If you can't find a baby, look for a precious little puppy (the smaller the better). Either a baby or a tiny dog always works fine. Want to really nail it? Put the baby and the puppy together. If the picture is so cute it makes you ill, you'll probably win first prize.

Send in your effort and see what happens.

Enter a contest even if you don't have any art training.

You may discover that when you feel a desire to succeed at visual expression, sometimes all you have to do is try. One possible outcome of this contest-entering effort: perhaps the judges may recognize you as an artist *before you accept that role yourself.*

Then, after you win, don't forget to thank the baby and/or the dog for doing all the work.

Returning to TEXTURE
Some background

TEXTURE will often serve as an interesting background upon which some other activity takes place.

This is a common assignment for TEXTURE and business art directors and commercial photographers sometimes search hardware stores and fabric shops just looking for unusual surfaces to use as backgrounds for their clients' products.

Also available are images and computerized collections of TEXTURES specifically designed for brochures, web pages and ads. These backgrounds include surfaces made of everything imaginable including rocks, buttons, clouds, coins, sand, grass and fabric. In advertising and marketing, the photography for cosmetics, jewelry, perfumes, fountain pens and similar items can be enriched with the sophistication that a TEXTURED background lends to the products.

TEXTURE is not usually the single strongest source of visual experience in a frame of reference. We might say, speaking generally, that COLOR, FORM and CONTENT are more common, and TEXTURE is the least common. Imagine you are shopping for a new car. Which would you prefer on the outside: a choice of COLORS or a choice of TEXTURES?

Of course, just about everyone wants shiny COLOR on their car, but this reminds me of two examples of TEXTURE on vehicles that were startling. One was a luxury car veneered with thin strips of wood. The car appeared to be *made* of wood in the familiar shape of that automobile. The wood TEXTURE was remarkable since our eye expects to see beautifully COLORED paint on an expensive car.

The second was created by someone really living visually. He covered its surface with thousands of tiny light bulbs. They flash in stunning patterns and are irresistible to look at. Seen at night, this car is an exciting TEXTURED FORM moving down the road.

And consider this: A California artist brought to electrifying life a real full-sized *kitchen*, with an adjoining outside patio, by completely covering it from floor to ceiling, including the furniture and fixtures, with *glass beads*. Millions (or probably billions) of beads make up the TEXTURED surfaces of everything in this three dimensional art. The beads even cover the household products and packages that fill the shelves inside cupboards. Millions of COLORED beads recreate the familiar graphics on each box or can.[52]

Finally, although TEXTURE may be called the least common strong lesson of light, it nevertheless plays a fantastic role in the history of art, especially in the work of Jackson Pollock, mentioned earlier. Pollock is a revered artist who created painting masterpieces by dripping, pouring and throwing paint into TEXTURES as his canvases lay on the studio floor.

A moo-ving experience of TEXTURE

I once had this experience with TEXTURE.

I was asked to design a county fair exhibit for a candy company. The exhibit's goal was to remind everyone that milk (which is, of course, good for you) is an important ingredient in the company's milk chocolate candy. Since milk comes from cows, I suggested the exhibit could be a life-size statue of a cow covered with the company's miniature chocolate candies.

When the idea was approved, we bought a fiberglass cow and covered her with 38,000 individual pieces of (M&Ms) candy. Since the TEXTURE of the candy was amazing to see, we expected that "Candy" (as we called her) would be a popular display. But we vastly under-estimated how famous she would become. For ten days, thousands of fair goers waited in line just to get a peek. Local TV news programs reported on the size of the crowd, and they then began reporting *how long the wait in line was expected to be.*

In addition, stories appeared in dozens of newspapers, and a national news magazine wrote about the exhibit as *news* (calling it "udderly amazing").

Finally, Candy was a live studio "guest" on the most popular American morning TV program. For ten minutes the host "interviewed" her as he talked about the candy, and how healthy milk chocolate can be for you. The wonderful and entertaining sight of a life-sized cow covered with a candy TEXTURE brought the candy company a million dollars of free advertising.

In marketing and business art terms, this was an impressive performance by a cow whose primary source of visual interest was the candy TEXTURE covering her. Candy was also a good example of how a business artist can help a company increase sales. She did what the client wanted, that is, she brought attention to the nutritional value of all the *fresh milk* used to make the company's candy.

This time, TEXTURE did the job.[53]

"Candy" was the first ever life-sized designed bovine, and she was the precursor to the exciting fund raising program called Cow Parade, which was born about six years later.

Maybe this story tempts you to look for nearby TEXTURES you may have missed. I felt the same way just re-telling it. So, as I wrote this page, I looked up and appreciated the pretty TEXTURE of some wicker and rattan baskets I use for storage in my studio.

Take a break from reading right now to look for interesting TEXTURES. (Get up and walk around if you have to.)

To see an image of Candy and read more about her, visit behindthescenesmarketing.com. (Bookmark this page.)

Just another day of visual living

Yesterday, while I was working, a visitor came in the studio.

We were discussing something when suddenly she gasped and said, "Oh my God! Look at *that*!" I looked up, and suddenly on the ceiling there were dozens of dazzling spots of TEXTURE that had somehow magically appeared, so it seemed, from *nowhere*.

Directly above began a show of dancing points of light that were sweeping around the room. They were moving in a rapid, random pattern. Some were brilliant white pin pricks of energy, while others had dashes of COLOR like the spectrum of a prism. There were dozens of these little visitors, darting back and forth with no apparent reason to be there. I was speechless and tried to make sense of them. What were they? A vision? An alien? A UFO? A sign?

What to do?

Pray, scream, run for cover? Call the army?

You can imagine how alarmed I was. I have sat in this room several hours a day for several years and nothing like this had ever happened. I searched my visual repertoire for an answer while the little lights continued their crazy ritual.

Then, as quickly, everything made sense. Actually it wasn't a vision, an alien *or* a UFO. It wasn't any of those things. The little dancers turned out to be only some tiny beams of extremely intense and brilliant sunlight, characteristic of this winter time of year, that were somehow streaking into my studio from a window that is high on a wall *in another room* about thirty feet (10 meters) away.

It was unusually luminous January sunlight and this is what made the show: These lost sun beams were racing into the studio, and then reflecting off dozens of silver sequins sewn on the front of my visitor's black sweater. Then they splash landed on the ceiling directly above us. As she moved, even the tiniest little bit, the reflections danced madly around, celebrating the dramatic end to their 93,000,000 mile (148,000,000 km) trip through SPACE.

The rays that reflected squarely off a sequin arrived on the ceiling as bright white lasers, while those that hit at an angle, like reflections through a crystal, were wondrously split into the COLOR spectrum of visible light. Like tiny rainbows, they came to rest (only to find themselves stranded on a ceiling!) The beautiful sight was made of nothing more than sun beams arriving on earth just a short distance above. Sunlight was teaching a lovely lesson of TEXTURE at the unfamiliar extreme of the visual boundaries.

For several moments I looked up as the sun, the earth, a patch of clear sky, a window, my studio, some sequins and the ceiling above all conspired to create a few fleeting seconds of amazing visual beauty.

Can you imagine?

It was another day of visual living.

* * * *

In review, remember that TEXTURES can be both decorative and useful, and re-read the lists on pages 246 and 247.

Before you continue to read, glance around your room.

Try to discover any TEXTURES that haven't yet caught your eye. If necessary, get up from reading and open drawers and closet doors before you finish your search.

Make a note of the most interesting TEXTURE you have discovered while reading this chapter:

The most interesting TEXTURE I have discovered is:

_____

Chapter Eight

SCALE as a source of visual experience

Dialog

I ONCE ASKED some design students,
"Do you all like abstract art?"
Some responses were:
"Abstract art is a joke," and,
"Letting worms crawl over a shoe isn't my idea of art,"
	and,
"I don't like things I don't understand," and,
"I don't know for sure, but I do sort of like it."

At the time, it seemed unusual that such a general question would draw such strong answers. After all, there are many kinds of abstract expression, so doesn't it seem odd that people would have an opinion without even narrowing down the question to a particular artist or a certain style?

But as it turns out, there really *is* a unique visual characteristic shared by all abstract visual work, regardless of who created it or what style or medium they use. It's a characteristic that just about everyone, including art students, is willing to judge without regard for details. This unique circumstance is the fact that, again generally speaking, most abstract visual expression presents our eyes with very little easily understood CONTENT.

And since CONTENT is by far the most common source of visual experience in our daily lives, it is natural for people to sense when it is missing.

You could compare this feeling that people have about abstract expression to the way some people might react to this situation:

Suppose that several photographs of beautiful bedrooms are shown to a group of individuals. Suppose that there are ten photographs, and each one shows a bedroom created by a different interior designer. Imagine that these are bedrooms like ones you see in expensive home decoration magazines. But also imagine that each bedroom is designed *without a bed*.

If you asked these people how they like the room designs, one response might be, "I don't like them because there's no bed to sleep on." On the surface, that sounds like a practical answer, but perhaps words are failing here. To see what I mean, read between the lines. Do you hear this question as, "How do you like these designs?" or do you hear the question as, "How do you like the idea of going into these rooms and trying to fall asleep?" If you think the question means, intellectually, "How do you like the idea of going into these rooms and trying sleep?" a practical answer could be, "I don't like them, because there's no bed to lay down on."

But if you understand the question more visually as, "How do you like the designs?," the beauty of that answer fades away. It's possible for someone to enjoy the visual excitement of a bedroom design, even if the bed is missing. The COLORS in the room, the TEXTURES of the fabrics, the FORM of other furniture, the SCALE of the SPACE, etc., are not less beautiful or less inspiring because there is no bed.

Furthermore, someone who is thinking on the other side of logic, without preconceptions (which is where many visual secrets are found) may tell you, ". . . even if the bed is missing, I can just sleep on the floor." That's why it's necessary here to say abstract art has very little *easily understood* CONTENT. Just as someone creative can accept a floor as a "bed," there are visual messages in almost all abstract expression that at least some people will understand to be CONTENT.

For example, there is nothing abstract about a painting that shows one man shooting another man. It is full of the easily seen human value CONTENT of murder or "hatred." But visually sensitive people may also see the CONTENT of murder or "hatred" in a second painting that shows only a mass of violently applied COLORS. To be more precise, if an artist has experienced the hatred of murder, and he then is able to express it on a canvas by violently applying a mass of COLOR (remember, there is nothing to keep an artist from expressing anything any way he or she wishes) then, true to the nature of visual expression, individuals who understand the visual language may sense that specific variety of visual CONTENT (hatred) when they encounter the painting. But it is usually only a person who is living visually, someone who understands the visual language, who will easily recognize that expression.

So, like most of the students in class that day, many people will say they don't like abstract art and, subconsciously, it's because it has little easily understood CONTENT. They have a sense, and again it's probably unconscious, that a visual image is not complete unless it has an amount of CONTENT perhaps similar to the CONTENT we find in daily life.

Just as a bedroom seems meaningless to them without any bed, visual expression seems meaningless without CONTENT.

You may at first agree with that thinking.

But I am asking you to separate, in your mind's eye, the *idea* of a bedroom, from the *visual experience* of a bedroom. The idea of a bedroom does need a bed to make sense. But the visual experience of a bedroom doesn't. And likewise, at this early stage of your interest in visual matters, you may still feel the idea of art requires CONTENT to make sense. That is, you may believe a painting must be a painting *of something*, that a statue must be a statue *of something* or that a photograph must be a photograph *of something*.

But as you progress in your understanding of how the visual language works, that preconception will gradually become less important. You will discover a new visual world speaking to you in eight other vibrant and emotional lessons, and each is just as powerful as CONTENT.

A role that abstract expression often plays in our visual life is to prove how exciting the other lessons of light can be, even without intellectual meaning. Abstract expression wants to free us from CONTENT. It invites us to share these secrets:

COLORS are magic! FORMS are awesome!
DEPTH is grand! TEXTURES are remarkable!
CONTRAST is startling! SCALE is majestic!
ANATOMIES are fun and SPACE is wondrous!

Furthermore, they each have stories to tell and questions to ask, stories and questions that go far beyond the ability of words, and CONTENT, to describe.

* * * *

Chapter eight continued
AN INTRODUCTION TO SCALE
The eighth lesson of light
The SCALE of Just Us

People are very conscious of their height, and particularly in comparison to other people. Individuals feel this way even though we are all pretty close to being the same size, if you consider how different we could be. After all, there is no reason men and women couldn't be 30 feet (10 meters) tall. But in an extreme case, it's possible for someone who is only a few inches (or cm) away from being average in height to spend their life feeling left out of something.

It may sound unusual, but skin COLOR is probably not as important to most individuals as their height is in relation to people around them. If very short people (or very tall people) could change their beauty, age, skin color or height, most would probably wish to be average height, even if they are unhappy about their appearance, their skin or their age.

Human height is a sensitive issue for millions of individuals, and unless you are close to being the most attractive height, there are probably times when it's a problem in your own life.

We all want to stay, or become, a size that allows us to fit neatly into a world where people have strong ideas about what size nearly everything should be. So, to begin understanding SCALE, it helps to keep this in mind: Our own height is a SCALE of sorts. And it's the basis for much of the SCALE we find throughout the world. Earth has a man-made SCALE, and we all want to fit neatly into it.

That's important, so let's repeat it for you to highlight:

> Our own height is a SCALE of sorts. It's the
> basis for much of the SCALE we find throughout
> the world. Earth has a man-made SCALE, and
> we all want to fit neatly into it.

Unlike COLOR, people aren't aware of SCALE from birth. Instead, it's an intellectual system that we learn.

SCALE involves measuring, in our mind's eye, the relative size of everything and then applying a judgment about how appropriate that size is. We "compute" these measurements, these value judgments, practically continuously, but the entire process usually takes place on a subconscious level. As we go about evaluating the world, deciding how comfortable we feel about it, the size of our own body serves as an unofficial unit of measure.

Although on the surface, the world appears no different to people who are living visually than it does to anyone else, visually alert individuals are generally more sensitive to, and more curious about, what they see, including SCALE. And more to the point, they know it's possible to manipulate SCALE to create engaging visual messages. Once a person is aware of this system called SCALE, it's then possible for her or him to adjust it within a frame of reference. Business artists and fine artists do this on a regular basis, but anyone living visually can tap this power of SCALE on a more personal level. This is something you might try in order to make a living room seem more cozy, or a garden seem more grand.

Big SCALE is next to Godliness

The fact that SCALE is learned as a visual sense means we can't see emotion in SCALE until we first understand the average sizes of things. For example, we must each learn that the oversized SCALE of a cathedral, synagogue or temple is more appropriate as a place where God lives than a normal house. Somewhere we have to learn, that is, to make the connection, that big SCALE has something to do with supreme spiritual power.

We have to learn, so to speak, that both cleanliness *and big SCALE* are next to Godliness. Like CONTENT, SCALE is filled with preconceptions like this.

Nothing forces us to believe that huge cathedrals or temples are better homes for God. But within the language of visual meaning, SCALE has come to have this role to play. Likewise, we are not terribly afraid of big dogs until we realize what size a typical dog is. A big dog may be more dangerous than a small dog. But it's the typical sizes of houses and animals that reinforces, in our visual sense, these learned emotions about churches and dogs.

Since SCALE is such an intellectual tool, it can be manipulated (just as CONTENT is often manipulated) to create a desired response to a visual experience.

SCALE can be expressed in familiar ways, or SCALE can be changed in ways that disobey, or defy, what is expected. There are four ways this can be done, and these are the conditions of SCALE, which are listed for you at the top of the next page.

The four conditions of SCALE that affect what we see:

> These are the four conditions of SCALE, that is,
> the four ways SCALE can modify visual impact:
>
> 1. Abstract balance
> 2. Appropriate SCALE
> 3. Manipulation of life-size (appropriate) SCALE
> 4. Dramatically good and dramatically bad SCALE

These are the keys to understanding how SCALE can dominate a frame of reference, and, by itself, be a strong source of visual experience.

Introduction to abstract balance

When we talked about abstract expression in class that day, it turned out that the students' ability to understand *and even agree on* the strength of abstract images was actually just beneath the surface of their thoughts. We discovered this was true when we drew three abstract compositions on the whiteboard and voted for the one we each liked the best, i.e., the one that looked most balanced.

Circle the sketch below that you like best, then I'll tell you how the class voted.

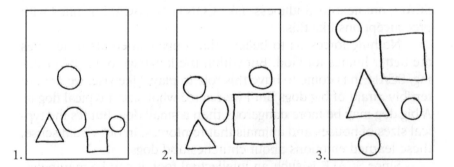

On the whiteboard, we drew sketches
similar to those shown here.
They were alike in two ways. First, each was drawn in a rectangular
frame of reference, the same size for all three. Second, each was composed
of the same FORMS, namely three circles, one rectangle and one triangle.
To see what was learned, look at the three sketches
and circle the one you believe looks the most normal.

The secret ballot came out like this: One student voted for number 1, three voted for number 3, and myself and the remaining nine students all voted for number 2. So among 14 people, ten said the second abstract sketch was more liked than the others.

The result indicated that there is, apparently, a value system people use to agree on what a balanced abstract composition is. It seemed to show that there may be an energy or emotional significance in images that have no CONTENT, even if they are sketches as simple as these three. Most of us decided that one sketch seemed to have more energy or emotional meaning than the others. But the voting also made us ask why the second sketch was more popular.

What value system did we use to judge it?

One answer may be that, only by chance, the second sketch appears to have better *abstract balance*. And, as the voting seems to suggest, the third sketch is partly balanced, and the first is not at all well-balanced. The unique and special visual quality called abstract balance is a version of SCALE we each have an unconscious understanding of. It's a tool visual artists rely on to inject a sense of rightness into every detail of the work they create.

Abstract balance
The first condition of SCALE

I said earlier that SCALE involves measuring, in our mind's eye, the relative size of everything and then applying a judgment about how appropriate that size is. In addition, SCALE is also a system we use to determine the *size of the impact* that each lesson creates in a frame of reference. This system, hidden within our understanding of SCALE, is called abstract balance.

Abstract balance is a characteristic of visual life we rely on continuously. It's a way of seeing SCALE that requires balancing the strengths and weaknesses of all nine sources of visual experience, the strengths and weaknesses of the nine lessons of light.

Abstract balance is the reference we use to judge how successfully the details of a frame of reference work together to create a unified whole. It is the tool we call on to decide if a COLOR is too bright, a person (a FORM) is too fat, a photo is too violent (CONTENT) or a room (a SPACE) is too empty, or too full of furniture.

It is the system we rely on to help our eye make an overall judgment about accepting or rejecting a frame of reference.

Does it have abstract balance or doesn't it?

Are we interested in what this is, or is it boring us?

Is this thing, this scene we're looking at, cool?

Or is it time for lunch?

It is impossible to say just where our sense of abstract balance comes from. But we know great numbers of people can agree that a frame of reference is properly balanced. In addition, there is evidence that visual standards such as this have remained constant through all of history. We know this, in part, because a set of geometrical relationships called the golden rectangle, first established thousands of years ago, is still recognized today as a standard of abstract balance.

This is a shape that visually active minds *and* mathematically active minds have both embraced over the centuries, a two dimensional FORM that is in abstract balance with itself, and people have always liked it.

If you wish, you'll see this important shape by searching internet images for "golden rectangle." (You can do this search now, and you may also read about the golden rectangle by searching web sites in addition to images.)

Because of the golden rectangle, along with other evidence, we know that judging abstract balance is not something that's open to general discussion. Unlike much of the opinion that surrounds visual expression, abstract balance is *not* something you are just free to accept or reject, as we are with preconceptions.

Abstract balance is *real*.

Usually, only visually active people develop an understanding of abstract balance enough to execute it perfectly in a frame of reference. But even among others, it is not uncommon to find a person with a sense of SCALE that is precise enough to recognize perfect abstract balance when they see it.

If not a fine artist or a business artist, a person with an ability like that may be otherwise involved in visual arts. It's a skill often possessed by gallery owners, art critics, successful art collectors, art dealers and museum curators. Even art historians.

If someone "has a good eye for art," it may mean simply that they have a natural understanding of abstract balance. The ability to recognize abstract balance is skill that's *not only* associated with actually creating art. To be an artist, you must create art. But *anyone* walking on your street might be a good judge of visual balance.

Even an excellent judge of it.

Because so many people understand and recognize abstract balance, it is reasonable to guess that our sense of it comes out of subconscious visual habits we all share. Leading those habits is the practice people have of always evaluating what we see. After years of processing billions of pieces of similar visual information, we arrive at a set of *averages* in our collective mind's eye. Again, history has shown that this sense of visual "averages" has not changed in thousands of years of known visual expression.

In fact, even today, architecture students are taught every lesson of abstract balance that can be learned from the ruins and reconstructions of the temples and architecture of ancient Greece.

But looking on the other side of logic, you might ask: if these values are so old, and if breaking rules (ignoring preconceptions) is such an important part of visual expression, what happens when you break the rules of abstract balance? Admittedly for an artist that is a very thought-provoking question. But looking at it closely only demonstrates, again, how incredibly important abstract balance is in its unchanging role. The reason is, if a frame of reference violates the rules of abstract balance, much like a frame of reference cluttered with too many lessons of light, plainly speaking, it will be simply ignored by everyone.

Just like frames of reference with too many strong sources of visual experience, frames of reference that have little or no abstract balance are just too tedious to catch our attention. They seem too busy, too cluttered and too complex. Or else, they seem too calm, too empty or too dull. Whatever their weakness, we may glance at them, but the sense of wrongness that radiates from a poorly balanced frame of reference causes us to immediately lose interest.

The "averages" that make up abstract balance are incredibly important, and their role cannot be successfully ignored.

The opposite of abstract balance is boring chaos.

The abstract balance goes on,
and on, and on

The following may explain just how important and universal abstract balance is as a condition of SCALE.

Imagine that this situation develops in your family: Suppose that your grandfather loves classical music and at the same time your little brother loves rap, your sister loves jazz, your mother loves top 40 and you love metal. Wow, that's a very diverse range of musical tastes. If this actually described your family, I'd bet it's also possible that your rap-loving brother could likewise *hate* classical music, while your mom hates metal, you hate jazz, your grandfather hates rap and your sister hates top 40.

Remember, this is explaining how all good visual expression has abstract balance in common, whether it's a famous painting in a modern museum or the plan you made for landscaping your front yard. It doesn't matter what the style or intent of visual expression is, it must have abstract balance before it communicates visually.

So, look back to your brother who loves rap and hates classical. When he is telling you how much he dislikes classical music, he may imply that rap music has nothing in common with classical. That's probably one reason he likes rap. He'll say it blows away everything that's respected in classical music. No violins, no French horns, no crescendos. In rap there's not even a melody.

Likewise, for those same reasons, your grandfather may hate rap and might even comment that rap is hardly music at all.

One night your brother goes to a rap show and your grandfather goes to a classical concert. Then at both performances something happens that shows how similar classical music is to rap (and how similar jazz is to top 40, or light FM, etc.). It demonstrates they all have something in common, just as all successful visual expression has abstract balance in common.

During the performance at both shows, the percussion player (the drummer at the rap show and the timpanist at the classical concert) drops the beat. At both shows, when it happens, the audience notices immediately and everyone looks up at the stage. The drummer and the timpanist are embarrassed. Everyone realizes an error was made in how they expect music to sound. And here's the error: No matter what kind of music we're evaluating, all successful music has a steady beat.

So what happens when a rap artist (or a classical composer) decides to violate that rule and write music that drops the beat on purpose? Is his music recognized as new? Is he credited for creating an innovative song writing approach?

Does he get rich? Does he get a Grammy? Actually no.

What happens is exactly nothing.

The reason is, just like visual expression that appears before us without abstract balance, when we hear music without a proper beat, we just simply turn away our ears and focus elsewhere.

Again it's time for lunch.

But on the other hand, when a frame of reference (or a new composition of music) *does* seem fresh and innovative or even revolutionary, it often means an artist has discovered, perhaps among other things, a new way to deliver abstract balance in a new frame of reference (or a musician has invented a new way to deliver the beat in a new composition).

Music and visual expression both have a basic and on going foundation. It's a foundation that is never changing. Music always needs a beat. Visual expression always needs abstract balance. In music you can not ignore the beat or defeat it. In visual expression, you can not dismiss abstract balance, and you can't outwit it.

In both cases, in order to explore new expression (musically or visually), your only option is to create a fresh new way to deliver these unchanging roots.

In my opinion, this was very nicely done by Dave Brubeck, Paul Desmond and Joe Morello on Desmond's innovative jazz cut *Take Five*. In visual expression, one of the great breakthroughs in abstract balance was brought to us by the genius Jackson Pollock in his breathtaking drip paintings, already mentioned. You'll see them by searching internet images for "pollock." To hear *Take Five*, search YouTube videos for "brubeck." (Bookmark this page.)

Abstract balance is a set of averages

To over simplify this, abstract balance is a set of visual averages. One artist, sometimes thought of as history's greatest portrait painter, said, "Everything in nature is harmony. A little too much or too little alters the SCALE, . . . makes discord."[54]

By "harmony" he meant abstract balance.

But defining this harmony, once again, stretches language to difficult levels. It is not simply a matter of saying that, after 15 or 20 years of unseeing COLOR, our sense of abstract balance computes the average COLOR, deciding this one COLOR by itself is in perfect balance. Of course, as you probably suspect, *any* COLOR can be part of abstract balance, as long as the other COLORS and lessons of light which share its frame of reference are adjusted accordingly.

That is, when a frame of reference has perfect abstract balance, it is because a fine artist or a business artist (or even Mother Nature) has adjusted the precise details of every FORM, TEXTURE, COLOR and SPACE (etc.) to work together in such unity that they bring us to realize we are seeing a rare example of the highest level of visual communication. One frequent goal of visual expression is to achieve perfect abstract balance such as this.

A photographer hired to capture a wedding is not only interested in catching a pleasing expression on the faces of the bride and groom, and a good picture of cousin John grabbing the bouquet. He or she is *also* concerned with composing the non-CONTENT details of each picture so that abstract balance is achieved. A sculptor may be dedicated to recreating the abstract balance suggested by the COLOR, FORM and TEXTURE discovered in a pebble on a beach.

A portrait artist will carefully arrange the composition of her props (FORMS) within the surrounding room (SPACE), as well the COLOR of clothing and even her distance (DEPTH) from her subject in order to achieve abstract balance. She's as much interested in these details as she is in capturing the likeness (that is, the CONTENT) of her subject. A department store window designer designs the composition of his window to be in abstract balance, even if it contains only a single group of vacuum cleaners placed at one end of an otherwise "empty" SPACE. He'll do this by balancing their FORMS and COLORS against the empty SPACE. A florist seeks abstract balance in the composition of flowers, using their FORMS, COLORS and TEXTURES, and the SPACES that separate them.

Virtually all product designs seek FORM that is in abstract balance. The visual appeal of a new automobile or toaster will catch your eye because its FORM demonstrates abstract balance in some exciting new expression. And just about every advertising layout, package design and interior design tries to attract the eye with this same balanced chord, this harmony. It's a perfect mixture of visual circumstances that evokes a sense of completeness, telling us that important visual expression, important visual *meaning*, is being presented in the clearest possible terms.

Although there is not any single COLOR or FORM that is perfectly balanced, there *are* studies that suggest humans do "compute" visual information to determine beauty. Researchers averaged together several dozen everyday human faces (a computer process called morphing). The resulting image was what you might describe as the image of an "average" face. In this research, they then shuffled the new morphed picture in with the original face photographs of real people, and then showed the whole collection to a group of volunteers. To their surprise, in practically every exercise, the volunteers selected the computerized face, which otherwise appeared as just another picture in the group, as the most beautiful![55]

A different lesson

Of the all the lessons you are learning here, this one about abstract balance has one unusual difference.

Although abstract balance is a condition of SCALE, it *represents* all the other sources of visual experience as well. In fact, it represents everything in nature. Before a frame of reference has overall balance, each of the lessons of light has to be under control; each must be in balance with the others. That means someone who has a good ability to recognize abstract balance probably has a good head start on understanding the whole visual language.

Lots of individuals who have no formal art training have a natural understanding of abstract balance. This is similar to another phenomenon, once again within music, where someone who has no musical training at all may have a perfect ear for tone.

But how do you know if you've got this visual knack?

In my experience, people are about as good at recognizing abstract balance as they believe they are. And that word *believe* is important. Like many elements of understanding visual matters, a critical issue in evaluating abstract balance is the truth in how you feel. Pretending that you recognize abstract balance won't cause it to happen. Fortunately, however, even if you don't already have a sense of visual balance, like each of the lessons of light, developing an appreciation for abstract balance can be learned.

The way to uncover this visual skill is to create visual habits that replace intellectual habits. We have said over and over that our most limiting intellectual habit is our unending addiction to noticing and evaluating CONTENT. So it won't surprise you to hear this: To improve your ability to recognize abstract balance, just follow the exercise we learned to unsee CONTENT. (It's found on page 226.)

If you recall, that exercise suggested that you to pick a lesson of light other than CONTENT and constantly notice it instead of CONTENT. Earlier, I suggested that COLOR is a good choice for this because COLOR is very easy to get excited about. But FORM or TEXTURE can work just as well. In fact, each of the other lessons of light can become your partner in this activity. Anything you do visually to stop thinking about and looking at CONTENT will move you toward a better understanding of abstract balance.

Right now, take a moment and decide which lesson of light you are willing to focus on in an effort to overcome your addiction to CONTENT, and to sharpen your perception of abstract balance.

Wherever you are now, look up and find two examples of it that you feel are especially interesting or exciting. Promise to begin looking for additional examples of this lesson of light.

I want you to *own* at least one of the nine lessons of light.

Do this before continuing to read, and write down your two examples on page 295, at the end of this chapter. Do this now.

So what's your eye Q?

To put this all simply, when a frame of reference has abstract balance, it looks good. But who is the judge? Actually we're working toward that moment when *you'll* be the judge.

In the meantime, let's look now at some everyday situations where abstract balance is playing a role.

Consider these questions: Have you ever glanced at a house and thought, "That just doesn't look right." Or noticed a friend wearing a new dress and announced, "Sorry, that's not quite your style." Or drawn a poster and said, "I better start over." Been disappointed about how a new chair changed your living room and told the store, "I'm bringing it back." Or have you ever: Had cosmetic surgery? Returned a bedspread? Hated your new hair cut? Painted over some old wallpaper? Changed your necktie? Criticized the design of a car? Redid your nails? Added more lights to your holiday tree, or more COLORful flowers to a backyard garden?

Even if you answered yes to all of these questions, you are not being temperamental. Each of these are observations about abstract balance. Each represents a situation where abstract balance is, in your opinion, out of whack. Read them again to see why that's true. Each of these statements represents a summing up of your visual opinion of something. Each is a visual judgement about the overall way something looks. Does this thing in front of me look ok, or not?

That's another way of describing abstract balance.

The more important these things seem to you, the more likely you have an elevated sense of it.

For artists and other visually sensitive people, these kinds of observations about how the world looks aren't trivial issues. Rather, they are some of the important concerns this book gives you permission to make a part of your life.

"OK great!," you may be saying. Perhaps you are even pleased with yourself after reading these last few paragraphs. You may be thinking, "I must be an artist because yesterday I saw a house that didn't look right. Last week I criticized my sister's prom dress and a month ago I fired my barber. It must be because I have a good sense of abstract balance."

Actually, on the surface, those kinds of observations *are* an indication that visual issues are being considered. But unfortunately there is a mistake sometimes made when these sorts of opinions are being offered. It's a mistake that has nothing to do with understanding abstract balance.

If the house you saw looked odd because it was Tudor style and you grew up in a Colonial house; or if the dress was annoying because, "She's my sister, and it was cut way too low," or if you quit your barber because you never wear your hair short (period, end of discussion), then your sense of abstract balance is not being tested, let alone confirmed.

When your personal preferences for architecture, dresses or haircuts (or anything else) are guiding your visual opinions, then CONTENT is once again limiting your vision.

All three of these opinions suggest "preconceptions."

When evaluating abstract balance, you can't say, "I only like Colonial style houses and that's that." or, "I don't care how pretty her dress is, no sister of mine will be seen in it." or, "I've always had shoulder length hair, and that barber talked me out of it."

As we learned earlier, these kinds of preconceptions are a big part of CONTENT. They are the fundamental pieces of information we "learn" all through life that help guide our intellectual thinking. Moreover, they are bits of information that we refer to over and over again to judge what we see. They are great for fixing a bicycle or balancing a bank account. But, aside from evaluating CONTENT, they are not useful in visual decision making.

Sensing and appreciating abstract balance is an ability that comes from another part of our understanding. And it happens at the moment something is seen. It sounds odd, but when you sense abstract balance, you are not relying on anything you have seen before. Or, perhaps this is the best way to put it: When you evaluate abstract balance, you are instead relying on *everything* you have seen before. Abstract balance doesn't rule out anything.

The part of our perception that evaluates abstract balance is separate from the part that stores our preconceptions. It's the visual part, and it guides us in evaluating the nine sources of visual experience. It guides us in seeing these nine special visual lessons in their own universe. To evaluate the abstract balance of a house, a dress or a haircut, you must see them as a combination of the nine lessons of light. Visually speaking, a house is not "a building for a single person or family to live in," as the dictionary says, or even "a dwelling design perfected by early American builders" (no matter how much you like the Colonial house you grew up in). Rather, (and put in visual terms), these things always, and most importantly, represent a combination of the sources of visual experience.

Your "eye Q" is your ability to honestly judge how things look without preconceptions. How would you rate yours?

Take a moment to think about that.

Looking at the sky
with visual curiosity

Since we're talking again about visual judgement, before going back to SCALE let's look at one more characteristic of visually sensitive people. I'm referring again to visual curiosity, which has been mentioned often in previous chapters. Visual curiosity doesn't mean a casual tendency to sometimes notice our surroundings. Rather, it's a specific habit. It means making an agreement with yourself to figure out why the information your eyes provide is either interesting or boring. Or why it's beautiful or ugly. Or why it's right or wrong. Or why one shirt looks so good on you, while another one doesn't. Or even why some things just don't seem to make any sense, visually speaking. Or why fine artists and business artists bother to show us the things they bother to show us.

As an example, in the first chapter, we talked about parallax and why, one hundred years ago, some 3D pictures of the moon were made. I asked you then to think about why anyone would go to the effort of making 3D photos of the full moon when, as we said, parallax is an effective way of evaluating DEPTH that is limited to a distance of perhaps only 100 feet (30 meters) in front of you?

I came across some of those double moon 3D pictures at an antiques fair once and was curious about that. (3D pictures look like two small photographs side by side on a piece of cardboard.) Unfortunately, there was no viewer available to see them in 3D.

So I put the cards back on a table and walked away.

But later I began to wonder about them.

My visual curiosity made me think about those pictures.

The question is, does it make any sense to take 3D pictures of something that's 250,000 miles (400,000 km) away?

Take a minute now to think about that.
Then I'll tell you how I arrived at an answer.

Here's how you can approach it:
As we said, parallax effects our sense of DEPTH to a distance
of about 100 feet (30 meters). However, there are some additional
factors that also affect our perception of DEPTH. Generally speaking, the more a large three dimensional frame of reference is filled
by one thing, the greater the sense of DEPTH it presents to the eye.
This is true because the action of scanning an object (by moving our
eyes around) helps our eyes to estimate how far away it is, and how
far away its *parts* are (like moon mountains or craters). If an object
fills a large frame of reference so much so that moving our eyes
helps to see it, then DEPTH is enhanced.

Of course, generally speaking, this does not normally impact
our perception of the moon, because the moon is not *that big* when
seen from earth with our unaided eye. In fact, with the unaided eye,
the moon is only a very small part of the frame of reference (the sky)
it appears in. And we do not need to move our eyes *at all* to take it
all in at a glance.

But what if DEPTH and parallax were somehow exaggerated in
those 3D moon pictures? Remember that exaggeration is a common
way that artists, photographers included, can give extra strength to
a frame of reference. In fact, artists often exaggerate the lessons of
light. When that fact comes to mind, there are some new possibilities to think about. New possibilities come into play.

I realized three things about 3D moon pictures.

First: the pictures were obviously magnified by shooting them
through a telescope. That means the telescope brought us perhaps
eight or ten times closer to the moon than our normal eyesight does.
Of course, even so, that still puts us about 25,000 miles (40,000 km)
away. (The distance to the moon divided by 10.)

And that is still quite a bit more than 100 feet (30 meters).

Nevertheless, when we see the moon through a telescope, we
are, for practical visual purposes, *closer to it.*

That leads to the second thing.

By magnifying the moon, it becomes bigger in its frame of reference. In fact, it becomes big enough (when seen through a telescope or a viewer) that you do need to move your eyes to take in the
whole image. That movement of your eye enhances DEPTH.

Finally, to understand what the third realization is, ask yourself: What else could photographers do to exaggerate the 3D effect of parallax? What else could they try in order to increase the illusion of DEPTH in those moon pictures? How could a photographer trick our eyes so that mountains and craters on the moon have very real-appearing height and DEPTH, even though the moon is actually very, very far away. Take a minute to think of your answer.

See if you wondered about this third observation:

It's found when you remember that artificial parallax requires two pictures, seen through a viewer. Normally, in 3D photography, those two pictures recreate what our eyes actually see. That is, the two cameras that take these pictures are usually set only 3"-5" (8–12 cm) apart, which is about how far apart our eyes are. The result is, in the viewer, we see a scene that looks much like reality.

But what happens if the cameras are set not inches apart, but *miles* apart? Of course, if you're looking up at the full moon, you could separate the cameras (which are attached to telescopes) by a huge distance. You'd still see the full moon, lit with even (reflected) sunlight, and captured as a complete circle.

If you separated your own eyes by that large distance, you'd get one bad headache. But with cameras, it's easy. Let's say, then, that a photographer set up his two cameras *30 miles (48 kilometers) apart*, and then aimed them at the moon through telescopes.

Are you following?

Now, divide 30 miles by 5" (the usual distance between 3D cameras) and you'll get a number that tells us how much "closer" to the moon the sense of DEPTH by parallax will appear to be.

If you do this math (try this on your paper), it shows that by standing the cameras 30 miles (or 48 kilometers) apart, you'd get a sense of parallax that is about *380,000 times stronger* than just looking at the moon with your own eyes. (30 miles = 1,900,800 inches. Divide that by 5 inches and you get 380,160.) If you then divide the 25,000 mile "close-up" view of the moon provided by the magnifying power of the telescopes by 380,000 (25,000 miles = 13,200,000 feet and then divide that by 380,000) the result seems to imply that the illusion of DEPTH in those 3D moon pictures is similar to the sense of DEPTH by parallax you might get while looking at something that is just around *35 feet (about 10 meters) away*. And that's well within the range of parallax. So slip a set of side by side photos like that in a viewer, and your eyes are tricked to believe the surface of the moon is only 35 feet away. A very wonderful illusion.

I eventually got a chance to look at moon pictures through a 3D viewer, and was happy to confirm that they do, in fact, present a beautiful image of the moon in three dimensions.

Quite a sight to see.

This is an example of visual curiosity.

If you have it, if you're curious about what you see, one way or another, at some time or another, you're going to wind up understanding art and design. And perhaps, one way or another, at some time or another, you'll end up making it yourself. There's no doubt you are already on a path that will lead you there. Just reading this book indicates that you already have very healthy visual curiosity.

The question is . . . *how much?*

And one more thing. The real truth is, I do not actually know if those 3D moon photos were taken in the way I described. For one thing, separating the cameras by 30 miles is maybe not necessary. If I researched a history of photography, or spent time on the internet, I could learn more about it. But that would miss the point. The important thing is that *I was curious* about how they were taken.

More about visual curiosity

Once in a while a student surprises me with a comment that is clearly preceded by visual curiosity. At those times, some of these things I am writing about and speaking about seem to be really getting through to people.

This kind of thoughtful comment was made by a student in a new class I began teaching just last week. He was interested when I showed the class the child's drawing that appears in chapter one. It's the drawing there that helps to illustrate how memory can be a condition of DEPTH.

After I reviewed that picture, holding it up for the new class to see and discussing the points that you, yourself, read in chapter one, this student surprised me with a very unique observation about the information hiding there. He observed that the second version of that picture, where the tree replaces the mountain, may hold an additional visual clue, one even I had never focused on.

He discovered something within that picture that might help us decide if the tree is closer to us, or further away, than the house.

If you like a challenge, look again at that picture (on page 68) for clues we missed in chapter one. Do this before you turn the page. Then I'll tell you what this perceptive student said.

Remember, the second version of the picture does not seem, at first, to offer any suggestions that help us determine if the tree is closer or further away than the house. Because of that, I said we might have only memories to assist us, assuming that we know the house and tree represent a real house and a real tree that the child was attempting to draw. And, you will recall, I left it at that.

But my student suggested this additional opinion: He noticed that the smoke coming from the chimney appears to be blowing briskly away from the house. That of course implies that the wind is moderately strong. If the wind is strong, he reasoned, then the tree must be sturdy, since it does not appear to be affected by the wind. If the tree is sturdy it is probably mature, and if it is mature, it is probably tall, and if it is tall, then it must be further away from us than the house, otherwise it would not appear smaller than the house. *That's* visual curiosity.

Of course, unlike solving a math problem (and just like the moon discussion), it doesn't really matter if any of this is true or if it's even plausible. What matters is questioning all the possibilities that are implied by the blowing chimney smoke. Good for him.

Now let's read about the second condition of SCALE.

Appropriate SCALE
(Life-sizeness, over-life-sizeness and under-life-sizeness)
The second condition of SCALE

Our reaction to the size of anything is related to how we feel the world should interact with the size of our own body.

In a nutshell, that's the basis for "life-size" SCALE.

Life-size SCALE is not very noticeable.

We do not pay special attention to a man five feet ten inches (1.8 meters) tall (that is, a man who is average or life-size) and, likewise, we'll ignore frames of reference that have predictable SCALES (and no other interesting lessons of light). We expect SCALE to be life-size, and when it is, as adults we are not impressed.

But life-sizeness is a value system we must learn, and learning it eventually provides all the information we need to judge the appropriate size of everything in relation to everything else.

For adults it's very long forgotten, but children look forward to the day they reach the physical size that the world seems custom made for. Kids look forward to being grown up, when they are themselves life-size or adult size. In children's experience life-sizeness of SCALE (the SCALE that basically fills our world) is a nuisance.

Chairs aren't comfortable, doorknobs are too high, stairs are too steep, steps are too wide, spoons are too long, and the list goes on. Our first visual experiences as children are crowded with convincing evidence that we are not yet life-size. As children, we know on a subconscious level that the sooner we become that way (the sooner we get physically bigger) the better off we'll be. The satisfaction that comes from finally fitting comfortably into the man-and-woman-made environment is one reward of growing up.

And by the way, the future will very likely see *robots* that copy the size, SCALE (and the ANATOMY) of adult humans for the same reason. Just as people are more "productive" in adult sizes, so will machines we build be more productive (as well as more lifelike and acceptable) when they precisely fit life-size environments.

This is already evident in ASIMO, a new robot under development by Honda. He (or she) is engineered to be life-size and to recreate human mobility. One goal is to assist handicapped people, but the possibilities are enormous. A startling preview of the future happened when ASIMO actually conducted a symphony orchestra.

To see a video of that amazing performance, for once I invite you to put aside the book and do an internet search now, *before* you continue to read: honda.com/asimo, and then click on "videos."

Dreaming an impossible dream. I am sure you will love it.

As children, we teach *ourselves* very much about SCALE.

As a result, during the process of growing up we become accustomed to everyday SCALE in three general formats. And we learn to accept that these variations are "appropriate."

This shows some of what we learn about appropriate SCALE:

There is "life-size,"	which might be a house, an automobile or cocker spaniel dog
There is "over-life-size,"	which, for example, is the cathedral mentioned earlier (a big house), a limousine (that is, a big car), or a Saint Bernard (a big dog)
And . . . There is "under-life-size,"	which could be a playhouse (or doll house), a subcompact car or a miniature poodle dog

Here is a simplified version of that same chart:

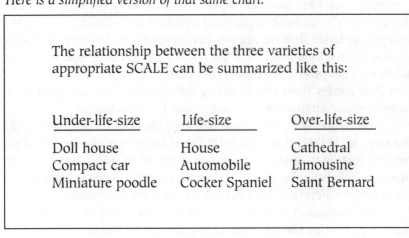

The relationship between the three varieties of appropriate SCALE can be summarized like this:

Under-life-size	Life-size	Over-life-size
Doll house	House	Cathedral
Compact car	Automobile	Limousine
Miniature poodle	Cocker Spaniel	Saint Bernard

From tiny to giant

Each possibility above shows a range of sizes from tiny (the doll house) to giant (the cathedral). But we are not very interested in the SCALE of any of these examples (even though cathedrals can be very big, and toy poodles can be very small). We are not interested in these things visually because we always *expect* that these things will be these sizes. It's usual. The *status quo,* so to speak. We have learned it is natural for these things to be these sizes.

The chart on the next page outlines some additional learned ideas about SCALE. It shows how we accept that many things will be either over-sized or under-sized. It shows how society has taught us when and where the SCALE of the world is supposed to be exaggerated. There is a SCALE for everything, and most of us agree on what it should be.

This chart is a more detailed assessment of the "appropriateness" of SCALE. Each item on the list is classified as either life-size, over-life-size or under-life-size. And, although over-life-size or under-life-size SCALE is possibly a bit more visually interesting than life-size, this is basically a list of common things that are, based on their SCALES, *not* strong sources of visual experience.

They're not strong sources of visual experience because we expect these SCALES to accompany these things. Look carefully at the list and decide if you agree with the description for each item that is provided.

A sampling of appropriateness in SCALE

The scene	We normally expect its SCALE to be:
A cathedral or church	Over-life-size
A public cultural center	Over-life-size
A theater auditorium	Over-life-size
A doll house	Under-life-size
An apartment or house	Life-size
A war memorial	Over-life-size
A toy poodle dog	Under-life-size
A hotel lobby	Over-life-size
A classroom	Life-size
A hospital room	Life-size
A movie theater	Over-life-size
A train station	Over-life-size
A bus station	Life-size
An airport	Over-life-size
A ballroom	Over-life-size
A sculpture	There is no preconception about this
A wall mural	Over-life-size
A miniature golf course	Under-life-size
A circus tent	Over life-size
A little person	Under-life-size
A bonsai tree	Under-life-size
A swimming pool	Over-life-size
A bathtub	Life-size

If you don't agree with these relationships, change them so you feel they are correct.

This list provides some basic information about appropriate SCALE. We need to be aware of this in order to understand how it's possible to create more meaningful expressions of SCALE by *modifying* these basic starting points.

That is, once we are aware that practically everything has an appropriate SCALE, we're on our way to understanding how it's possible to create greater emotional tension within visual expression by changing those SCALES on purpose. That's done by assigning some *un*-appropriate SCALE to almost anything, assuming it's done in an imaginative or creative way.

Manipulating appropriate SCALE
The third (hidden) condition of SCALE

In other words, this kind of engaging SCALE is brought to life with the help of the third and fourth conditions of SCALE, as we'll see in the following paragraphs.

Our childhood years, during which our own bodies are out of SCALE, contribute to a special sensitivity to SCALE that remains within us throughout life. Visual artists can take advantage of this sensitivity by changing expected (that is appropriate) SCALE in subtle ways that are sometimes almost invisible.

For one example, architects and set designers often "manipulate" life-size SCALE to lend atmosphere to dramatic SPACES they create. By manipulating life-size SCALE, an architect can modify the emotional appeal of an environment, and as a result, a SPACE can gain (or loose) a sense of warmth, prestige, elegance or importance.

This process usually includes adjusting SCALE and SPACE.

Consider these thoughts: you might assume that the design for a small beach cottage will be warm and cozy. After all, normally these are two common and appealing characteristics of small beach cottages. These are characteristics of small beach cottages that are appropriate. You could say it this way: *warm and cozy* are *expected* (under-life-size) characteristics for a small beach cottage.

Nevertheless, when trusted to the imagination of a talented architect, a small beach cottage can instead be designed to express ambiance that's more *inspiring and magnificent* (manipulated).

At the same time, the design for a large mansion might bypass being inspiring and magnificent. Even though being inspiring and magnificent is *expected* for a large mansion, in the hands of an imaginative architect, a mansion can instead be made more warm and cozy (manipulated).

Manipulation of appropriate SCALE operates on the same emotional level as our reaction to large dogs and small dogs. You'd probably agree that, speaking generally, people will react with fear to large dogs and with amusement to small dogs. In both cases, we are making intellectual judgments based on the size and ferociousness of a typical dog. This kind of built in value system which we all possess can be manipulated in order to create a variety of emotional responses to SCALE, based on the typical size of *anything*.

This can be accomplished by professional artists, or by anyone who is living visually.

In fact you, yourself, can very likely accomplish this manipulation, even if your plan is only to renovate a dining room in time for an important birthday.

How would you approach this?

In any interior SPACE, any of the doorways, moldings, base boards, step heights, windows, ceiling height, sill levels, and rooms themselves can be adjusted (even slightly) so the imagined emotional feeling becomes a reality. These variations in SCALE can be so skillfully created they seem to be felt rather than seen. They are often accomplished by making very minor adjustments to the size and dimensions of interior details. Visitors to the room sense only that the SPACE is comfortable. But they likely will have no idea *why*. As a result, this condition of SCALE may seem invisible.

Manipulation of life-size SCALE might therefore be called the *hidden lesson of light*.

That's a bit of a revelation, so let's repeat it:
Manipulation of appropriate SCALE could
be called the hidden lesson of light.

Goofy SCALE

A popular place to experience "hidden" SCALE is at Walt Disney World, where brilliant examples of all nine lessons of light are found practically everywhere. Artists with many different talents work to create the visual environments in Disney theme parks. They include architects, interior designers, landscape artists, sign painters, stage and set designers, photographers, cartoonists, illustrators, costume and vehicle designers and animators.

But some of the magic in the Magic Kingdom is only a clever use of the manipulation of life-size (appropriate) SCALE. This happens throughout these parks. On Main Street, designers adjust the architecture of some buildings. At street level, doorways and windows, etc., are often slightly smaller than life-size in SCALE, while at the same time, the second, third and fourth floor exterior of each building is slightly larger in SCALE than the floor below it.

Visitors feel special in this environment. The small SCALE of street level architecture gives us a feeling of importance, a feeling that we are bigger than life. And the larger SCALE of upper floors overcomes perspective (DEPTH), and makes windows and rooftops seem to be within reach. They seem accessible, which makes visitors feel comfortable. If you have visited Main Street at a Disney park, you were probably curious about what is behind the upper floor windows. The ability of SCALE to capture our imagination in Disney environments is impressive anyway, but even more so when you realize, in many cases, *nothing at all* is behind those windows.

And the reverse is true also

As you might imagine, it is also possible to manipulate life-size (appropriate) SCALE in the other direction, and that creates an environment that may subconsciously intimidate us.

The design of a courtroom may be just over-life-size enough to create a disciplined feeling, but not enough to make the room as inspiring as the over-life-sized SCALE of a church, library or museum. That is to say, the inside of some courtrooms has a slightly over-size SCALE. The result is, we feel not quite as important as the judicial system which operates in the room. In addition, of course, the judge's desk is high up and oversized to help carry on the illusion. These manipulations of SCALE create the intended effect, making the process of law and justice more impressive and dignified, as it should be in civilized society.

Manipulated life-size SCALE is usually experienced as feeling, not something that is easy to see. If an artist manipulates life-size SCALE in an environment, usually a three dimensional SPACE (like some of the examples we have been discussing) or with a three dimensional FORM (for example a building design or a large sculpture in a park), part of its success lies in not being obvious. That is, manipulated life-size SCALE can make a difference in our feeling about a place, but only someone familiar with the visual language, someone who enjoys living visually, can usually understand how SCALE is working to create this sensation.

Summarizing the second and third conditions of SCALE
Nothing expected is surprising

To put this in other words, explaining the second and third conditions of SCALE: we know we are supposed to react in a certain way to the size of certain things. Mother says to baby, ". . . look how big this apple is," and the baby learns that there must be some emotional difference between an apple and a *big* apple.

In summary, the second and third conditions of SCALE, discussed in the paragraphs above, are usually weak sources of visual experience. They usually don't anchor visual expression.

Appropriate SCALE is expected, and has little impact.

So if a man, a house, a spark plug, a cat or a waterfall is the size we expect it to be (appropriate), then our visual interest in the SCALE of these things is less than our interest in other SCALES that surprise us with originality. It's true that a giant waterfall does have its appeal, even though we expect waterfalls to be giant. But in the end, nothing that is expected is ever very surprising.

As an alternative, the third condition of SCALE (manipulated SCALE) may be slightly more interesting and it is often satisfying to come across a new feeling brought about by manipulated SCALE. However, because manipulated SCALE is hidden, it may often pass with little commotion.

We learn that we are supposed to laugh and be amused at tiny dogs, to feel impressed by big muscles, to marvel at miniature computers, to be humble in gigantic cathedrals* and patriotic at the Grand Canyon.

Henry Moore, the famous 20th century sculptor (who was also mentioned earlier in chapter two), once summed it up. He said, "The very small or the very big take on an added size emotion."[56]

Like the rest of us, he had learned his lessons very well.

Please glance again at the chart on page 285.

It is intended to remind us that, throughout life, especially in childhood, we learn it's normal for certain things to be bigger or smaller than average. From that moment, and continuing for the remainder of our lives, when these things appear that way in a frame of reference, it is no surprise that their visual impact is not especially powerful or moving.

Another huge and massive over-life-sized downtown city skyscraper, a powerful FORM that is soaring into clouds and towering majestically above everything else within sight is, visually speaking (let's face it) nothing new, special or unexpected.

To explore visual expression that *is* new, special and unexpected, we need to move ahead and become familiar with the fourth condition of SCALE as a lesson of light.

---

*Nevertheless, Frank Lloyd Wright, often named the greatest 20th century architect, said in a 1959 interview that when experiencing SPACE within a great cathedral he felt, not humbleness or size emotion, but rather "regret." That's true, he explained, because it doesn't represent the "sovereignty of the individual." From *Between You and Me*, Mike Wallace, Hyperion, 2005. p 139.

Dramatic SCALE:
Visual impact that's new, special and unexpected.
The fourth condition of SCALE

SCALE that *is* particularly noticeable in a frame of reference must violate, or strongly exaggerate, learned ideas about what size something should normally be. Dramatically good and dramatically bad SCALE, as these fourth conditions of SCALE are called, can be the foundation for visual experiences with very strong impact.

Dramatic SCALE happens when a major change is made in the direction of *either* over-lifesizeness or under-lifesizeness. But it must be a change we've not learned to expect. An artist who understands how, when, and to what degree this change in SCALE can be made can create visual expression with dramatic SCALE.

These two types of SCALE *aren't* appropriate SCALES.

They wouldn't fit in the previous chart.

Referring to them as "dramatic" means they *are* very noticeable in a frame of reference, and have the potential to add impact to visual experience. Dramatic SCALE is so powerful because it suggests something is greatly exaggerated in size (it's either waaaaaaay too big or waaaaaaay too small) when compared with its own usual size, or with the usual size of other things (the memory of which we keep in our "mind's eye," or in our visual repertoire).

If widely held preconceptions about SCALE (many of which are mentioned on the last several pages) are ignored, the result is dramatic SCALE.

What does dramatically good SCALE
and dramatically bad SCALE look like?

Dramatically *good* SCALE is a tool for creating images people will respond positively to. When we come across dramatically good SCALE, we are agreeing, in effect, that an unexpected SCALE which appears suddenly is original or exciting.

On the other hand, dramatically *bad* SCALE can appear just as suddenly, but we call it "dramatically bad" because people do *not* judge it to be original and exciting. Rather, dramatically bad SCALE is ugly, rude, wrong or annoying.

As a case in point, some frame of reference (an illustration, let's say) may show us two things that are very out of proportion to each other when evaluated against what we know to be true.

An example of this appeared once in a magazine where an article about a famous baby doctor was illustrated with a retouched photograph showing the doctor standing next to an infant child.

Dramatically good SCALE is the source of visual impact in the image because the baby, which is normal in every other respect, *stands equal in height to the doctor.* That is, imagine a healthy, normal seeming baby who is six feet (1.8 meters) tall and posing with his doctor (or sketch this on your paper). The reader's eye is stopped at the full page "doctored" picture, and interest in the article is dramatically increased. The picture is an example of how a business artist (in this case a magazine art director) expressed dramatically good SCALE to make a magazine layout special and unexpected.

Dramatically good SCALE gains strength because it is not typical in its expression of the relationship between the sizes of two typical things. Or, it can startle us by suggesting that some thing or object is very much out of SCALE with the size of our own body.

On the other hand, dramatically bad SCALE can result when something about the size of a visual element clashes strongly, in a negative way, with what seems correct, based on preconceptions about SCALE. Dramatically bad SCALE may provide a strong visual impact, but the wrongness it projects leads people to reject the emotional meaning that tries to accompany it. A built-in warning system we have goes off when something is out of agreement with learned ideas about SCALE, and is also without any special visual payoff (like the giant baby) to help us overlook the wrongness.

Returning to the example of a cathedral, it would be almost impossible to build one so big that people feel it honors God *too much.* In fact, from the dawn of civilization until the twentieth century, architectural history was basically the story of societies inventing newer and better construction methods, just so bigger and bigger temples and churches *could* be built.

So, the bigger a cathedral becomes, then (usually) the more intimidating and awe inspiring it is (a learned feeling). But we *expect* a cathedral to be intimidating and awe inspiring. One way we judge an architect's skill is to evaluate *how* intimidating and awe inspiring a cathedral's SPACE is (using SCALE to help us do it).

But there is a point where some things (but not cathedrals) get too big. There may be a point where the size of a billboard, for example, has gotten out of hand, no matter how effective it is for delivering an advertising message. At a certain point, people may begin to resent its size, leading to dramatically bad SCALE.

If they resent its size they perhaps ignore its message.

A situation like this may exist in Boston, Massachusetts, where a gigantic lighted sign for a gasoline company rises more than a hundred feet (30 meters) into the air. As a sign, it's beautiful, but it's visible from just about every section within the city, and can be seen nationwide on U.S. television when games are broadcast from the nearby baseball stadium. It can even be seen through a window behind guests who are interviewed on a national news program.

When seen as simply a huge billboard, the opinion that it is *very* dramatically bad in SCALE is difficult to argue with. It's a sign that is just too big for its environment. It's taller than anything for a distance of a mile or two, and it is the center of attention in that part of the city. If we rely on a learned sense of SCALE to evaluate this sign, it's reasonable to conclude that signs are not supposed to be that huge, or that important.

But because it is nicely designed (it's really just a big logo) people who like the sign defeated an effort to have it removed. They argued the sign has become part of the cultural environment, so it apparently doesn't violate laws that limit the size of billboards. One could say that maybe people misjudge the sign's dramatically bad SCALE, believing it is, instead, dramatically good SCALE.[57]

This gasoline sign discussion illustrates one of the complex ways we react to SCALE. The question seems to be is it a billboard? Or is it a symbol of the free enterprise system we live in? If it's a gas sign, it's dramatically bad SCALE. If it's a monument to our way of life, it's dramatically good SCALE.

In any case, apparently it's here to stay since recently the sign was restored with high tech lights and electronics. But some people probably still think it's too big. If you'd like to see this sign, search images for "kenmore square sign." (Bookmark this page.)

Another example of
dramatically bad SCALE, or was it?

Since opinion about SCALE is learned, there's some weakness in any rules about it. First, as the gasoline sign suggests, people have different opinions of what is dramatically good SCALE and what is dramatically bad SCALE. And second, no matter what people believe, there is always the chance that opinions will *change*.

The interesting story of an iron tower that was erected long ago describes a situation where the opinion of just about an *entire nation* changed. The following story is true even though it occurred more than one hundred years ago,

When the tower was built it was part of a large exhibition planned to last just a few months. It was approved as a temporary structure, intended to demonstrate how strong iron is.

The tower's design was criticized even before the first sections were assembled, but the work went forward because the owners promised to dismantle it when the exhibition was finished. Even so, when the tower began to rise, practically everyone, and especially nearby artists, was ashamed of how ugly it was.

For one thing, people were embarrassed because it was visible from a huge distance away. People were outraged. They could even see it from outside the city. It was the worst case of dramatically bad SCALE ever. Again, some people protested:

"Things in cities are not supposed to be *that big!*"

But when the exhibition was over the sponsors were broke, with no money to remove the tower. So weeks and months went by as people continued to complain. Then the months turned to years, and years turned to decades (and decades recently turned to centuries) and now no one can imagine Paris without the Eiffel Tower.

Yes, that's right. The Eiffel Tower was meant to be temporary!

Of course, now it has become a much loved, respected, and even revered symbol of Paris. This became even more true after the Year 2000 New Year's Eve celebrations. I say that because, on that beautiful night, the Eiffel Tower was magnificently lit with millions of twinkling lights and fireworks.

It was breathtaking and I believe it was the most stunning of all the New Year 2000 millennium light shows broadcast around the world that memorable night.

A wonderful night to be living visually.

Nevertheless, the early protests about the Eiffel Tower were understandable not only as anxiety about it's design, but also about the first example of what eventually happened to all 20th century cities. That is to say, today, giant structures within a city, and on a city skyline, are considered normal (even though plenty of artists still find some of them to be ugly).

For more recent examples, bring to mind any skyscraper, or or else think of the London Eye, the Gateway Arch above St. Louis, Missouri, or the Space Needle in Seattle, Washington. Search internet images for these landmarks, or search for the Burj Dubai, one of the world's tallest buildings. (Bookmark this page.)

In our generation these expressions of SCALE are expected, and we've learned to accept them. But years ago, most people considered the Eiffel Tower to be very dramatically *bad* SCALE.

Apparently it may be illegal to
ignore what I'm telling you

I am trying to convince you to begin a life of visual living so I'm providing as much evidence as I can to persuade you to give it a try. For example, next time you see a picture of the Eiffel Tower, maybe you will look closer, imagining it as *temporary*.

Nevertheless, although I'm sure you'll never regret bringing the lessons of light to your life, it never occurred to me that it might be *illegal* to ignore them.

That's why I laughed once when I heard something interesting on one of those people's court TV programs, a show where folks come to complain about their landlord or their noisy neighbor.

There was apparently a dispute because a man was careless about noticing some of the details of a minor traffic accident. When the judge questioned him, he admitted he had probably overlooked something that might have made a difference in the judgement. He said, "Your honor, I guess I looked but I didn't see," which sounds pretty harmless. But to my surprise, the judge replied,

"Well, looking without seeing is *negligence!*"[58]

Of course, on one level that's just a figure of speech.

But it turns out that when a sitting judge uses those words, he is by law referring to the specific legal principle called negligence, which is defined as follows:

> Negligence: The failure to use the care a reasonable and prudent person would use *under similar circumstances.*

So don't say I didn't warn you: According to that judge that day on TV, apparently it's against the law for a reasonable and prudent person to look . . . *but not see.*

Now all I have to do is get them to include *unseeing.*

We need a law that says it's illegal to look but not unsee.

The SCALE of just us

As your visual life blossoms, watch for examples of SCALE.
Keep in mind that many frames of reference you encounter will have some visual expression that you'll subconsciously relate to the size of your own body.

* * *

For review, here are the four conditions of SCALE:

> Abstract balance
> Appropriate SCALE
> Manipulation of lifesizeness
> Dramatically good and dramatically bad SCALE

Take a moment to look for these conditions of SCALE.
You'll find they are all around, no matter where you are.

Review the exercise on page 276,
and then fill in these three blanks:

The lesson of light I promise to explore is: _____

These are two examples of that
lesson of light that I found while
doing the exercise on page 276:

1. _____

2. _____

Chapter Nine

SPACE as a source of visual experience

Dialog

APPEARING ONCE ON TV, a famous architect was asked by an interviewer, "What is the first rule of architecture?"

Normally, you'd expect his answer to be a summary of how to create well-designed buildings. Instead he said,

"The first rule of architecture is get the job."

I was a young business artist when that interview took place and, at first, I was practically offended. Like so many young artists, I had the conviction that maintaining visual principles and artistic integrity were the first rules guiding *every* visual occupation, including and especially architecture, which as mentioned earlier is often considered one of the highest visual professions.

If artists, young and old, don't stand for principles and artistic integrity, then who will?

Unfortunately, however, and although he was a well-known and talented architect, it turns out he wasn't in the least bit joking. But as I have gotten older myself, and more experienced, I can now understand why he said that.

He knew that every art and design profession is, aside from its creative character, a *job*. No matter what creative skills an artist has, they are meaningless, in financial terms, until someone hires you or commissions you, and this is particularly true for business artists. I'm sorry to say, for business artists, business sense is much more valuable than artistic skill when it comes to getting (and keeping) work. That's unfortunately true even if the work itself requires excellent visual abilities.

The result is, in terms of earning money and paying the rent, it is not unusual for a business artist to discover that business skills and *people skills* are often more valuable in the long run than visual talent. In fact, and again I'm sad to say it, this is one theme of the important novel called *"The Fountainhead,"* by Ayn Rand, a well-known book that explores artistic integrity. (Plus, it's a very romantic, adventuresome story, and you might enjoy reading it.)

Artists work in a very real world, and much of it is operated by people who are not living visually. Much of it is operated by individuals who have little or no understanding of people who *are* living visually, and what we do. That means a genuinely creative and financially successful artist must thoroughly learn both sides of the profession, the visual part *and* the people part.

As a result of this, it sometimes happens that "artists" working in business, that is, people who may actually have the title of architect, art director or designer, may possess an alarmingly poor understanding of the lessons of light, even though they are financially very successful. Their success may be anchored in the skill of "getting the job." (Or getting *their* job.)

As a way of incorporating creative thinking, including visual expression, into business problem solving, big business art firms, including ad agencies and marketing companies, often divide their staff in half. In ad agencies there are often two departments, called the creative group and the account group. The creative group carries out the creative work. But the account group, staffed by people who are trained in business skills and *people* skills, generally meets clients, and gets the assignments.

If an artist is satisfied working at the bottom of the creative group, these people skills can be sidestepped. But to rise up toward senior levels of success and income, even creative-side people need to begin meeting clients, and bringing business to the firm.

Sometimes, that's not easy for a visually sensitive individual because, again unfortunately, these kinds of people skills are different from and unrelated to art skills.

So for many artists they must be seriously studied.

Furthermore, business skills and people skills are in some ways the opposite of art ability. That means artists who are also successful at business have usually learned to be at least a little flexible in their emotional principles. They sometimes look the other way, even when they know some valid or important artistic principle is being compromised. That's the only way to play the business game according to established rules, especially in our current cultural and economic era. I say that because the times we are living in are dominated by technological revolution, and regrettably *not* by aesthetic or visual revolution, which I believe is very long overdue.

This is yet another difference between fine artists and business artists. To be successful, a fine artist would be foolish to look the other way when a visual principle is being compromised. After all, as we have said before, it is the genuine honesty of fine art that makes it worth doing. That's why it's always amusing to hear rumors about some great and talented but nevertheless furious fine artist (perhaps temporarily down on his luck) who is persuaded by some rich housewife to create a painting that matches her favorite sofa.

In a similar way it was amusing to hear many years ago that one of our great sculptors was justifiably annoyed when a reporter asked him to pose for a picture that showed him looking through a hole in one of his large abstract figures. Obviously the "hole" is an important element of SPACE in the work, and for someone to stick their head through it (God forbid it's the artist himself) shows a total *mis*understanding of the visual questions being asked.

But in everyday business life, there are unfortunately factors beyond visual integrity that need to be seriously incorporated into the daily workload. These issues sometimes include teamwork, delegating responsibility and, it should also be said, in some cases it's important to simply please the client. In business art, we try hard not to reduce work to just pleasing the client, but the truth is, it's sometimes necessary to at least take a quick look at his sofa.

Sometimes that's part of getting the job.

Anyone entering any visually creative profession (including architecture, illustration, photography, stage design, fashion design, art direction, or interiors) should know, just as that architect once said on TV, the first rule *is* get the job. (And incidentally, the second rule is keep the job.) So, if reading this book is a step for you on the road toward becoming any kind of business artist (especially a self-employed business artist), for you, if you want to survive, that's the most important lesson in this book.

However, "Help Yourself to a Blue Banana" is not primarily about how to earn your living using the visual language. Rather, it's showing you how to see (or unsee) like someone living visually.

It's showing you how to awaken your eyes to art and design and how to either experience the visual world for your own expanded enjoyment, or how to begin actually making art.

So, with that specific goal in mind, instead of the admittedly practical *get the job* rule described above, a much better answer to the question, "What is the first rule of architecture?" is this one:

What is the first rule of architecture?

The first rule of architecture is *master SPACE* –
otherwise known as the ninth lesson of light.

Lost in SPACE

Although this short and pithy statement advises you to "master SPACE," it's important to realize we're not talking here about space travel and aliens. We're not talking about outer space where rockets and astronauts go. SPACE as a lesson of light is more magical than the "emptiness" that fills most of the universe.

Much more magical.

Nevertheless, I confess here that, at some level, this chapter struggles with introducing something that is, by some definitions, invisible. For some individuals, especially those who are not accustomed to being visually active, learning to see SPACE creatively is a process much like learning to see something that is *not there*.

Experienced artists may be sorry to see such a thing written about SPACE. In fact, SPACE is as real and as visible as a red stop sign. However, any careful examination of commercial business art, including advertising, graphic design, packaging, or even architecture itself, presents a disappointing body of evidence. Our everyday environment is filled everywhere you look with visual messages and designs that are crippled by the poor expression of the SPACE that accompanies them.

Often *fatally* crippled.

Obviously SPACE is still invisible to many individuals who call themselves artists.

Many otherwise visually alert and talented people carry on their daily work as though SPACE is not there, even though SPACE is a very powerful source of visual experience.

It has the strength to attract attention to a frame of reference and create emotional meaning when it is controlled successfully.

Or, like each of the other eight sources of visual experience, SPACE can also destroy the impact of a frame of reference if it's misused or ignored.

Seeing trees, not SPACES

A familiar proverb helps to explain why SPACE sometimes seems invisible. It's the proverb about a man who can't see a forest because the trees get in his way.[59]

It may sound funny, but a simple sounding mistake like this sometimes happens when SPACE is being ignored. Sometimes people who are otherwise knowledgeable about visual matters don't see SPACE because something else gets in the way. And what gets in the way frequently are the very things that give SPACE its dimensions.

Just like trees can "hide" a forest, it is likewise possible that when someone overlooks SPACE, it's because the details that actually define the SPACE, and the details that define its frame of reference, are more easily noticed than the SPACE itself.

Just as someone may look carefully at trees without seeing the forest, someone else may look carefully at pictures on walls, but not see the three dimensional SPACE the walls are enclosing. A man may look closely at a computer in an advertisement layout, and not see the SPACE in which the ad's designer has displayed it. Someone may rush to read captions under magazine pictures, without pausing to see how the (two dimensional) SPACES on the page helped capture his attention, how it *led* him to the captions. To learn about SPACE, allow yourself and your feelings to be captured and *entertained* by every visual curiosity within view, including SPACE.

In this chapter, we'll investigate SPACE in both two dimensions and three dimensions, looking for the secrets within its power and impact. With help from your eyes, and "Help Yourself to a Blue Banana," SPACE can take its rightful place in your visual world.

SPACE, we're all in it together

For an architect, three dimensional SPACE is *the* source of visual experience. It's *the* lesson of light. We all live, work and play in SPACES, and architects are responsible for inventing the SPACES that help us do these things easier and better.

Architects enjoy a special place among artists because they often have the artistic vision to speak to us with SPACE in ways that go far beyond the visual talents of others.

After years of practice, an architect knows, for example, that SPACE (with the help of SCALE) is frequently responsible for the comfortable feeling we have when we are walking through a carefully planned building, or relaxing up in the loft bedroom of a well-designed apartment. In addition, architects know, along with anyone sensitive to the visual language, that SPACE can also be a very important part of other events.

Consider the significant contribution that SPACE can make to these experiences (imagine yourself on location at):

    . . . . a memorable theater performance,

    . . . . a visit to an English castle, or

    . . . . a stroll on deck aboard a Caribbean cruise ship.

At this minute, SPACE is *unifying* an outdoor plaza in Rome, Italy, *separating* grocery store shoppers in Chicago, Illinois, and at the same time *ruining* the layout of advertisements in Hong Kong and Sydney, Australia. We're all in SPACE together. And like it or not, see it or not, SPACE unites and/or separates everything.

But what are the special powers of SPACE, and why do people, artists included, have such a difficult time managing them?

These are very important questions.

The source of choice: Picking red,
and not green, from a big box of crayons

As we've said many times, you understand English (in other words, words) better than you understand the visual language.

So we're using words to help tell you about these things.

However, using words to describe SPACE is much harder to do. There just aren't any good explanations that go straight to the point. I can tell you SPACE is magical, wondrous and awe inspiring, and hope you believe me.

But that does not tell you *why* SPACE is magical, wondrous and awe inspiring. And if you are one of the millions of people who do not yet see SPACE that way, how can it be explained to you? Making the problem more difficult is this: Long before our eyes open for the first time inside our mother's womb, SPACE (or the lack of SPACE) is something we are already very aware of.

As soon as we're conscious of being alive, we are aware we are somewhere. Even though it's tiny, that somewhere is a SPACE.

That means, unlike other sources of visual experience, such as SCALE and CONTENT, which are primarily learned sensitivities, SPACE is something we are all aware of constantly from our first moment of consciousness.

When an infant crawls under a blanket, or she hides inside a cardboard box, the security she feels is the beginning of the same secure feeling about SPACE that an architect develops throughout a whole lifetime of work.

If you continue to look for something else in a three dimensional frame of reference, after the "objects" are accounted for, what you see is SPACE. You might say three dimensional SPACE is a sort of substance that fills the area that is left over after everything else has been considered.

"Everything else" can mean many different things.

In different frames of reference, "everything else" can be the furniture and walls of a room, the clouds and mountains seen from an airliner, the trees and bushes in a backyard, or the pews and the columns found inside a gothic cathedral, to name just a few possibilities among billions.

To become skilled at ignoring all these physical parts of the everyday world is a first step in learning to see SPACE.

Once you begin to ignore these physical objects around you, you are free to consider this fundamental truth about SPACE, which although it may sound unusual is nevertheless *true*: as simple minded as it sounds, visual artists actually *care about* how SPACE takes up an area that's left over when everything else is accounted for. We care about the *shape* of SPACE that's left over when everything else is accounted for. We care about the *size* of SPACE left over when everything else is accounted for. And we care about the *SCALE* of SPACE that is left over when everything else within a frame of reference is accounted for.

When you are comfortable with all those possibilities, then you're approaching a very big milestone in visual understanding. You're beginning to grasp how it is possible that an artist may actually care *more* about SPACE that is left over when everything else is accounted for within a frame of reference than he or she cares about *anything* or *everything else.*

You are beginning to understand this: creating a SPACE that visually and meaningfully communicates may actually completely replace an artist's *entire* interest in "everything else."

Again: Imagine: Creating SPACE that visually
           communicates in a meaningful way can totally
           replace an artist's interest in "everything else."

This ambition to express visual meaning within SPACE can replace someone's interest in DEPTH, FORM, ANATOMY, COLOR, CONTRAST, CONTENT, TEXTURE and SCALE *all put together.*

A single SPACE may express, nearly all by itself, more visual meaning than all the possible combinations of all the other lessons of light combined.

Architecture students are (hopefully) taught to comprehend this goal. When it's within reach, it means that someone who is living visually has the specific choice, the conscious option, to express SPACE as the central visual statement in his or her work. It's as liberating as a young child's freedom to pause for a moment, consider his possibilities, and then choose red instead of green from a big box of wax crayons.

Throughout centuries of architectural history, over and over, artists have chosen this special path, this freedom to communicate using SPACE, as a fundamental source of visual expression in the design of everything from cities and parks, to cathedrals and temples, to churches, stadiums, shopping malls, skyscrapers, stores and homes. You might say SPACE is the source of choice for the most significant visual expression imaginable.

Can you understand how incredible that is?

I would like to repeat the last ten paragraphs because they are *that* essential. Please re-read those important words before you continue. And highlight them with your marker.

Tunnel vision

An architect can expand this choice by relating one SPACE to other SPACES.

As we learned earlier, two COLORS side by side have a dramatic effect on each other. They change in appearance separately, and at the same time, create a new emotional tension by working together. In the same way, three dimensional SPACES which exist near one another also have an effect on each other. There can be an energy transfer between SPACES that is almost physically felt. You might discover this feeling when driving down a highway into a tunnel. You can't help notice the drastic change in your sense of SPACE as the car enters and leaves the enclosed environment.

An architect knows this same sensation, perhaps on a more subtle level, can enrich the experience of strolling through a park, or hurrying through a train station.

Even simply *looking into* beautifully designed SPACES can be satisfying. A line of sight from your front door through the SPACE of several rooms may give visitors a warm sense of welcome even before they step into your home.

In that kind of environment, the magic of SPACE (which is a magic quality that brings to life the satisfying feeling that you have *arrived* somewhere) is felt by everyone, even people who have never heard of visual living or lessons of light. Becoming aware of how your home appears to visitors, and also how it moves visitors emotionally, is a fun part of visual living.

Even if you're reading this book with no interest in creating serious visual expression, if you can, make a plan to evaluate your home or apartment when it's empty. Notice how you feel walking through rooms with no furniture, curtains, carpets or decorations. Just about every environment has at least one SPACE that is gratifying, visually speaking, if it's left that way, with nothing in it.

Many elements can invest an otherwise empty SPACE with this kind of unique power. For example, the light from a window, the TEXTURE of a wood floor, the SCALE of the ceiling's height, the COLOR of walls or the peek-a-boo elegance of French style doors.

These are each interior designs all by themselves.

Each can magnify both the expression of a SPACE and also the *experience* of a SPACE.

They help a person experience an emotional connection to SPACE probably without realizing it. These kinds of visual details *cause* a person to experience a SPACE.

Sometimes, nothing else is needed.

SPACE can single-handedly create this variety of very special atmosphere, an atmosphere that will speak beautifully through the visual language sometimes in very unexpected ways.

Consider this right now:

Look up from reading. Perhaps the room in which you are sitting at this very moment, even if it's not empty, has some of these special characteristics that enhance or modify SPACE. Wherever you are sitting, take a moment to experience SPACE in these special ways. Overlook every *thing* that is in the room and allow yourself to notice only the SPACE itself. Sense the SPACE in three dimensions, noticing the width of the room in both directions, and the SPACE as it fills the room from floor to ceiling.

Get more familiar with SPACE.

Do this right now before you continue to read.

Remembering SPACES

Everyone's first surprise about SPACE comes when it suddenly expands at our birth. We must be pleased to find it's possible to
survive without our mother's womb surrounding us. If we could talk,
we might ask, "How much bigger is this new SPACE, compared to
the crowded one I've been living in?"

Although we can't remember our birth, artists do sometimes
remember other childhood moments or successes which may have
indicated visual progress. Some of these are memories of SPACES.
If you have visual talent that has not yet blossomed, remembering
creative moments from your childhood may provide clues. You may
have quietly embarked on a journey to visual living many years ago.

I remember examples of my own. When I was about nine, I
made a calendar. I wrote "JUNE" on top of a page with outlined letters. Then I drew sides for each of the letters so they appeared three
dimensional. I was surprised to see what I'd done. I believe that was
the first time I tried to draw DEPTH (perspective).

I once rearranged all the furniture in my bedroom, including a
bookcase, so the room was divided in two. It made SPACES for
sleeping and for working. How the SPACES flowed into one another was nice. It gave a sense of security and was practical, a kid's try
at creating a centered SPACE (a process we'll read about shortly).

Here's another memory: While attending college, I went to
Europe with fourteen classmates. They were music students, invited to perform for overseas American military personnel. I was an
amateur drummer and had the opportunity to travel with them. This
was a special thrill for me because I was raised in the U.S. military.

We visited several countries.

In one city, our host took us sight-seeing in a motorcoach. We
stopped near a church and she explained it was a special place of
worship. We were all friends, talking about things we saw.

So without thinking I said sincerely, *"It's an ugly church."*

My music friends, more interested in music than visual living,
forgot I was studying architecture. Even so, they were embarrassed
and confused. I'm sure they wondered,

"What difference does it make even if it *is* ugly?"

I don't think she heard me, but I had been rude to our tour
guide. However for anyone who is living visually, if a church, a temple or mosque doesn't show the significance of God in a beautiful or
meaningful visual and emotional way, it *does* make a difference.

Of course that's no excuse. My comment was still out of line. And furthermore, looking back, I assume it's likely that church *was* visually meaningful, even beautiful, but in a way or style I didn't yet understand. Nevertheless, whatever that church was or wasn't, I'm still very proud those things mattered to me at a very young age.

Many artists recall experiences at earlier ages. A famous fashion designer remembers, at five years old, being somehow magically influenced by a pair of his mother's red shoes.[60] And consider this: I suspect almost everyone has memories of thoughtfully organizing school books inside their desk, or else in that little storage area under the seat. Or of customizing the inside of a hallway locker.

These are early adventures in "designing" (small) SPACES.

I was frequently distracted by the desk thing, always setting up small compartments for pencils and other supplies. I used school books (especially those big flat geography books) as dividers and shelves, which made them conveniently unavailable for studying.

Searching your childhood memories may hint that some ideas you're reading about in this book are not completely new to you.

The opposite can be true as well. Looking back, I can see my young journey was sometimes *way off track*. For example, for a time I was very confused by abstract expression. I couldn't understand what it said, so I assumed it said nothing. I wondered if it could just be a joke, as one of my students suggested years later. I made up a dumb rule. I agreed (with myself) that nobody's abstract expression had meaning unless that person could also create lots of good non-abstract work (that is, work I felt I could comfortably evaluate).

Of course that's ridiculous. An artist can legitimately work for an entire lifetime using *nothing but* abstractions.

It's not necessary to *ever* create non-abstract work.[*]

And yet another error in my thinking:

For a time I believed visual expression had to originate from the isolated imagination of the artist. If someone was a real artist, then no copying or tracing or borrowing or "cheating" of any kind was acceptable. No drawing or painting from life, no referring to photographs (let alone actually using them) and no looking at *how to create art* books. Real art was done all from memory and feeling and instinct, using only your personal visual repertoire as a guide.

Otherwise, or so I believed, it was all bogus.

[*] However, I'm not the only person who ever gave this some thought. Andy Rooney, the American TV commentator, likewise suggested that artists should be required to demonstrate some proficiency in non-abstractions before exhibiting abstract work. The examples he used *did show* that many amateur "artists" are in fact incompetent in abstractions. From *60 Minutes*, television broadcast of July 6, 2008.

However, as you may guess, that's even more laughable.

All artists (even great artists), copy everything, including one another. And may I add, *constantly*. (Even so, the hard part doesn't change. It's still necessary to find new questions while taking inspiration from someone else.)

But again, even though those were all misguided ideas, I am proud these things mattered to me at a very young age, stupid rules included. No matter how old you are, cherish what visual opinions you have, even if they turn out wrong. They are part of the process, part of the discovery, and hopefully part of the fun of becoming a person who is living visually.

Trying to work in a warm environment

Eventually I overcame all those wayward ideas. But even as an adult professional artist, I had other slip-ups now and then, and some were about how to behave in a business environment. This is a frequent problem for business artists, as business practices sometimes seem tedious, illogical or even bizarre. So here's how I once bounced off business procedures in a curious sounding way:

I was offered a position at a large ad agency and they gave me an office whose walls needed to be painted. One wall in particular was very dirty and scratched. On my first day, someone apologized saying that if I was patient, they planned to paint the whole agency. I wasn't comfortable with it but I held out for a while. Then, as things started going very well for me there, and since dirty walls don't mix well with visual living, I got the idea that I might come in on a Saturday and paint the wall myself.

Using hindsight, it would have been much *(much)* smarter to lobby my boss to get it done. That would have demonstrated a (non art) skill that most businesses (and most bosses) admire.

But it's a skill I unfortunately did not yet have.

So I painted the wall a warm white and it really did the trick. It was a light blush COLOR (white with a touch of red in it) and, like some COLORS I mentioned earlier, it was more felt than seen. It made the SPACE very lively and my spirit picked up. The following Monday morning people definitely noticed, saying something in my office was different, and better. But they couldn't say what until I directed their attention to the freshly painted wall. I was happy and I got busy in the new glow that surrounded everything.

But the next Monday morning, it was *me* who sensed something different. Over the weekend, the maintenance man had paint-ed over my new warm wall with regulation white. At that odd com-pany, apparently a dirty wall was ok but a refreshing COLOR, even barely noticeable, was not.

Although it is becoming less common, there are still some ad agencies that encourage art directors to show imagination in their cubicles and work stations. But in our technology-and-business ori-ented economy, logical as it sounds (because art directors probably work better in creative SPACES) that liberty is often not granted. In any case, for whatever reason, the agency that painted over my nice wall shortly went out of business.

One more thought about working as a business artist: A few years ago there was a theory circulating, based in part on truth, and in part on fiction. It went like this: All the male writers and art direc-tors at big advertising agencies were giving up long hair and blue jeans in order to look and dress like bankers. They were hoping to impress their new bosses, a new generation of *real* bankers who, so it seemed, were then taking over the advertising industry.

But, so the story goes, in just a few short years this was no longer necessary. The reason was, by that time all the writers and art directors in the big agencies *were* bankers.

* * * *

Chapter nine continued
AN INTRODUCTION TO SPACE
The ninth lesson of light
I challenge you to experience it

As young children, we don't learn about SPACE in the same way we learn about SCALE, for example. There is not a moment in youth when a comment from your father makes you aware of the importance of SPACE. SPACE is such an enormous part of visual life, that it is, for practical purposes, taken for granted by everyone, including parents. Since it is always there, it becomes, in a way, *invisible*. And as a result, finding a way to bring SPACE back to con-scious awareness is a major challenge on the path to visual living.

There is no easy way to do that. Getting into the habit of notic-ing SPACE, and then perhaps speaking through it as one lesson of light, may well take years of gradual progress. But as an introduc-tion, it will help you to know that SPACE exists in two basic ways.

If you are conscious of these distinctions, you won't be confused or surprised to hear an interior designer (or an architect) talk about SPACE quite differently from the way an artist who creates oil paintings or advertisements talks about SPACE.

The reason is, an interior designer is concerned with SPACE in three dimensions, which, as we have already discussed, is that kind of "nothingness" that remains when everything else is accounted for (like the air inside your living room remains after you have accounted for the furniture, walls, ceiling and floor).

On the other hand, an oil painter, advertising art director or a designer of internet pages will be more sensitive to SPACE in two dimensions, as the area of a surface (like a page inside a magazine or the screen of a monitor) that isn't occupied by anything else. (For example, the margins on this page are, visually speaking, simple two dimensional SPACES within the frame of reference of the pages you are reading.) Two dimensional SPACE is also any empty area inside the frame of reference of any photograph, painting or printed design, including brochures, advertisements, posters and signs.

That doesn't mean an interior designer is never interested in two dimensional SPACE, or a painter is never interested in three dimensional SPACE. As artists they'll find both important.

To do their work, interior designers need to know about two dimensional SPACE when they choose art for the walls of their interiors, and painters need to know how to recreate the impact of three dimensional SPACE on a flat surface. (To do that, they can call upon the conditions of DEPTH we learned earlier.)

There's no end to
three dimensional SPACE

I heard several years ago that all the gold everywhere would fit inside an area, a storage vault let's say, that's only fifty feet (15 meters) in each direction. That's the size of a small building that is fifty feet across the front, fifty feet deep, and about five stories high.[61]

I like that statistic because it helps make it easier to understand something that seems unknowable, that is, how much gold there is. It means, if we could gather together all the gold, we could actually see it at a glance. To put it another way, all that gold would fit inside the White House. (There's a thought.)

It makes you aware of just how special, and *rare*, gold is.

In the same way, I'd like to be able to glance at all the three dimensional SPACE in the world. That way, we'd have a feeling for how special this ninth lesson of light is also. That's something everyone needs to know, because we commonly take SPACE *too much for granted.* Since we're born into SPACE and never leave it, we never think it over. SPACE always was and always will be. You can close your eyes to stop seeing SCALE or FORM or COLOR, but there's no getting away from SPACE. Even when we're sleeping, we're experiencing SPACE. Even when you're asleep, you're still *in* SPACE.

Unfortunately, however, we can't say all the SPACE in existence would fit in the White House. All of SPACE wouldn't fit inside *anything.* The reason is, unlike gold, there is no end to SPACE, starting with all of the air that's around our planet. In order to grasp how important this is, it helps to realize that even when there doesn't seem to be anything else to see, there will always be SPACE. Even if you are lying on your back on a football field, looking straight into the blue sky of a cloudless afternoon, SPACE is still filling the "emptiness" above you. And in that situation, with your eyes wide open, SPACE would be the source of your visual experience, along with the COLOR blue.

But just like other lessons of light, there is a place we "put" SPACE when we want to express with it. That place is, of course, a frame of reference. But, consider this odd sounding fact: unlike the other sources of visual experience, such as COLOR for example, it's not necessary to move SPACE from one place to another when it's needed in a frame of reference. The reason is, speaking generally, SPACE is always created, in either two dimensions or three dimensions, *every time a frame of reference comes into existence.*

That needs to be repeated (and highlighted):

> SPACE is always created, in either two
> dimensions or three dimensions, *every time*
> *a frame of reference comes into existence.*

That's to say, with very few exceptions, the act of defining a frame of reference produces SPACE. But the problem is even bigger. Here's why. If one decides to use COLOR, that is, if we decide to express with COLOR, we can just pick up a paint brush, a marker, a package of pansy seeds or our computer mouse and *put* COLOR where we want it. If we don't want COLOR, we can simply put the brush or the pansy seeds away. But not so with SPACE.

The reason is SPACE exists everywhere *already.*

In the creative process, we don't actually create SPACE.

Rather, we only move it from here to there.

A fallout of this is that the explanation for poorly designed SPACES is often not very complicated. They usually occur because someone has focused too strongly, too exclusively, or just too carelessly, on the other lessons of light, while SPACE is ignored. When an artist, or anyone else, makes that mistake, crummy SPACES are what we're left with.

This can happen to anybody, not just to artists. Even in your home, you have to keep an eye on SPACES as you add furniture (FORM) and other lessons of light to your environment.

Here are some common enemies of SPACE: wall paper, carpets, framed pictures, and light fixtures. We said earlier that these things can, at times, enhance a SPACE, especially an empty SPACE, but they can likewise destroy it. (Only your eyes can tell you which is happening.) They can all easily overwhelm the magic that is trying to live in the open SPACES you begin with.

Again, these are not trivial things to anyone living visually. An architect who conceives four walls, a floor and a ceiling *knows* he is bringing to life a frame of reference for a room that already has three dimensional SPACE in it. And in the next section, we'll also see how the same is true for artists who work in two dimensions.

This relationship that exists between SPACE and frames of reference explains why there are always so many SPACES to worry about in practically any visual process. Whatever our decisions and goals are about the emotional impact we hope to create, no one has the luxury of deciding beforehand how they will introduce SPACE into a frame of reference. Every visual statement must actively deal with SPACE from the moment its frame of reference is identified or conceived. Therefore (and this is set apart here for you to highlight):

If we decide to subdue SPACE, we must *actively* subdue it.
If we decide to express with it, we must consciously assert it.

That's why it's important for anyone who is exploring visual expression, especially professionally, to learn about SPACE not only to speak through it in a frame of reference, but more importantly (especially for beginning professionals) to prevent it from crippling the strengths of the other sources of visual experience.

Forgetting to consider the impact, good or bad, of SPACES within a frame of reference is one of the most common weaknesses throughout all visual arts.

What that means is, we cannot allow automatic SPACES to simply remain unattended. Like each lesson of light, SPACE has to be consciously controlled or it will detract from the visual expression trying to be born. It will distract from the impact of the visual information being communicated.

That's one particularly bothersome problem in architecture, where three dimensional SPACE frequently *is* the visual information that is being communicated. For example, another architect once explained how the huge SPACE that visitors walk into, after touring a presidential memorial he designed, *is* the monument to the president. There are no busts or statues of the famous man, and no photographs or paintings of him either. The majesty and power of the SPACE *alone*, the architect says, serves as a profound memorial to the deceased man and his accomplishments.

If you saw this environment after gaining an understanding of three dimensional SPACE, you would agree it does communicate that message perfectly. However, true to the nature of the architect's vision, the message is presented in the visual language, not an intellectual language (for example, through the CONTENT of a painting of the president). And, of course, if you wish to fully experience it, you must be familiar with that language. In this case, it means having an understanding of the emotional power that SPACE can deliver as a source of visual experience.

The same architect explained that his design for an entrance and reception building, which is basically a huge glass pyramid, in the courtyard of a well-known older museum, is appropriate. There is controversy about it because the existing museum buildings were designed many years earlier in a classic style, very different from the new addition. The new building has open and sun filled SPACES, ready to psychologically prepare visitors for the crowds in the existing museum galleries. He said the first experience guests should feel is one of openness and "SPACE-iousness," even though the remainder of the museum (built years before) cannot and does not carry on that same feeling.[62]

Centered SPACE and three dimensions

But how can someone who is living visually evaluate three dimensional SPACE? How do we judge that a SPACE is successful, and is doing "visual work" in a frame of reference? To put it simply, how do we know a SPACE is communicating emotional meaning to us through the visual language? One answer is this: we often judge SPACE by evaluating how *centered* it seems to be.

Trying to exactly define a "centered" SPACE is yet another exercise where words won't fully cooperate. But there are two characteristics that come to mind. First, a centered SPACE is in abstract balance with the other lessons of light. And second, we sense we can control it. Allow me to repeat:

> A centered SPACE is in abstract balance with the other lessons of light. And a centered SPACE is one we sense that we can control.

A centered SPACE has a rightness that is seen and felt.

This rightness can be sensed from a distance or can be experienced as we walk, stand, sit, fly, drive, pray, swim, run, kneel, lay down, dance or sleep within it. A successfully centered SPACE can bring the human senses to a higher level of experience. For example, in a centered SPACE, COLORS are just right, CONTENT is not overwhelming, and there's a sensation of correctness that can be felt through all five of our senses.

There is a feeling of truthfulness through the SPACE that is anchored within its relationship with the other lessons of light.

As a result of all this pleasantness, in a centered SPACE you might feel the taste of food is more satisfying, the smells of perfume are more pleasing and music is more exciting to hear, or seems to be more soothing to your ears.

There are many three dimensional SPACES that can offer a "centered" feeling such as this. Some examples might be the thrill of sitting in the front row *center(ed!)* at a concert. Or standing on center stage yourself, facing into the theater. You might also find centered SPACE at a table by a window in a well-designed restaurant, or near the bandstand in a club.

In addition, this kind of SPACE is what we love about the carpeted area directly in front of a roaring fireplace or about standing on a balcony that overlooks a park. In fact, you can experience centered SPACE on just about any mountain or hill that overlooks everything else. Architects and interior designers bring these environments to life intentionally, or mother nature can surprise us with centered SPACES created by natural geography.

At one time I lived in an apartment whose large rooftop deck was open on three sides. It was an ordinary apartment house on an ordinary street. But by chance, the building was located at the center of a horseshoe-shaped range of low mountains. The ANATOMY there was very similar to the giant open theaters you may have read about in ancient times. The feeling I experienced while standing on that deck was much like standing on an immense stage. The sensation was created because centered visual energy filled the SPACE all around it, all the way to the hilltops. I loved that roof deck.

Other experiences of centered SPACES might include standing at the altar of a church while getting married, or the excitement of water skiing or swimming across a still lake. These special feelings about three dimensional SPACE are experienced by everyone, not just artists. But an architect, to be sure, is interested in bringing these benefits into *every* SPACE he or she creates, whether it's a new athletic stadium, the conference room in an office building or even the checkout counter at your local supermarket.

Loft in Space

A second characteristic of "centered" SPACE is:
We feel it is under our control.

When a SPACE seems "centered," you'll sense that you *can* control it (which is something your eyes judge) and that you *do* control it (which is something your intellect will tell you). People love SPACES such as this where there is a glow of pleasant and secure emotional energy. A child rushes into a cozy play house and is overcome with glee. A sports fan hurries into a huge stadium where electricity fills the air. SPACE is working its magic.

An apartment that I know of has a loft bedroom with a lower than usual ceiling. In the loft, there's a corner for sitting, plus an area for lounging, and a double bed with shelves next to it. One wall of the loft opens to the living area in the apartment below. It's a very comfortable SPACE, with many "places," but except for the stair landing, there's no other area there high enough to stand up in.

You might describe the loft as cozy, and people who have visited there don't miss the higher ceilings found elsewhere in the apartment. There's something satisfying about the reduced SCALE. It makes people feel larger than life, like "goofy" SCALE at Disney World (see page 287). The SPACE in the loft is centered and everyone who goes there seems to like it.

That's why I was surprised when I heard the young woman living in it had once been reading a frightening novel in bed, and felt a need to leave the light on in the stairway up to the loft. My visual curiosity was awakened. I wondered: how can someone be scared in a SPACE that's so visually comfortable? Can a nice feeling created by a centered SPACE be ruined by bad thoughts? I wondered the opposite also. Can someone's mood (or courage) be improved by a visually comfortable SPACE? I suspect both answers are yes.

When talking about it a few days later, she said a book she was reading *was* frightening. As a result, she wanted the light on all night. It's true, she said, the feeling of security in the loft was comforting no matter what she was reading, as long as she stays in the bed. But things change if she has to get up during the night. Anxiety starts if she needs to leave the loft, to *move through* the SPACE, and return, "not knowing," she said, "what may have crept up there."

When she returns to bed, she inspects the loft to be certain that nothing has moved in with her. Then she gets back in the bed, which ends the worrying. The interesting thing is that no real danger ever exists in that loft. People will feel safe and comfortable in a SPACE designed to be that way. But intellectual doubt, brought by an active imagination, or a scary book, can change that feeling.

Maybe it's possible for people who scare easily to overcome some fear by relying more on visual senses, because visual information is not as easy to distort in our mind as intellectual thought.

This not a new idea, or even close to it.

2000 years ago, Julius Caesar said, "As a rule, what is out of sight disturbs men's minds more seriously than what they see." And Leonardo da Vinci himself was even more specific when he told us, "the eye makes fewer mistakes than the mind."[63]

No matter who you are, where you are, what you're doing or when you're alive, three dimensional SPACE is *always* part of every moment. Since it is so incredibly important, and always around, it's understandable why architects and interior designers have the habit of noticing exactly what makes a SPACE enjoyable or what makes it unpleasant. They notice why a table by the window in a café is so satisfying, and what makes it different from another table that's *not* by a window. An architect might investigate why it's such a pleasure to sit on the 50 yard line at a football game, and *not* a pleasure to sit behind the end zone. If we can learn what power those places possess, and *why*, it can be captured and brought to life again, anytime and anywhere.

That means with just a little bit of collecting, you can actually recognize, yourself, this special energy SPACE has. I'm sure you can find it even in places you visit everyday. Then, once you "get it," you can purposefully bring it into your own home, just as an architect brings it to a high speed rail station she designs. This transformation within SPACE might be accomplished by simply opening up a wall in your living room, or moving a bookcase, rearranging some furniture, adding a window, or raising (or even lowering) a ceiling.

At your next opportunity, bring visual curiosity into play as you explore a centered SPACE like those described. You'll discover lessons of light exist in a sort of harmony when a SPACE seems centered. These special SPACES are in abstract balance with the other sources of visual experience.

Wherever you are right now, take a moment once again to evaluate your SPACE, this time to see if it is centered. What's the verdict? Take a moment away from reading to wonder about this.

Two dimensional SPACE

As its name suggests, two dimensional SPACE is expressed on flat surfaces. It is big part of every printed page, painting, postage stamp, book jacket, poster, parking ticket, diploma, business card, party invitation or advertisement to name just several of the many places you'll find it. As you would imagine, two dimensional SPACE shares many of the powers and characteristics of the other sources of visual experience, including those of her three dimensional sister.

However, there is a significant difference worth noting.

Whereas three dimensional SPACE has the magic power to replace an artist's complete interest in the other lessons of light (see page 303), two dimensional SPACE does not have such special status. There's no way I have seen to muster the strength of two dimensional SPACE on a canvas or a web page so that it easily dwarfs COLOR, TEXTURE and DEPTH or the other lessons of light. And there are not any masterpiece paintings in the museums that I am aware of whose emotional life comes mostly from the expression of pure two dimensional SPACE (partly, yes, but not mostly).

Although that is a difference between these visual relatives, there is likewise a similarity that they share. That's the problematic issue, already discussed, about how SPACE is always created whenever a frame of reference comes into existence. When we are working with two dimensional visual expression, this reality needs to be constantly addressed.

It is such an issue in two dimensions,
that I repeat here what was written earlier:

This relationship between SPACE and frames
of reference explains why there are always so many
SPACES to worry about in practically any visual
process. Whatever our decisions and goals are about
the emotional impact we hope to create, artists do not
have the luxury of deciding beforehand how they will
introduce SPACE into a frame of reference. Every
visual statement must actively deal with SPACE from
the moment its frame of reference is identified or
conceived. If we decide to subdue SPACE, we must
actively subdue it. And if we decide to express with
it, we must consciously assert it.

In two dimensional expression, this means that a fine artist
who stretches a canvas is creating a "frame" (of reference) that has
an automatic amount of SPACE inside it. This action *creates* SPACE.
Likewise, a business artist who drags a rectangle on a computer
monitor, to serve as frame of reference for a poster or a coupon, creates a rectangle that already has two dimensional SPACE in it.

The effort needed to control all the two dimensional SPACE
that is created in the process of bringing visual expression to life is
sometimes overwhelming.

Pain in Spain

For example, here's the story of a design that was ruined by
two dimensional SPACES. Even though many years have passed
since this happened, I was still defensive about it just two weeks
ago as I retold these details to a friend.

Early in my career I was the business artist for a hotel located
off a highway. The manager asked me to design a big sign for the
highway at the exit to the hotel. At first, I thought my layout looked
good, but then, after the billboard company enlarged it to 30 feet (10
meters) across, something was drastically wrong.

Overall the sign was not in good abstract balance and, also,
dramatically bad SCALE appeared from nowhere. That's sometimes

a problem when a sketch is enlarged so much. But beyond that, and again overall, I felt the sign had a visible weakness about it.

When the layout was enlarged, the type and COLORS were not as impressive as I felt they should be. Even more troubling was one more difficulty. Many awkward two dimensional SPACES crippled the design. They made it very hard to read, especially in the few seconds it was visible as cars whizzed by.

There were uneven SPACES around the words and pictures, and other SPACES were also awkward and not balanced. You could say the finished sign had the *Curse of Graphula,* which is a kind of visual disease made out of SPACES. The Curse of Graphula gives people the urge to ignore, *to turn their eyes away from,* something that has it. It's a problem that often affects graphic design.

I knew that huge sign had it. I was sure drivers coming down the road were ignoring the information because the SPACES confused the message. Plus the sign was too wordy and I thought it was obvious that it didn't have effective marketing impact.

I expected to be criticized.

But to my surprise, although I wanted to redesign it (to simplify it), when I made that suggestion to the manager, he ignored me and even said, "Don't worry, it's a job *well done!"*

The compliment fell on (my) deaf ears. I was annoyed and I knew the sign was unsuccessful.

Then a few days later, the manager called me again.

I hoped he was ready to agree but, after a warm greeting, he explained how he was planning to put up six more signs just like it! When I protested again, we agreed to disagree, and of course he put up the new billboards anyway.

The result is, even today I am happy those seven signs were in a remote part of Spain, where I left them far behind. Despite what Caesar and Leonardo said (see above), in this case something out of sight was definitely *less* disturbing to my mind.[64]

As I retold this story to my friend, he was surprised I felt so strongly about it. "That was many years ago," he said, "and besides, what was so wrong? Your client was happy."

But his comment just reminded me how someone who is living visually can feel *very* strongly about things that aren't important to other people. There are times you'll have an inner voice that suggests what is ok and what is *not* ok.

It's separate from other people's opinions.

And, of course, my advice is: *listen to that voice.*

The Curse of Graphula

The billboard story is about a design that suffered from the Curse of Graphula. The Curse of Graphula is the gigantic mass of cluttered and unorganized two dimensional SPACES that just ruin visual meaning practically everywhere you look. It's why plenty of advertisements never get noticed, and it affects just about every situation in which words need to be read, including everything from packages on a store shelf to the menus in a restaurant to billboards along highways. This single weakness is responsible for more lost communication than any other problem in graphic design.

It results from the difficulty people have, artists included, of seeing two dimensional SPACES, which are just as "hard to see," as their three dimensional sisters. So it's not very surprising that many artists pay no special attention to them. But, unfortunately, even people who can't see them react by ignoring any messages that busy SPACES clutter up and destroy.

I'll try to explain why.

Just like all the paragraphs you see printed on this page, any written words have necessary SPACES around them that help guide the eye. The first lines of paragraphs are indented to show us where a new thought begins, and whole blocks of copy are separated from each other by SPACES that help clarify the message.

At first, it may seem these SPACES are not important in our understanding of information. After all, you may say, "people read words not SPACES, so what real difference does it make how the SPACES look?" But an art director or business artist who works in advertising or publishing will testify that people do "read" SPACES. And the more simple the SPACES appear, and the fewer meaningless SPACES there are, the easier it is for people to read the words.

And even more important, the more simple the SPACES are, the more likely it is that people will *think* the words will be easy to understand. That is typically an evaluation that people make even before they begin to read. To put it as directly as possible: people are more willing to read a simple looking message than a busy looking message, and this is often a totally unconscious evaluation.

In fact, by carefully organizing SPACES in a two dimensional layout, a designer hopes people will begin to read the words *even before they have decided to read them!* That's why work of one graphic designer may be worth more than the work of another designer simply because the first knows how to organize SPACES in this way.

A poster or advertisement designed by an artist who is familiar with SPACE will be read by many more people. This process of making two dimensional SPACES "work" is part of the "magic" of visual expression, a power hidden within the visual language that we discussed in the first chapter. (If you are already a graphic designer, or want to become one, highlight this paragraph because it can earn you lots and lots of money.)

Although these characteristics about SPACE affect all varieties of printed graphic design and electronic communications from advertisements to postage stamps (as well as paintings, drawings, web pages and photographs), they're especially important on a billboard. A person driving a car must make a quick judgment. He must decide to begin reading as he drives past. He may even need to decide to actually turn off the road (remember the hotel sign). That means that if a sign, an advertisement, a business card, a brochure cover, a logo, a clock face, a computer screen, a book jacket or a billboard looks too complicated, *people will simply ignore it*. And messy SPACES, the Curse of Graphula, is usually why it happens.

You can prove this by reading a newspaper. Try to become conscious of an advertisement after you begin reading it. Then look around on the same page. Usually, you will discover that the ad you unconsciously began to read is more simple looking than other similarly sized ads seen on the same page. You will probably notice its SPACES are more even and clean than the SPACES in other ads around it (meaning the words are organized more neatly also). As you look at the other ads, remember that most people who are reading that newspaper are *also* ignoring those ads, just as you did.

Students can demonstrate how any unorganized web page, for example, has the Curse of Graphula. They first put see-through plastic (like kitchen plastic wrap) over the monitor's screen and then use a red marker to draw circles around all the SPACES on the visible page. If a SPACE flows smoothly into another SPACE, the two SPACES are included together in one odd-shaped circle. But if there is a SPACE lost somewhere by itself, at the end of a short sentence, let's say, that SPACE gets its own red circle. When all the SPACES are recorded on the plastic, a line is drawn around the frame of reference (the edge of the screen), and then the plastic is laid upon a sheet of white paper.

What's left on the plastic is a kind of graphic "map" showing all the SPACES. A beautiful and effective page will usually have only four or five circles inside it's frame of reference. But a cluttered page, that is, a page people may never seriously read, can have as many as fifteen or twenty circles (SPACES). In addition, an effective page will usually have SPACES that display abstract balance, which means the scribbled red circles on the plastic look almost as well organized as the page itself. A page that suffers from the Curse of Graphula will have a "map" that is as unorganized as the mess it represents. You can evaluate any newspaper or magazine ad in the same way by putting plastic (or tracing paper) on top of the ad.

You will see what I mean if you try these experiments.

By the way, the cover of this book has fairly good abstract balance and no curse of graphula.

Small print about negative
SPACE in two dimensions

Those of us working in visual arts hear about it all the time.

But despite the misconception, allow me to clarify that there is *no such thing* as negative SPACE.

SPACE is not negative, and it's not positive either.

It just *is*.

The idea that artists should be sensitive to "negative" space in two dimensional visual expression has been around forever. But this unfortunate use of words only serves to suggest there is something deficient about SPACE (i.e. it's *negative*) when compared to other lessons of light. In fact, if anything is true, the opposite.

Given the right circumstances, all lessons command extraordinary and equal visual power. So it is more useful you to be sensitive to nine varieties of visual impact, and to them as equals. Then you can politely correct anyone who that SPACE is negative because there is *no such thing* as negative SPACE, just as there is no such thing as negative COLOR, or negative FORM or negative TEXTURE.

Nothing's anything unless
it's in SPACE

Our human lives are defined by the time that we individually occupy SPACE. Of course, before the womb, before we "are," we take up no SPACE. Then, small as it is, our mother's womb is our first SPACE, and then at birth we find a much larger SPACE.

In turn, what happens when we die?

We are taken from a large SPACE and usually put in another small SPACE, where we may be for a while (or forever). But eventually each of us again stops occupying any SPACE whatsoever.

Ashes to ashes and dust to dust.

Ashes become dust, and dust becomes nothing.

That seems to mean that SPACE justifies everything.

No matter if someone or some thing is living or not living, from the vantage of human visual perception, there's no more fundamental requirement for existence than a need to occupy SPACE.

That helps to validate the leading role played by SPACE as the most preeminently visible actor within a world that's majestically teeming with visual expression and the nine lessons of light.

* * * *

For review, remember:

SPACE exists in two dimensions and three dimensions
SPACE is always created whenever any frame
    of reference comes into existence
There's no such thing as negative SPACE

Please take time to re-visit the exercise on page 255, searching magazines and books for pictures to describe, using the lessons of light. You should now be able to identify each of these important sources of visual evidence within everything you see. Take time to practice identifying the lessons of light in random images, and in the actual world that surrounds you as you carry on your daily life.

If you've resisted searching for the internet images referred to throughout the last nine chapters, now is the time to revisit your bookmarks and study those examples. To make this easier, I have relisted all of those suggested searches on pages 332 – 339.

❖

Some great news:

NOW THAT YOU HAVE FINISHED "HELP YOURSELF TO A BLUE BANANA," YOU HAVE PERMISSION TO AWAKEN YOUR EYES TO ART, DESIGN AND VISUAL LIVING. TAKE ADVANTAGE OF IT! OPEN YOUR EYES TO THE LESSONS OF LIGHT. LOOK UP FROM READING AND WELCOME YOURSELF TO A WORLD OVERFLOWING WITH LIFESTYLE POSSIBILITIES THAT ARE VISUALLY ABUNDANT AND FULFILLING. WHAT A WONDERFUL MOMENT!

Don't re-read this book

You have probably been told or taught that one way to gain better understanding of new material is to review it right after your first experience with it. That happens to be true, but it can also be boring. Who wants to go back into a book the minute it's finished?

I know another way to do it, *an easy way to review this book.*

I give this assignment to my art students who are using this book to study the lessons of light. But it works even better, I think, if you read "Help Yourself to a Blue Banana" *without* attending art school, even if you found it in a library, or received it as a gift.

Here's what I mean. Don't review each chapter. Instead, find one friend or family member you can explain the lessons of light to.

Explain this to your brother, sister, roommate, best friend, mother or father. Ask if they wouldn't mind listening as you review some information. You should have no trouble keeping their attention as you explain how visual expression is made of nine elements called lessons of light. Give details of what you mean. Find a picture to evaluate, or look out a window, with your "student" beside you. It shouldn't take long. You can do this in as few as nine minutes, taking one minute for each lesson of light.

Don't overlook anything important.

As a guide, use the summary that appears on page 330.

Some readers have remarkable success with this.

At times, because your explanation is so engaging, your student may ask to borrow or purchase the book. They'll thank you!

When you become a teacher of the lessons of light, you give this information a special place in your heart, a place reserved for knowledge you'll cherish the rest of your life. And you'll help someone else discover the enjoyment of visual living.

You can teach your mini art class before you check out the suggested internet searches (to help out, a review of them begins at the bottom of page 332), or else, invite your student to do those searches with you. Then, if you decide to re-read the book anyway, or to spend time reviewing chapters you liked, you will be ahead of yourself in allowing the lessons of light permanently into your life.

If you'd like, you can write a report on how successful your teaching experience is and email it to me. I'd love to read about it!

Plan your class now. I have provided a place to keep some brief notes about your experience on page 339. If you'd like to teach the lessons of light to more than one person, email me first.

A F T E R W O R D

What you haven't learned
in the previous nine chapters

Earlier I said the lessons of light are how artists see, but I also said they are far from being *why* artists see. Likewise, they are also far away from explaining the individual style in which an artist expresses, or the individual talent he or she demonstrates.

Any effort to create visual expression is uniquely influenced by the hand of the artist. The result is that one painting that finds meaning in DEPTH, FORM and CONTENT is not necessarily equal to another that also expresses meaning in the same three lessons of light. The same can be said for two brochure designs, two labels for a peanut butter jar or the layouts for two party invitations.

In their own way, they may all express with DEPTH, FORM and CONTENT. But even so, it's very possible that one will exhibit breathtaking genius, while the other ones waste our time. The difference may be nothing more than talent. The lessons of light are the best way to describe visual expression regardless of the ability of the artist. But talent itself is a different issue.

There is a work of art in the history of painting that helps us to explain this. Let me tell you about it.

Leonardo da Vinci (also mentioned earlier) was a great artist and inventor who lived five hundred years ago. Fortunately many of his works are still surviving to demonstrate his extraordinary talent, including the *Mona Lisa*. But another, earlier, painting allows us to compare Leonardo's work, side by side, with work of another artist. It gives us a comparison of Leonardo's talent with the talent of a fellow artist who was painting almost the same subject, and at the same moment in history.

I'm referring to a painting called *The Baptism of Christ* which came to life in 1472. As was very customary in that era, *The Baptism of Christ* is a collaborative effort, painted by a famous artist named Andrea de Verrocchio, with help from his younger studio assistants, among them Leonardo.

Within this painting, the central figure of Christ was painted by Verrocchio, who also painted a small angel standing at Christ's side. However, it is known that Leonardo painted a second angel in the picture, also at Christ's side. And that is where we can see the comparison between the mature, lesser talent of Verrocchio, the teacher, and the young genius of Leonardo, his student.

Each of the angels is an expression of (organic) FORM along with CONTENT and COLOR. However, even though both angels represent the same lessons of light, the angel painted by Leonardo, the "student," can easily be seen to be superior.[65]

But this clear difference in talent, the superiority of the angel painted by Leonardo, is not accounted for in the statement that both angels are created of FORM with CONTENT and COLOR.

And of course, that appears to diminish the value of the lessons of light. You might say, "What good are they if they don't provide a measure of talent?"

What you have learned

But that is hardly a shortcoming at all.

The reason is, the lessons of light are tools that help us genuinely see the visual expression we find around us in everyday life and also within the great museums. At the same time, they help us unsee the CONTENT that restricts just about everyone's appreciation of visual experience. And that's their magic. It's the process of genuinely seeing, or genuinely unseeing, that frees your ability to judge and appreciate visual talent. That is the power the lessons of light transfer to anyone who embraces them.

I can write here that both angels in *The Baptism of Christ* are expressions of FORM, CONTENT and COLOR, a statement that by itself does not suggest that Leonardo's angel is more inspiring. But, by recognizing these three visual lessons in the work, you will make that discovery *yourself*. It is the truthfulness and trustworthiness of your own beliefs that allow you to become a good judge of serious visual expression, or perhaps a good or even great artist yourself.

That is what you have learned in this book.

To demonstrate this, find a picture of *The Baptism of Christ* online by searching internet images for "leonardo baptism."

Do this now.

When you see the two angels, you will know which is which. (Close-ups are shown on the internet, and also compare the other figures in the picture, mostly painted by Verrocchio.)

At that moment, and maybe for the first time, you will evaluate visual experience for yourself. You'll see which of these angel images expresses with more visual authority. That's the exceptional, emotional moment I referred to in the introduction when I wrote:

> " . . . believe it or not, you'll
> finally begin to understand."

Where do you go from here?

How do you progress in your visual life now that you have finished "Help Yourself to a Blue Banana?"

There are many possibilities, covering many options.

If you've read this book as part of a study program in art or design, that's where you belong. You can carry on toward your certificate or degree using the lessons of light to broaden your understanding of the material presented in your classes.

On the other hand, if you have not enrolled in art study but are considering it, maybe this book has convinced you to take that action. Studying visual art is a rewarding way to expand your education, and it leads to many opportunities as life unfolds.

If you are a visual arts educator, librarian, curator or collector, I would appreciate your support. I believe the information here will improve art and design understanding in many ways.

If you are a working professional in the visual arts, perhaps you'll discover that the nine lessons of light are a tool that can help enrich your skills, while you communicate more meaningfully with other professionals.

Lastly, if you are just a curious bystander to visual expression, you'll find your new knowledge may open an inspiring area of pleasure. As you welcome the visual language to your life, new satisfactions will present themselves.

Even if you never aspire to create serious visual experience yourself, or to participate in the visual professions, you'll get a more enriching visual reward from living your everyday life.

The beginning – Some people are right about art

Understanding that everything you see is a vibrant interaction of visual building blocks is the key to helping yourself interpret visual expression in an advanced way.

It's the secret to understanding art, design and visual living.

Of course, throughout history, millions of artists and other visually sensitive individuals have led the fullest and most creatively productive lives without understanding the visual language in this re-organized way. But all artwork, even art that is centuries old, represents an orchestration of the nine lessons of light.

Look in a museum at an ancient canvas, or out your window at an unusual pile of trash at the side of your street today. In both cases you can now understand what you are seeing. Even though artists and visually sensitive people have always recognized important visual expression, you now know how a pile of trash at the side of your street might be as visually engaging as a famous painting.

We now know how a pile of trash, a pebble on the beach, or perhaps a struggling sapling that's clinging to a mountainside, may actually *inspire* a visually important work of artistic expression.

To decide correctly if something is art, all you need do is to look at it. Now that you understand the visual language, translated into English throughout the last nine chapters, *your eyes will tell you* if what they see is meaningful and truthful visual expression.

However, once your confidence has reached the level of recognizing what art is, your need to understand it as a blending of the nine lessons of light will probably cease to matter.

. . . . And in all likelihood, as it has for millions of
visually curious people before you, it may even cease to exist.

Appendices

The nine lessons of light and the conditions that help define them:

> First, here are the four conditions of frame of reference:
> focus, light, preconception, intention

1. The seven conditions of DEPTH as a source of visual experience:
    parallax   perspective
    circumstance   advancing or receding COLOR or tone
    memories   lightness and darkness of COLOR or tone
    shadow

2. These are the two conditions of FORM:
    organic   geometric

3. The conditions of ANATOMY are:
    comparing similar looking objects
    substituting similar looking objects
    creating new objects by combining familiar objects

4. There are four conditions of COLOR:
    appropriateness of COLOR
    side by side variation of COLOR
    the additive primary COLORS
    the subtractive primary COLORS

5. The two conditions of CONTRAST:
    opposites   conflicts

6. These are the six conditions of CONTENT:
    human values   civil values   self values
    typography   humor   it's of something

7. In review, remember that visual TEXTURE
    can be both decorative and useful.

8. These are the four conditions of SCALE:
    abstract balance
    appropriate SCALE
    manipulation of life-size (appropriate) SCALE
    dramatically good and dramatically bad SCALE

9. For review, remember that SPACE exists in both two dimensions
    and three dimensions, and is always created when
    a frame of reference comes into existence.

Below are six references found in this book to visual design and marketing work carried out by Michael Adams. You can see examples of his work at behindthescenesmarketing.com

Page 127
Armitron Watches point of sale display. Refers to a department store display created for Armitron Watches by the author.

Page 150
The Ritz Taipei Hotel and The Lai Lai/Sheraton Taipei. Refers to work performed at these hotels by the author in Taipei, Republic of China.

Page 153
Philip Morris Company. Refers to new product marketing development carried out by the author and by Wells Rich Greene Advertising, NYC.

Page 195
The Central Park Conservancy. NYC. Refers to a fund raising brochure designed for the Conservancy by the author.

Page 259
"Candy," the M&M Chocolate Candy Cow. Refers to a marketing promotion created by the author for M&M Mars candy company, in association with Rowland Worldwide, an event marketing firm.

Page 318
The Sotogrande Hotel, Costa Del Sol, Spain. Refers to work performed by the author.

Beginning here, and on the following pages, is a summary of 33 internet searches suggested in the text. Please read the book before exploring these searches. Excepts are taken from the text on the pages referred to.

Page 58 INTERNET SEARCH REFERRED TO IN THE TEXT:
3D photographs are made by setting two cameras side by side, about 5" (12 cm) apart. The cameras recreate what each of our two eyes would see. To see the DEPTH in a 3D picture like this (which is actually two pictures), a special viewer is needed. The viewer lets each eye see a separate picture. When that happens, our eyes are fooled into seeing a normal lifelike view of that scene, including 3D DEPTH.

For more information about the principles involved, or to see examples, search "stereoscope" on the internet.

Page 60 INTERNET SEARCH REFERRED TO IN THE TEXT:
You can find examples of magic eye illustrations to practice on, and
guidelines about how to see the pictures they hide, by searching pages
and images on the internet for "magic eye." I just now did this internet
search myself, and I can report that the three dimensional effects work
perfectly even on a computer screen.

For more information search pages
and images on the internet for "magic eye."

Page 62 INTERNET SEARCH REFERRED TO IN THE TEXT:
In the meantime, if you are curious, there is of course more detailed
and technical information about parallax on the internet.

If you are interested, search "parallax," or "parallax examples."
Be sure to select "images" on your search engine, not "web pages."

Page 65 INTERNET SEARCH REFERRED TO IN THE TEXT:
As with parallax, there's much information about
perspective also on the internet.

If you are interested, search "perspective" or "perspective examples";
be sure to select "images" on your search engine, not "web pages."

Page 76 INTERNET SEARCH REFERRED TO IN THE TEXT:
Referring to a lunar eclipse: Wonderful, wonderful night.

You can search images for "lunar eclipse" to see a picture of the
moon in total eclipse. Or to see a 3D photo of the normal full moon
go to http://www.astrosurf.com/cidadao/qc_moon_3d.jpg.
You'll need some standard red and blue 3D viewing glasses.

Page 81 INTERNET SEARCH REFERRED TO IN THE TEXT:
Empire State Building crash, 1945. Soon after I read a historical
account of the accident, I mentioned it to an illustrator I know.
He is also the owner of a penthouse near the Empire State Building,
where, like the artist in the story, he also maintains a studio.

You can read about the Empire State Building crash
by searching the internet for "empire plane crash."

Page 90 INTERNET SEARCH REFERRED TO IN THE TEXT:
Louise Nevelson. Many of her sculptures are complex arrangements
of common wooden boxes she found and painted black. Her work
is a magnificent expression of abstract balance.

You can see examples of the work of Louise Nevelson
by searching images for "nevelson."

Page 112 INTERNET SEARCH REFERRED TO IN THE TEXT:
ANATOMY in the movie *Men in Black*. The visual idea worked
because the top parts of the towers are sort of round and flat,
just as we imagine flying saucers to be. "Men in Black" is a movie
about aliens on Earth, so the writer, who is obviously living visually,
wrote a plot twist based on this similarity between those tower tops
and UFOs (flying saucers).

> *You can see what he saw if you search internet*
> *images for "New York World's Fair pavilion."*

Page 116 INTERNET SEARCH REFERRED TO IN THE TEXT:
I once used a more visual example of ANATOMY in a logo design. When I
worked in the Republic of China, I designed the name for a tourist magazine
called "TAIWAN." I designed normal letters, but substituted a Chinese pagoda
(a building that has sort of a pointed top) for the second letter "A." It works
because the letter "A" actually looks somewhat like a pagoda.

> *You can see this logo if you visit behindthescenesmarketing.com*
> *Click on the "Our Work" link, and then on # 96.*

Page 123 INTERNET SEARCH REFERRED TO IN THE TEXT:
Picasso's *Bull's Head*. As you become more familiar with modern visual
expression, and visual living, you may discover a picture somewhere
of that remarkable bull's head sculpture. In fact, you could make a plan
to look for it in your library, a bookstore or find it on the internet.

> *Search images for "picasso bull's head" (with quotation marks).*

Page 126 INTERNET SEARCH REFERRED TO IN THE TEXT:
Skull / woman poster. That poster was created on purpose to look like
a skull, but it is possible for unwanted "pictures" to creep into a frame
of reference by accident. To prevent this, every detail of a frame of
reference needs a second look.

> *If you're curious, and I bet you are, you can see*
> *that illustration by searching images for "skull mirror."*

Page 127 INTERNET SEARCH REFERRED TO IN THE TEXT:
Harvard Lampoon Building, with a face on it.
> *You can see the Harvard building by searching*
> *images for "lampoon building."*

Page 128 INTERNET SEARCH REFERRED TO IN THE TEXT:
A wrist watch display and ANATOMY. As I started to work I held the watch
in my hand. On my work table was a plastic triangle with the center cut out.
I glanced at the triangle, and then looped the watch strap through it. Instantly
the ANATOMY of a miniature kite appeared. I could see the possibility of
making the display look like a kite.

> *You can see this display if you visit behindthescenesmarketing.com*

Page 129 INTERNET SEARCH REFERRED TO IN THE TEXT:
If you have ever seen the Halloween parade in New York City you
may know how evil and unfamiliar things can get. In fact I might even
say the New York City street scene on Halloween is sometimes almost
out of control, visually speaking.

> *You can see some of that scary chaos by searching images
> for "New York Halloween parade." or visiting halloween-nyc.com*

Page 154 INTERNET SEARCH REFERRED TO IN THE TEXT:
American flag illusion. As a result, since red is the complement of green,
for a few seconds their eyes automatically see a normal red and white flag
in the blank space. It's really just the afterimage of the green flag, which
lingers on the light sensitive part of our eye.

> *You can see this illusion if you search
> internet pages for "flag illusion."*

Page 168 INTERNET SEARCH REFERRED TO IN THE TEXT:
To define it visually in words, *The Goddess of Democracy* did not *express*
CONTENT as a source of visual experience. Rather, it *became* CONTENT
as a source of visual experience. Unfortunately, however, it was smashed
by Chinese troops. When you see that sculpture in historical news accounts,
remember what it meant as important visual expression as CONTENT
and as a call for freedom from repression.

> *You can see it, and Michelangelo's David, if you search "goddess
> of democracy" and "michelangelo david" images on the internet.*

Page 169 INTERNET SEARCH REFERRED TO IN THE TEXT:
Chinese tank man image. Who can forget the stunning photograph of
a single man who stood motionless in the path of that armored column
of Chinese tanks advancing on the crowds? What a phenomenal image,
an image I believe was broadcast worldwide, even as it was happening.

> *You can see this picture by searching images for "chinese tank man."*

Page 187 INTERNET SEARCH REFERRED TO IN THE TEXT:
The Trylon and Perisphere. For an example of this conflict in action, see
pictures of the famous 610 foot tall theme building at the *1939 World's Fair*
in New York City, which was unfortunately demolished long ago. It was a
tall pyramid next to a big sphere. The visually appealing thing about the
Trylon and Perisphere is that they visually conflict with each other.

> *Search internet images for "Trylon and Perisphere."*

Page 192 INTERNET SEARCH REFERRED TO IN THE TEXT:
Monet paintings and conflict. I am referring to two pictures by the artist
Claude Monet, a French painter who lived about 100 years ago. Both
paintings provide examples of CONTRAST (conflict) that are easy to see.

> *If you're curious, you can see these paintings by searching
> internet images for "monet haystacks" and "monet poppies"*

Page 192 (continued) INTERNET SEARCH REFERRED TO IN THE TEXT:
Refers to Katsushika Hokusai's iconic Japanese print called *The Great Wave.*
You can see that print if you search images for "hokusai wave."

Page 195 INTERNET SEARCH REFERRED TO IN THE TEXT:
Fund raising brochure for the Central Park Conservancy. The slot separated
the *natural* part of the park (the trees, etc.) from the *manmade* part of the park
(the stone staircase, etc.). And the cards sticking up from the slot seem to say
"Your donated money will help the park managers take care of both."

> *You can see this design if you visit behindthescenesmarketing.com*
> *Click on the "Our Work" link, and then on #64.*

Page 219 INTERNET SEARCH REFERRED TO IN THE TEXT:
TEXTURE dominates Jackson Pollock's *One*, perhaps
the world's most extraordinary abstract painting.

> *You can see that painting if you search images for "one pollock."*

Page 220 INTERNET SEARCH REFERRED TO IN THE TEXT:
The Hindenburg. Try to remember seeing pictures of the explosion of the
great Hindenburg, the giant hydrogen filled airship which flew in the 1930s.
The Hindenburg was moored. Passengers were unloading. All was safe.
The dangerous ocean crossing was over. Then, unprecedented disaster.

> *To see pictures of the terrible explosion,*
> *search internet images for "Hindenburg."*

Page 222 INTERNET SEARCH REFERRED TO IN THE TEXT:
The Challenger disaster. Then such unspeakable irony. The maiden voyage
of the "new era" came to an unbearably abrupt and almost incomprehensible
conclusion. I was shattered by the incredible symbolism of destroyed hope,
and the death of innocents and innocence.

> *Normally I'd refer you here to an internet search of*
> *"Challenger" images, but I am not willing, even now,*
> *to re-visit those pictures or to ask you to revisit them.*

Page 233 INTERNET SEARCH REFERRED TO IN THE TEXT:
When he created the pipe painting, that artist (Magritte) probably didn't understand the CONTENT value of writing (in words) any better than you understand
it, right now, after simply reading the last few paragraphs. But he decided to
question it anyway. He questioned it by adding some writing to the bottom of
his picture. Just like that, a masterpiece was born; not by knowing any remarkable secrets about visual expression, not by having extraordinary drawing skills,
not by reading "Help Yourself to a Blue Banana," or any other art or design
book. Instead, this masterpiece came to life just by questioning something. And
remember, this man didn't even answer the question. He only asked it. In fact,
I'm sure it's fair to say he didn't *know* the answer. Art does not have to answer
questions. It only has to ask them.

> *You can see the painting by searching images for "pas une pipe."*

Page 251 INTERNET SEARCH REFERRED TO IN THE TEXT:
A marathon race image that demonstrates TEXTURE. Visually speaking,
there is little difference between TEXTURES we can feel and those like
the marathon picture that are simply too big to feel.

> *You can see similar helicopter views of marathon*
> *races by searching images for "verrazano runners."*

Page 254 INTERNET SEARCH REFERRED TO IN THE TEXT:
The Gibraltar catchments. The solution was a gigantic project that smoothed
out part of the eastern face of The Rock and covered it with concrete tiles.
It was a flat slope that at one time covered 34 acres (14 hectares).

> *In 2001, the rain tiles were removed, and the terrain was returned*
> *to it's natural vegetation. However, you can still see a picture by*
> *searching images for "gibraltar catchments."*

Page 260 INTERNET SEARCH REFERRED TO IN THE TEXT:
The M&Ms candy cow. This was an almost unbelievable performance by a
cow whose primary source of visual interest was the TEXTURE of the candy
that covered her. Candy was also a good example of how a business artist can
help a company make money. She did just what the client wanted her to do,
that is, bring attention to the large amount of nutritious milk used to make
milk chocolate. Candy was the first ever life-sized designed fiberglass bovine,
and she was the precursor to the interesting municipal fund raising program
called Cow Parade, which was born about six years later.

> *You can see Candy and read more about her if you*
> *visit my web site, behindthescenesmarketing.com.*

Page 270 INTERNET SEARCH REFERRED TO IN THE TEXT:
The golden rectangle is a two dimensional FORM
that is in abstract balance with itself.

> *You can see this important shape by searching images*
> *on the internet for "golden rectangle."*

Page 273 INTERNET SEARCH REFERRED TO IN THE TEXT:
Jackson Pollock and abstract balance: In jazz, new balance was nicely
done by Dave Brubeck and Joe Morello on their innovative cut called
Take Five. In visual expression, one of the greatest breakthroughs in
new abstract balance was brought to life by the genius Jackson Pollock
in his breathtaking drip paintings.

> *You can hear "Take Five" by searching YouTube for "brubeck"*
> *See Pollock's paintings by searching images for "pollock."*

Page 283 INTERNET SEARCH REFERRED TO IN THE TEXT:
A startling preview of the future happened when ASIMO, Honda's
human-SCALED robot conducted a symphony orchestra. See a video:

> *Search honda.com/asimo and click on "videos"*

Page 294 INTERNET SEARCH REFERRED TO IN THE TEXT:
That is to say, today, giant structures within a city, and on a city
skyline, are considered normal (even though plenty of artists still
find some of them to be ugly).

> *For recent examples, think of the London Eye, the Gateway
> Arch above St. Louis, Missouri, or the Space Needle in Seattle,
> Washington. Search internet images for these icons or search
> for the Burj Dubai, one of the world's tallest buildings.*

Page 294 (continued) INTERNET SEARCH REFERRED TO IN THE TEXT:
For example, maybe next time you see a picture of the Eiffel Tower
you will look a little more closely, trying to imagine it as temporary.

> *Search images for "eiffel tower."*

Page 327 INTERNET SEARCH REFERRED TO IN THE TEXT:
To see what I mean, you can find a representation of *The Baptism of Christ*
by searching internet images for "leonardo baptism." Do this search right
now. When you see the comparison between the two angels, I am certain
that you will know which angel is which. (There are close-up views of the
two angels provided on the internet.)

> *You can see a representation of* The Baptism of Christ
> *by searching internet images for "leonardo baptism."*

* * * *

About the writer

Designer Michael Adams was born in Canonsburg, Pennsylvania,
and was raised as a military brat in the U.S. Air Force. He studied
painting in Germany under Ernst Krupp, architecture and economics
at Catholic University, and graphic design at the School of Visual Arts.

He has held senior creative positions at top design studios and advertising
agencies and traveled internationally as design director for three leading
hotel corporations. He is the owner of Behind the Scenes Marketing (.com)

He is professor of art and design at Montclair State University and
lives visually in New Jersey, on the east coast of the United States.

Contact him with comments or suggestions at:
ma@behindthescenesmarketing.com

To purchase additional copies, send an email to:
info@behindthescenesmarketing.com

If you would like to teach the lessons of light,
please email info@behindthescenesmarketing.com

Note page (for use when teaching the nine lessons of light)

When you speak to your "student" about the nine lessons
of light (see page 324), keep notes of the experience here.
Write down what your student said, and record
how well you performed as a teacher.

Teacher (you): _____

Student: _____ Date: _____

How did the lesson go?: _____

_____

_____

_____

_____

_____

_____

_____

This is what my student said: _____

_____

_____

_____

_____

_____

_____

_____

_____

If you need more space, continue writing on the blank pages between chapters.
If you would like to teach the lessons of light™ to more than one other person, please email the publisher.

Index – The nine lessons of light are shown in **bold face**

Endnotes (footnotes). Artists in **bold.**

---

[1] P 42. The iMac personal computer, an Apple computer. The iMac is a mass market computer that incorporates the processor into the monitor. Much of this book was written on an iMac personal computer.

[2] ***Grandma Moses*** *– (1860-1961) – painter - p 49*
One successful artist whose style on some paintings suggests an under-developed ability to draw, especially a primitive use of perspective. Grandma Moses started painting at age 77. You can see examples of her work by searching images for "grandma moses."

[3] ***Mark Kostabi*** *– painter - p 51*
An artist who sometimes signs art that is created by his staff. You can see examples of his work by searching images for "kostabi."

[4] ***Andy Warhol*** *– (1928-1987) – artist - p 51*
The artist known for, among many other things, manipulating existing photographs of famous people. You can see examples of his work by searching images for "warhol."

[5] ***Matt Hotch*** *– motorcycle designer - p 52*
"I'm not much of a drawer." Paraphrased quote from *The Great Biker Build Off* – The Discovery Channel, broadcast of August 4, 2004.

[6] P 57. Story Musgrave, US Astronaut, referring to comments he made about the size of a UFO: "I do not know how large this object is because I do not know how far away it was." Paraphrased from information found at http://www.spacestory.com/extraterrestrial.htm.

[7] P 61. *Uncovering the Secrets of the Red Planet* - Paula Raeburn and Matt Golombek, National Geographic Society, 1999, an illustrated book which includes 3D photographs of the landing area around the Mars Pathfinder lander.

[8] P 61. *Sports Illustrated*, 3D Swimsuit issue – Winter 2000

[9] **Robert Weaver** – *(1924-1994)* – *illustrator* - *p 81*
"He must not have been a very good sculptor." Quoted from a
humorous conversation following his class at the School of
Visual Arts. Weaver pioneered a journalistic style of illustration.

[10] **Pablo Picasso** – (1881-1974) – *painter* - *p 82*
Refers to *"Le Reve,"* Picasso's oil painting of his mistress Marie-
Therese Walter. In 2006 the owner of the painting, casino developer
Steve Wynn, accidentally poked his elbow through the painting's lower
right corner after arranging its sale for $139 million, a record price
at the time. The sale was called off, and after a $90,000 restoration
the work was revalued at $85 million. From askmen.com, 10/15/07

[11] **Louise Nevelson** – *(1899-1988)* – *sculptor* - *pp 76, 90, 153*
"Many of her sculptures are complex arrangements of common wooden
boxes she found and painted black, including her very first "discovery":
a wooden linoleum shipping crate that measured 6' x 6" x 6". This
reference, and others found on pp 76 and 153 (referring to shadow and
the COLOR black), are taken from recorded comments that accompanied
a catalog for her show at the Pace Gallery, NYC, May-June, 1980. You
can see examples of her work by searching images for "nevelson."

[12] **Vincent Van Gogh** – *(1853-1890)* – *painter* - *p 98*
Refers to the artist's depression which is sometimes blamed for the
act of severing his own ear (and his eventual suicide). You can see
examples of his work by searching images for "van gogh."

[13] P 101. Quoted from comments made by Mikhail Baryshnikov on the
Charlie Rose program, Public Television, broadcast of April 15, 2008.

[14] **Henry Moore** – *(1898-1986)* – *sculptor* - *p 103*
"I like women more than men," quoted from the artist's comments
in *"The Real Henry Moore,"* a video documentary of the artist's
sculptures. You can see examples of his work by searching images
for "henry moore."

[15] **Antonio Gaudi** – (1852-1926) – *architect* - *p 108*
Refers to his architectural work in Barcelona, Spain, especially the
Cathedral of Sagrada Familia, Barcelona, which is partly inspired
by organic plant life. You can see examples of his work by
searching images for "gaudi."

[16] P 108. *"The Oval Portrait,"* by Edgar Alan Poe: His short story describing a painter who captures his wife's energy so well on his canvas that when the portrait is finished, the poor woman dies.

[17] **Roger Ferriter** – *graphic designer - p 115*
"There's something wrong with the ANATOMY of this letter. It doesn't have 'M'ness." Quoted from his class in typography design at the School of Visual Arts. Ferriter is the creator of the naming and identity for L'eggs pantyhose and other well-known brands.

[18] **Paul Rand** – *(1914-1996)* – *graphic designer - p 116*
Refers to his logo for the IBM corporation. *You can see examples of his work by searching images for "paul rand."*

[19] P 120. A snowflake designed from five airplanes: broadcast art which appeared during the report of major snowstorm. CNN Headline News – broadcast of January 5, 1999.

[20] **Pablo Picasso** – *(1881-1974)* – *artist - p 123*
This refers to his sculpture *Bull's Head*, in the collection of Galerie Louise Leiris, Paris, France, and to his title as "The most influential artist of the 20th century" conferred by Time Magazine, 1998. You can see examples of his work by searching images for "picasso." You can see the bull's head sculpture by searching images for "picasso bull's head."

[21] **Al Hirschfeld** – *(1903-2003)* – *illustrator - p 124*
A brilliant artist whose drawings of famous personalities frequently appeared in *The New York Times* and *TV Guide*. Hirschfeld hid his daughter's name "NINA" in the folds and trusses of many of his pictures. You can see his work by searching images for "al hirschfeld."

[22] **Joan Steiner** – *sculptor - p 125*
Refers to her book *Look Alikes*, a collection of photographs of miniature rooms, each created by the artist entirely by using alternative tiny objects, assembled to represent every feature of the rooms and their contents. Little Brown, 1998. You can see examples of her work by searching images for "joan steiner."

[23] P 128. Armitron Watches display. Refers to a point of sale display created for Armitron Watches by the author. You can see this display if you visit *behindthescenesmarketing.com.*

[24] ***Norman Rockwell*** *– (1894-1978) – painter - p 129*
Artist who painted friendly illustrations for magazine covers including the *Saturday Evening Post.* You can see examples of his work by searching images for "norman rockwell."

[25] ***Thomas Kinkade*** *– painter - p 129*
Copies of his paintings of cozy and friendly settings are sold in shopping malls around the world. His art is sometimes criticized for lack of unique artistic expression, but much like some scenes imagined by Norman Rockwell, many of Kinkade's paintings are magical examples of CONTENT, visual experience that is firmly anchored at the totally familiar extreme of the visual boundaries *on purpose.* You can see examples of his work by searching images for "kinkade."

[26] ***Jean-Michel Basquiat*** *– (1960-1988) – painter - p 129*
Referring to his images of strange beings and quietly disturbing details. You can see examples of his work by searching images for "basquiat."

[27] ***Gustav Klimt*** *– (1862-1918) – painter - p 133*
Refers to a print of his oil painting *Freunddinnen,* an image of two girls, one naked. In 2006 Klimt's painting *Adele Bloch Bauer* became the most expensive artwork ever sold to that date ($135 million). You can see examples of his paintings by searching images for "klimt."

[28] P 137. In 1962, the beige-colored Crayola brand wax crayon called "flesh" was renamed "peach" in part because of the US Civil Rights movement. See http://www.crayola.com

[29] p 137. In 1912 Robert Ridgway published *Color Standards and Nominclature,* which named 1115 colors. A vast majority of his names were variations of each other, like "Pallid Grayish Violet-Blue." From http://www.colorsystem.com and http://books.goggle.com

[30] ***Donna Karan*** *– fashion designer - p 138*
"It's the color. It's the vegetable, delicious, wonderful color!" A comment made by the designer describing her work after a Spring 2004 runway show. From Metro TV, *Full Frontal Fashion,* broadcast of February 15, 2004. Search images for "donna karan."

[31] P 143. Len Sudol, president of a textile company, NYC
"These are living things we're talking about," referring to textile
dye colors. Quoted from a conversation with the author, 1989.

[32] P 144. Slogan for television programming: *In living color.*
National Broadcasting Company, NBC

[33] P 144. Centuries ago, purple dye was expensive
to produce. From *Loose Cannons & Red Herrings*,
Robert Caliborne, Norton, 1988. "Born to the purple."

[34] P 150. The Ritz Taipei Hotel and The Lai Lai/Sheraton Taipei.
Refers to work performed at these hotels by the author in Taipei,
Republic of China.

[35] *Auguste Renoir* – *(1841-1919)* – *painter* - *p 152*
"I've been forty years discovering that the queen of all colors is
black." A comment made by the artist referring to the color black.
Taken from *Hodge Podge Two*, J. Bryan III, Atheneum Books, 1989.
See examples of his work by searching images for "renoir."

[36] P 153. Philip Morris Company. Refers to new product marketing
development carried out by the author and by Wells Rich Greene
Advertising, NYC.

[37] P 167. Teri Horton purchased a painting for $5 at a California
thrift shop in the early 1990s, and came to believe it is a Jackson
Pollock original. She has apparently been offered $9 million for it.
The New York Times, November 9, 2006. You can see the painting
by searching images for "pollock thrift"

[38] *Alvar Aalto, Harry Bertoia* and *Charles Pollock* - *p 172*
Three 20th century furniture designers. Refers to an Aalto bent wood
dining chair, a Bertoia "Diamond" chrome easy chair, and a Pollock
leather office chair, found for $1-3 each in nearly perfect condition
at a thrift shop and yard sales. Two of these chairs are in the permanent
collection of the Museum of Modern Art in New York City. You can
see examples of their work by searching images for "bertoia," "aalto"
and "charles pollock chair." A different artist by the same name was
the brother of the genius Jackson Pollock.

[39] *Leonardo da Vinci* – (1452-1519) – *artist - p 172*
Refers to daVinci's painting *"Saint Jerome"* painted in 1480 or 1481.
From *Leonardo. Discovering the Life of Leonardo da Vinci* by Serge
Bramly, Harper Collins, 1991 – p151. Search images for "da vinci saint
jerome." Notice how the cut away portrait section of the picture (Saint
Jerome's head) has been reunited with the balance of the painting.

[40] *Roy Lichtenstein* – (1923-1997) – *artist - p 179*
"I don't think artists like myself have the faintest idea what we're
doing, but we try to put it in words that sound logical." Quoted from
the *New York Times* obituary of the artist in 1996. This quote by Roy
Lichtenstein was also paraphrased by Michael Kimmelman, chief art
critic of *The New York Times,* appearing on the *Charlie Rose* program,
Public Broadcasting Television, October 2, 1998 during a discussion of
his book *Portraits,* Random House, 1998. You can see examples of
Lichtenstein's work by searching images for "lichtenstein."

[41] P 195. The Central Park Conservancy, NYC. A brochure designed by
the author was a Caples Awards finalist, the direct marketing "oscars."

[42] *Andrew Wyeth* – *painter - p 207*
"You never know how influences come in. If they come with me, they
come in casually. I'm certainly never conscious of them, if I am truly
interested in what I am doing. Knowledge of the works of certain others
is, of course, important. But that doesn't mean that you should think
about it. These things should go into your bloodstream and disappear."
From *Two Worlds of Andrew Wyeth*, by Thomas Hoving, Houghton
Mifflin, 1978 – p17. You can see examples of his work by searching
images for "andrew wyeth."

[43] P 210. A hiker named Aron Ralston amputated his own right hand
in May, 2003, to escape a ravine after he was trapped by a large rock.

[44] *Andrew Wyeth* – *painter - p 212*
"I tell them I don't give a damn. I'm painting for myself. If my
paintings are worth anything – if they have quality – that quality
will find a way to preserve itself. I paint for myself within the tenets of
my own upbringing and my standards." From *Two Worlds of Andrew
Wyeth,* Thomas Hoving, Houghton Mifflin, 1978 – p23. You can see
examples of his work by searching images for "andrew wyeth."

[45] **Roy Lichtenstein** – (1923-1997) – *artist - p 218*
Refers to Lichtenstein's paintings which were inspired in part
by comic book art. You can see examples of his work by searching
images for "lichtenstein."

[46] **Jackson Pollock** – (1912-1956) – *painter - p 219*
Refers to his abstract painting *"One"* in the collection of the
Museum of Modern Art, New York. You can see examples of
his work by searching images for "jackson pollock."

[47] P 230. Alan Prescott, typography designer, NYC. Refers to
a conversation with the author about an Elvis Presley book.

[48] **Rene Magritte** – *(1898-1967) – painter - p 232*
Refers to his painting *"Ceci n'est pas une pipe,"* which shows a pipe
above the words (written in French), "This is not a pipe." You can see
examples of his work by searching images for "magritte."

[49] P 234. Norman Cousins was cured of an illness by forcing himself
to be constantly amused. *Anatomy of an Illness*, Norman Cousins,
W.W. Norton & Co, 1979.

[50] **Cindy Sherman** – *photographer - p 237*
" . . . there was nothing more to say (through painting). I was
meticulously copying other art and then I realized I could just use a
camera and put my time into an idea instead." From cindysherman.com.
See examples of her work by searching images for "cindy sherman."

[51] P 244. "The 11 o'clock news."
A comedy routine which suggests that weather turns to light in the
morning. George Carlin, *FM & AM*, Little David Records, 1972.
Carlin passed away in the summer of 2008.

[52] **Liza Lou** – *artist/sculptor - p 259*
Artist who created a life-sized kitchen and patio, each surfaced entirely
with glass beads. *The New York Times Magazine*, July 11, 1999. This
work by Liza Lou was also featured on *The Guinness Book of Records*,
ABC Television, broadcast of December 1, 1998. You can see examples
of her work by searching images for "liza lou."

[53] P 260. "Candy," the M&M Chocolate Candy Cow. Refers to a marketing promotion created by the author for the M&M Mars candy company, in association with Rowland Worldwide, an event marketing firm. This promotion was the precursor to the ongoing phenomenon called Cow Parade. You can see this promotion on the author's web site at behindthescenesmarketing.com

[54] *Jean Auguste Dominique Ingres – (1780-1867) – painter - p 273* "Everything in nature is harmony. A little too much or too little alters the scale, . . . makes discord." An early reference to the relationship between abstract balance and SCALE. Ingres was a French painter of the nineteenth century, considered by many to be possibly the finest portrait painter ever. From *Ingres: Slaves of Fashion,* a video of the artist's work. Home Vision, 1982.

[55] P 274. Studies show most people select a computerized "average" face as most beautiful. *Discover Magazine*, The Discovery Channel, broadcast of December 18, 1999.

[56] *Henry Moore – (1898-1986) – sculptor - p 289* "The very small or the very big takes on added size emotion." From the book *Modern Artists on Art*, "On Sculpture and Primitive Art," Spectrum, 1964. You can see examples of Moore's work by searching images for "henry moore."

[57] P 292. Refers to a large Citgo gasoline company sign in Kenmore Square near Fenway Park in Boston, Massachusetts.

[58] P 294. "Looking without seeing is negligence." Quoted from a decision by Judge Joseph Wapner, *The People's Court,* tv broadcast of Thursday, March 9, 1989.

[59] P 301. "Too much light often blinds gentlemen of this sort. They cannot see the forest for the trees." An observation by Christoph Martin Wieland, English writer of the 18th century, 1768.

[60] *Isaac Mizrahi – fashion designer - p 307* Fashion designer who, as a child, claims he was inspired by his mother's red shoes. From *Unzipped*, a documentary movie about the fashion industry, Miramax Films, 1995. You can see examples of his work by searching images for "mizrahi."

[61] P 310. The amount of gold in the world, a statistic taken from a Blanchard & Company advertisement for American Eagle gold coins, broadcast on CNBC television, June 10, 1999.

[62] *I.M. Pei* – *architect - p 313*
Referring to additions to the Louvre Museum, Paris France and the JFK Center, Washington D.C., from comments he made in a video docume ntary which appeared on Public Television You can see examples of his work by searching images for "pei."

[63] *Leonardo da Vinci* – *(1452-1519)* – *artist - p 316*
"The eye makes fewer mistakes than the mind."
From *Leonardo. Discovering the Life of Leonardo da Vinci* by Serge Bramly, Harper Collins, 1991 – p261.
You can see examples of his work by searching images for "da vinci."

[64] P 319. The Sotogrande Hotel, Costa Del Sol, Spain.
Refers to work designed by the author including a large billboard.

[65] *Leonardo da Vinci* – *(1452-1519)* – *artist - p 326*
Refers to daVinci's work within the painting called
"The Baptism of Christ." From *Leonardo. Discovering the Life of Leonardo da Vinci* by Serge Bramly, Harper Collins, 1991 – p105.
You can see examples of his work by searching images for "da vinci."

BOOK DESIGN, COVER DESIGN
AND COVER ILLUSTRATION
BY THE AUTHOR
© MICHAEL ADAMS MMV - MMVIII

Please contact the publisher at: info@behindthescenesmarketing.com